Timeshare
Resort
Operations

Timeshare Resort Operations

A Guide to Management Practice

Randall Upchurch
Conrad Lashley

AMSTERDAM • BOSTON • HEIDELBERG • LONDON
NEW YORK • OXFORD • PARIS • SAN DIEGO
SAN FRANCISCO • SINGAPORE • SYDNEY • TOKYO

Butterworth Heinemann is an imprint of Elsevier

Elsevier Butterworth–Heinemann
30 Corporate Drive, Suite 400, Burlington, MA 01803, USA
Linacre House, Jordan Hill, Oxford OX2 8DP, UK

Library of Congress Cataloging-in-Publication Data
Lashley, Conrad.
    Timeshare resort operations: a guide to management practice/Conrad
Lashley, Randall Upchurch.
        p. cm.
    Includes bibliographical references and index.
    ISBN 0-7506-7904-2 (hardcover: alk. paper)
    1. Hospitality industry—Management.   2. Resorts—Management.
    I. Upchurch, Randall S.   II. Title.
    TX911.3.M27L377 2006
    647.94068—dc22
                                                                2005027693

British Library Cataloguing-in-Publication Data
A catalogue record for this book is available from the British Library.

ISBN 13: 978-0-7506-7904-6
ISBN 10: 0-7506-7904-2

For information on all Elsevier Butterworth–Heinemann publications
visit our Web site at www.books.elsevier.com

06   07   08   09   10   10 9 8 7 6 5 4 3 2 1
Printed in the United States of America

Contents

Preface   vii

Chapter 1:   Evolution of the Timeshare Industry   1

Chapter 2:   Timeshare Resort Development
             and Financing   25

Chapter 3:   Real Estate Development   59

Chapter 4:   Timeshare Markets and Consumer
             Behavior   89

Chapter 5:   Relationship Marketing, Selling,
             and Beyond   125

Chapter 6:   Consumer Finance   149

Chapter 7:   Managing Human Resources in
             Timeshare Operations   171

Chapter 8:   Managing Service Quality in Timeshare   197

Chapter 9:   Home Owners Associations and
             Stakeholder Management   227

Chapter 10: Business Ethics and Ethical Practice 251

Chapter 11: The Future of Timesharing: A Matter
of Strategy 275

References 299

Index 311

Preface

The timeshare industry is a new but fast developing business activity across the world. Timeshare properties are now found in over 95 countries and on all of the world's continents. In the last couple of decades, timeshare business activities have become increasingly branded as large hotel, resort, and leisure attraction developers have added timeshare offers to their portfolio of accommodation provision. The entry of large corporate, branded, global players has done much to increase the professionalism of timeshare operations and management. It is against this culture of increasing professionalism that this book emerged. It is intended as text to support management programs at undergraduate and postgraduate levels in higher education, and professional management development programs delivered in industry for practitioners.

In higher education provision, the authors were increasingly aware of a need to establish timeshare as a consumer option with a place in the curriculum of those destined for careers in resort, hospitality, tourism, and leisure management. In particular, timeshare needs to be treated as a business format with specific operational requirements, but ultimately as a business requiring the application of an array of business concepts, models, and theories. The presence of visitors who need to be entertained, accommodated, and nourished while they reside on the property ensures that the operational skills needed are more than those for property development and investment appraisal. At the same time, the nature of the purchase, the potential length of the relationship, and the life cycle of the customer over the period of the purchase mean that timeshare is more than another consumer service experience in the hospitality and tourism sector. Property development and investment appraisal and the management of the hospitality experiences of tourists are vitally important dimensions of the sector. Timeshare operators therefore need to exercise a broad cluster of skills and concepts in the management of the business. Hence, one of our aims is to present a text that prepares those destined for timeshare resort management.

The authors reviewing current training and management development programs among industry practitioners saw the need for a text that discussed practical steps in managing the timeshare operation within a conceptual, theoretical framework. The timeshare business is just that, a business, and general business principles usually apply. Successful practitioners need to be reflective; developing a set of business skills is not enough in itself. Managers need to be able to understand the wider picture, to see principles at work, and to be able to critically evaluate the contexts in which they work.

The book is organized around themes that broadly follow issues related to resort development and resort operations. The first three chapters describe the timeshare business in general and current international trends. They also discuss timeshare resort development and financing, as well as estate development. The next three chapters seek to develop an understanding of the marketing issues related to timeshare, consumer behavior, and the development of a long-term relationship with resort owners and visitors. Consumer finance as an element of the marketing offer to customers aids the purchase decision, but it also provides an additional stream of business income. The last half of the book is concerned with a number of specific resort operational issues, through the management of resort visitor and owner service quality experiences as they are delivered through resort employees. Chapter 10 includes a discussion of business ethics, as it applies to timeshare business operations. The development of ethical business practice through industry associations such as the American Resort Development Association (ARDA) and Organization Timeshare Europe (OTE) has been significant in mitigating the negative effects of unscrupulous business practices in the past, and future management practice can benefit from ethical issues. Finally, the last chapter examines future trends and developments in the sector.

Many of the examples and statistics included in the book tend to be North American or European. We make no apology for that, for as

Chapter 4 shows, six of every ten timeshare owners are citizens of the United States, the United Kingdom, and Germany, and over 70 percent of resorts are located in the United States and in Europe. Timeshare ownership is very much a First World activity. In addition, we expect readers at this level to be able to recognize the general principles involved regardless of the immediate national context. Accordingly, we do not attempt to mechanistically apply a common formula of examples and international case studies to every chapter. The examples drawn from North America and Europe themselves create an understanding of timeshare as an international phenomenon, though skewed to a small number of international locations.

We assume that the book will be used largely as a support to management development in industry, and in the final year of undergraduate or postgraduate programs. As a consequence, it is written in a style that attempts to expand and explore concepts and theories. To make the text an effective learning tool, we provide chapter learning outcomes at the beginning of each chapter. We also identify key learning points throughout the text. In addition, to aid reflection we invite the reader to actively consider the issues of cases provided in each chapter. It is our belief that effective learning takes place from active learning. Thus, we encourage readers to take time to think about the key points and reflective learning issues provided. We hope the book is helpful and stimulating. Good luck!

Professor Randall Upchurch
ARDA Professor of Vacation Ownership
  and Resort Development
Rosen School of Hospitality
  Management
University of Central Florida
United States

Professor Conrad Lashley
Director, The Centre for
  Leisure Retailing
Nottingham Business School
Nottingham Trent University
United Kingdom

CHAPTER
• • • • 1

Evolution of the Timeshare Industry

Learning Objectives

After studying this chapter, you should be able to:

- understand what the concept of resort timesharing means.

- differentiate between the different timeshare products in terms of products and amenities offered.

- apply resort life-cycle theory to the timeshare industry.

- critically discuss factors that influence the growth of timesharing in an international market.

Introduction

Timesharing, a term that combines the words *time* and *share*, is simply that—the act of sharing vacation time at a luxurious resort facility in a geographical location of choice. As such, the timeshare sales representative promotes the timeshare product to interested consumers with the primary belief that the purchaser can achieve a higher level of intimacy by means of "sharing quality time" with people important in his or her life at a private resort that pampers consumers with recreational and leisure services that are unparalleled in quality.

The timeshare industry, otherwise known as vacation ownership, first appeared in Europe in the 1960s. One of the early entrants, a ski resort in France known as Superdevoluy, developed the first ownership program in the world. The purpose of the program was to give the owners of Superdevoluy a guaranteed opportunity to ski in the Alps (Baiman and Forbes, 1992). Not very long after the concept had taken hold in Europe the concept of sharing time at a resort was quickly adopted in the United States. The expansion was so pronounced that since the 1970s, the timeshare industry has recorded double-digit growth, which no other service sector has been able to do for this same period of time.

Many owners consider the timeshare industry to be a viable alternative vacation product to more traditional short-term and long-term lodging arrangements such as hotels, motels, bed & breakfasts, and condominiums (Upchurch and Gruber, 2002). Since the 1970s, the timeshare product has evolved in the metrics of sales volume, number of owners, and independent and brand-name developers that have entered the field. In addition, the range of product lines as well as the diversity of product designs has expanded over time.

A Short History of Timeshare

From a consumer perspective, purchasing a timeshare entails the purchase of access to a condominium style of accommodation for a designated period at a vacation resort that appeals to the purchaser's lifestyle and vacation interests. This type of purchase means that the timeshare consumer is granted exclusive occupancy rights to a vacation home type of experience in increments of a week or more (Upchurch and Gruber, 2002). Because the timeshare product is typically sold in week increments, the buyer is not burdened with the daily upkeep costs normally associated with full home ownership. As such, the timeshare owner is free from the daily maintenance concerns of the resort and is therefore able to maximize his or her recreational and leisure experiences while the developer or a property management group maintains daily operational functions.

Key Point 1.1

Timeshare is defined as the right to purchase a specific time period in which to use a property at a geographical location of choice.

Product Registration: From Fixed Weeks to Float Weeks to Vacation Clubs

Another way to define the industry is through the process of product registration. To the novice consumer, the timeshare product is sold in increments of weeks with individual access being granted to a specific villa at the resort with open access to the resort's common areas. This is true, but what exactly does the consumer own? The answer to this question depends on how the product is registered in the state in which the resort operates. In the 1960s, timeshare resorts were sold in "fixed-week" increments, which simply meant that the consumer was entitled to use the resort's facilities at a set week, each week, every year for the length of the agreement. This fixed-week structure still exists, but it is not as prevalent as in the 1970s. A fixed-week purchase works as follows: if a consumer purchases week 32 at resort "X," then this consumer is granted usage rights for week 32 for as long as the legally binding agreement remains valid.

Key Point 1.2

Timeshare developers have responded to consumer demands for product flexibility by changing the product offering to a more consumer friendly format. The product offering has progressed from a fixed week to a float week to a vacation club product that is sold based on points.

In the 1970s and 1980s, consumers began demanding more flexibility in how they could use their purchase, and the industry answered this concern with a "float week" offering. Simply put, a floating week offering means that the consumer is entitled to resort access rights within a specified range of weeks within a calendar year or as specified within the contract. The advantage of this format is that the consumer is offered more flexibility in product access versus that of a fixed-week structure. This flexibility in selecting a vacation week clearly is of benefit for the consumer who might be challenged in scheduling his or her annual vacation leave. Later in the 1970s to early 1980s, the timeshare consumer became more demanding in product use and access, which led to the creation of a float system (Upchurch and Gruber, 2002). Under a float system, the consumer had two options at her disposal depending on how the agreement was originally drafted. Under the week float option, the consumer was given use of a specific unit (also called a villa) while the week "floated" throughout the calendar year or within a given season. Under the unit float option, the consumer's interval (i.e., week) remained the same while her choice of unit (same type in terms of one-bedroom, two-bedroom, etc.) location varied as long as the unit type was the same as the one she had originally purchased. Clearly, either float schedule offered the consumer a higher degree of week or unit flexibility that heretofore did not exist under a fixed system (Trowbridge, 1981).

In 1992, Disney was the first to roll out another legal format whereby consumers were not restricted to a fixed- or float-week structure; instead, consumers could purchase points within Disney's vacation club. Under this legal format, a timeshare product is registered under a vacation club structure, which means that the consumer purchases points instead of weekly increments. The purchased points, in turn, have a pre-determined equivalent value of timeshare resort usage rights. Under this legal plan, the consumer has a greater degree of control over the type of product that best meets his or her needs. For instance, a vacation club owner could purchase enough points for a single-unit, a two-bedroom, or three-bedroom villa for X number of days. In addition, vacation clubs offer much more flexibility in the range of services consumed in that club membership is not restricted to villa usage rights. For instance, some vacation club plan offerings allow the consumer the option of purchasing cruise line experiences, hotel stays, golf packages, or other appealing recreational and leisure experiences using their point structure to do so (Baiman, 1992; Gruber, 1999a; ARDA, 1999b; Suchman, 1999). Under a vacation club points system, the consumer simply purchases enough points to satisfy his annual vacation needs. From the consumer perspective, this system is touted to offer the maximum amount of flexibility, while in contrast this system is quite complex for the developer to manage relative to inventory management purposes (Sherles and Marmorstone, 1994). From the developer perspective, a very robust reservation management system must be in place to track factors such as unit size, length of stay, location availability, seasonal issue, point allocation, and remaining point allocation. Basically, the point type of interval schedule, sometimes referred to as a vacation club, offers the consumer the highest degree of vacation options in contrast to either a fixed or a float type of interval arrangement (Burlingame, 1999 and 2001).

Reflective Practice

Survey current trade literature to determine who the major timeshare developers are in your region; include both branded and independent operators.

Basic Legal Forms of Conveyance

Another way to define the industry is to classify the timeshare product into the legal form under which it is sold. The three most common types of conveyance are (1) deeded interests, (2) right-to-use, and (3) leasehold agreements. Under the deeded interest method of conveyance, the purchaser receives title for the real property that is being purchased from the timeshare developer. If a consumer purchases a timeshare under a deeded arrangement, he or she has obtained legal ownership of the villa for a weekly interval that grants the owner the right to use the property for the week specified in the deed. Under this deeded type of conveyance, the purchaser has the legal right to: (a) use the real property (villa) in perpetuity, (b) will the real property to a family member, or (c) sell the real property at a point in which he or she no longer wants to use the property.

The right-to-use type of conveyance is not associated with deeding the underlying real property to the purchaser; instead, the individual is given contractual rights to use the timeshare facilities for a specified period of time. Upon expiration of this specified period (e.g., twenty years), the purchaser's rights of usage terminate unless he or she purchases additional time.

Key Point 1.3

The timeshare product is categorized into three basic legal modes of conveyance: (1) right-to-use, (2) deed, and (3) leasehold agreements.

The conveyance mode known as a leasehold agreement is similar to a right-to-use contract in that the purchaser holds a leasehold interest or other interest that is less than a full ownership interest. In practical terms, this means that the purchaser has the right to inhabit the timeshare unit for a specified period of time, and at the termination of the lease, the property reverts to the timeshare developer. One of the fundamental differences between a leasehold agreement and a right-to-use agreement is that the leasehold is of shorter duration than the right-to-use contract (Suchman, 1999; ARDA, 2002b).

In practical terms, the vacation ownership product comes in either a deeded or a nondeeded version (often referred to as a right-to-use arrangement). Under either arrangement, the consumer, also known as an owner, is given use at a

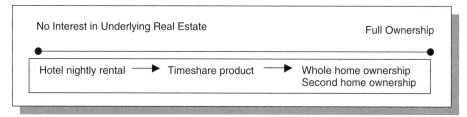

Figure 1.1 Product ownership continuum

specific resort, a specific unit, and exclusive occupancy for a specified period of time. In short, this means that a given developer can build and sell an individual unit for fifty-one or fifty-two weeks out of a year, depending on whether a week is held out for general maintenance purposes (Upchurch and Gruber, 2002).

From a product perspective, the vacation ownership concept holds a unique position within the leisure product continuum owing the fact that either via a deed or a contract the consumer owns the right to use a specific unit at a specific resort, at a specific period of time. In comparison, under a hotel arrangement the consumer is given the opportunity to rent a unit by the day without any kind of underlying deed or right-to-use/contractual arrangement, whereas whole ownership connotes a legally binding interest in the underlying real estate (see Figure 1.1).

A Macro View of the Timeshare Industry's Growth Cycle

A common question asked is, "Where did the concept of resort timesharing begin?" Many in the United States would trace the roots of timesharing to the most popular geographical destination market located within the U.S. borders: Orlando, Florida. Although the state of Florida has a rich history reaching back to the 1970s, it would be logical to conclude that it is the home of the first-ever timeshare development, but that would be an error of judgment. Actually, the site that originally spawned the growth of the timeshare resort concept is not within the United States at all. As noted earlier, the first timeshare resort was located in Europe. In 1964, a European developer known as Superdevoluy began offering timeshare intervals at a ski resort in the Alps for ski resort enthusiasts (Trowbridge, 1981). The basic concept proffered by Superdevoluy is not largely different from the core timeshare definition in that Superdevoluy sold individual units to multiple owners for a specified period of time. This vacation offering allowed the ski devotee who wanted to own real estate at a premium ski resort location a guaranteed right to vacation at that resort at an affordable price (Trowbridge, 1981).

In less than ten years, this concept of selling individual resort units (villas) to multiple owners gained momentum in the United States. Indeed, the first reports concerning time-sharing began to appear in publications in the 1970s (Trowbridge, 1981). In the 1970s, the timeshare concept migrated to the United States. During this time it was not uncommon for a timeshare resort development to be nothing more than a converted hotel project. This approach failed because many of these converted hotel projects were distressed properties and therefore were also not successful as timeshare resorts. The net result was that the concept of time-sharing in the United States had a very difficult startup process owing to high failure rates and the resultant negative press. Other negative influences during this time centered on inflation and the economic downturn of the U.S. economy.

One of the less glamorous outcomes of the 1970s was that a few unscrupulous developers took advantage of unknowing consumers by selling a product that did not exist. As a result of such dishonest actions, state lawmakers began to consider extensive product registration and licensing for timeshare enterprises. Many in the industry therefore refer to the 1970s as the birth of timeshare's negative image. It took years to counteract this bad image.

By the early 1980s, the practices of such unscrupulous developers were out of control. The net result was that Florida's state legislature passed the state's first timeshare law in 1983 that put an end to such unethical selling practices. This first timeshare law imposed strict restrictions on timeshare developers that in principle put the bad developers out of business. These initial regulatory actions saved the industry from an early demise. After the 1980s, the industry's image improved significantly owing to the fallout of these scam artists, the entrance of hotel brands, and implementation of quality control procedures (Gruber, 1999a, 1999b).

Key Point 1.4

The timeshare industry's image has been strongly influenced by consumer protection legislation and the entrance of hotel brands into the timeshare market.

The entry of major lodging companies into the timeshare industry during the 1980s and the 1990s exerted a strong influence on increased consumer acceptance of the timeshare product. What lodging companies were early entrants into the timeshare market? In 1984 Marriott entered first, followed by Disney and Hilton (in 1992). These developers brought considerable brand-name recognition and elevated consumer acceptance levels through strict standard operating procedures, organizational performance standards, organizational views toward civic responsibility, and adherence to strong business ethics. By the end of the century and continuing onward, other branded lodging companies followed Marriott, Disney, and Hilton's entrance into the realm of vacation ownership. For instance, Starwood purchased Vistana Resorts (1999), and in 2000 Cendant added Fairfield Communities (now called Fairfield Resorts) to their long list of hospitality-related companies. The entrance of these major developers demonstrate that timesharing had gained widespread acceptance in the hospitality arena (Pryce, 1999).

The 1990s also evidenced public trading of timeshare companies on the stock market. As of 2003, seventy-five companies were operating timeshare operations on the open market (Vacation Ownership World, 2003). Thus, the timeshare industry had become a viable and legitimate alternative to traditional resort vacationing. This sustained increase in the number of timeshare resorts is supported by a benchmark study conducted by Ragatz Associates in 2003. This report, titled "A Study of the Timeshare and Vacation Ownership Industry" conducted in 2003, reported that forty-seven states (U.S.) and ninety-five countries reflected this growing timeshare

Aggregate Resort Profile		Key European Locations		US State Profile	
Location	Frequency	Location	Frequency	Location	Frequency
Worldwide	4,325	Europe	1,452	USA	1,590
		Spain	512	Florida	366
		Italy	186		
		France	142	California	125
		UK	139	South Carolina	119
		Portugal	124	Colorado	75
		Austria	55		
		Greece	45	Hawaii	73
		Turkey	38	North Carolina	59
		Germany	38	Nevada	56
		Switzerland	37	Missouri	49
		Finland	31	Texas	49
		Malta	23		

Source: ARDA (2003) A Study of the Timeshare and Vacation Ownership Industry: 2003, American Resort Development Association, Washington, DC.

Table 1.1 2003 Timeshare Resort Profile

phenomenon (ARDA, 2003a and 2003b). Furthermore, these forty-seven states accounted for 1,590 timeshare resorts in the United States alone, while the worldwide number increased to 5,425 timeshare resorts (see Table 1.1 for details). According to Ragatz, the number of timeshare resorts in the United States has increased approximately 3 percent since 1994, and the total number of timeshare resorts since 1997 has grown 4.7 percent. These longitudinal statistics indicate that the timeshare industry has come of age.

Design Shifts and Developments

A quick review of the literature finds that the vacation ownership product has been impacted by consumer preferences, legal mandates, destination market factors, and industrywide product quality standards (McMullen, Zanini, Fugleberg, and Donovan, 2000). In particular, this group of industry consultants, architects, and interior designers showed that the industry is not truly a non-sought good by the mere fact that consumers had, and still are, exerting an influence upon how the vacation ownership product is designed, built, and tailored to their ever increasing demands. The following summarizes design changes that have occurred over the past twenty years as reported by McMullen, Zanini, Fugleberg, and Donovan, 2000).

Consumer-driven Influences

In the 1970s, timeshare developers typically catered to the family market, which influenced unit design in a variety of tourist destinations ranging from beachfront to mountain, ski, and entertainment areas. The campus-style resort at that time was designed as a two-bedroom, two-bath unit that gradually evolved into a two-master suite unit. In addition, during this period resorts were designed to appeal to the sports-minded enthusiast. In golf-oriented resorts, the product was commonly sold to foursomes. With so many occupants, the design necessitated the presence of two beds in each bedroom. In this type of market, the designer typically built the units with additional space to accommodate luggage, equipment, and other personal items. The standard configuration for these campus style structures was the two- to three-level condo-style structures with surrounding onsite recreational activities. In the twenty-first century this campus style of timeshare resort has gravitated toward townhouse and single-family units with individual pools. Timeshare resort projects of the 1970s were typified by a small number of units (e.g., 50 units), whereas projects of the twenty-first century are markedly larger in scale. For instance, projects with 900 or more units are not an anomaly in the present day, yet these mammoth projects are not without design and service challenges. In line with the construction of these multiphase timeshare projects, the developer builds each residential accommodation in stages whereby the next phase is started with each successive stage being sold out at a level of 50 percent or higher. The reason for this is to make sure that sufficient capital and demand are present before the next residential building is constructed. The residential units are built in phases because the sales pace often falls behind construction of the units. This rather challenging fact means that the developer must engage in a rental program to defray the costs associated with each additional building while waiting for sales activity to catch up with construction. The basic process is to use the initial building phases as long-term rentals, then to phase to short-term rentals of six months or less, and finally to convert the remaining inventory to timeshare units, after all residential phases are complete. Furthermore, the growth in the number of residential units coincides with the size of the individual unit from less than 100 square feet to over 2,000 square feet per unit/villa.

Key Point 1.5

> Resort design has changed over the years to reflect the lifestyles and recreational preferences of the intended target market. This is reflective of an industry that actively uses segmentation theory and is in a growth mode.

During the 1980s timeshare resort units were commonly designed with two bedrooms and two full baths for a maximum bedroom capacity of six to eight people; urban resorts featured one-bedroom units that typically slept four or six people; and studio units accommodated two to four people. By and large, this capacity pattern per type of unit has changed very little over the years (Upchurch, 2002; ARDA 2003a and 2003b).

The international consumer has always been a preferred target market in tourist destinations such as Orlando, Florida. The unique factor relative to this market is that the length of stay pattern is longer (up to four weeks), therefore necessitating extra space for luggage and personal belongings. This market is always interested in onsite recreational services for the pleasure of the entire family ranging from golf to tennis, basketball, shuffleboard, and other activities.

A smaller but influential market segment that also began in the 1970s to the 1990s was the unmet need for timeshare units in urban locations. To satisfy this need, the developer entered this market by purchasing existing hotels or condominiums that were either in primary or secondary markets. The primary physical difference between urban timeshares and leisure destination timeshares is that the urban timeshares are configured as high-rise facilities with limited recreational amenities available to the owner.

Evolution of Industry Standards

The trade literature implies that the entrance of the branded hotel companies such as Marriott, Hilton, Hyatt, and Disney in the 1980s and 1990s immediately enhanced design standards and service standards. There is no doubt that these companies did bring standardization and credibility to the timeshare industry. But more importantly, the exchange companies implemented a resort rating system that placed all timeshare resorts on an equivalent measurement system. The two major exchange companies, Resort Condominiums International (RCI) and Interval International (II), have devised a rating system to gauge the "quality" of resort furnishing and service levels. These systems classify resorts based on particulars such as ease of guest flow, presence of private sleeping areas, bathrooms that are accessible without walking through the bedroom, kitchen amenities based on the size of the unit, and other amenities considered mandatory (e.g., partial or full kitchen, with a coffeemaker, small refrigerator, microwave, oven, and four-burner stove). Additional, particulars are wet bars, larger televisions, or VCRs, depending on the unit and market. The outcome of RCI's and II's rating system is that the higher the level of amenities and services offered, the higher the resort's quality rating will be. The benefits of these rating systems are numerous, ranging from elevated product quality to the most important being that consumers now had a means to learn what level of product and service quality existed at any number of resorts that they could potentially exchange. Hence, these ratings systems strongly influence the initial marketing encounter when a prospect is trying to determine the credibility and value of purchasing at a given site, and after-the-sale the newly minted owner has a means by which to gauge resort quality with a global perspective.

The Product Life Cycle and the Timeshare Product

The growing industry evolves from introduction of a concept to growth, maturity, and eventual decline. The initial stage of exploration is typified by a newly found curiosity in traveling to the area. The next stage reflects this newfound interest in traveling to the area in that services begin to be established that serve the needs of this traveling public. The third stage, the most robust in terms of physical development of the area, is typified by rapid product and service development. However, this rapid development becomes an issue to the residents and to policy agents relative to the impacts of tourism on the community. Hence, it is in the development phase that economic, sociological, cultural, and ecological impacts become an issue. In addition, this development phase is commonly associated with considerable advertising and promotional efforts aimed at attracting tourists and in maintaining a balance with available resources. The last phase is strongly impacted by positive or negative events that have occurred during the development phase. Hence, the final stage of decline is largely contingent on the tourist destination's ability to cope with the identified tourism impacts. If the issues are insurmountable, then decline follows with a concomitant drop in tourist arrivals to the area. However, if policies are enacted that sustain the balance between precious resources and tourist demands, then the probability of decline is averted.

Richard Butler is a noted expert that developed a life cycle model explaining tourism product development. In general terms, at the early stages of the development of tourism, the exploration stage and the involvement stage, minimal facilities are provided for the tourist and the region is visited by only a few tourists. During the development stage, infrastructure and services grow rapidly. In the consolidation and stagnation stages with high-class and abundant facilities, the main emphasis is on maintaining a targeted approach to tourist marketing in a highly competitive environment. It is this competitive environment in the stagnation phase that slows down product expansion rapidly (see Figure 1.2).

Following Butler's model, it can be ascertained that the vacation ownership industry is still entrenched in the development

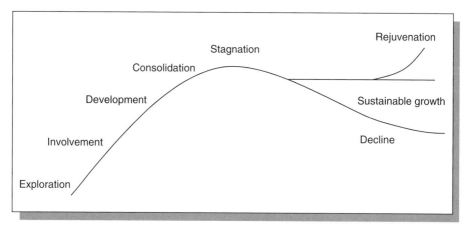

Figure 1.2 Butler's Product Life Cycle

phase of the tourism product life cycle (Butler, 1980). This is supported by the prevalence of timeshare resorts in commonly accepted tourist destinations such as Orlando and Las Vegas. According to ARDA, 24 percent of the timeshare industry is located in Florida, with Orlando being the most concentrated city. The breakdown of the timeshare industry in the United States is Florida (36%), California (12%), South Carolina (12%), Hawaii (7%), Colorado (7%), North Carolina (6%), Nevada (6%), Texas (5%), and Arizona (4%) (ARDA, 2003). The growth of vacation ownership resorts within these states and others is indicative of an industry that is deeply entrenched in the development phase. Therefore, an argument can be made that the industry is in the early stages of Butler's development phase for two reasons. First, there is evidence of economic, sociological, cultural, and ecological impacts of vacation ownership in the main media stream.

Applying Butler's Resort Life Cycle to Timesharing

Relative to Butler's product life-cycle theory, tourism progresses through the stages of exploration, involvement, development, consolidation, stagnation, and finally decline (Butler, 1980). The initial stage, *exploration*, is typified by a newly found curiosity in traveling to the area. In this phase, product branding and quality levels are established; pricing is set at a level that appeals to the consumer price point and therefore builds interest; distribution is selective by focusing on primary markets such as areas of high tourist flow; and promotional efforts center on those that fit the profile of early adopters.

Key Point 1.6

In the context of Butler's resort life-cycle theory, the timeshare industry has progressed out of the exploration phase into the early stages of development/growth.

The *involvement* stage reflects the developer's desire to refine its marketing and sales efforts to better attract potential consumers in the resort's geographical location. During this stage, the timeshare developer refines its marketing channels and engages in various onsite and offsite marketing programs that present messages appealing to individuals with a profile similar to that of the early adopters of the timeshare product.

The *development stage* is the most robust in terms of physical development of the area and is typified by rapid product and service development. The resort product quality is maintained and improved upon, and other features and support services are added to the offerings. Along with these quality enhancements the developer is driving consumer demand, with the result that the price points begin to move upward. The marketing and sales engine during this phase is robust owing to further refinement of marketing strategies that differentiate the lifestyle needs of existing and potential consumers for existing consumers. This phase is often marked by the creation of differing resort products, thus being representative of differing market segments. However, this rapid development becomes an issue to the residents and to policy agents relative to the impacts that tourism is having on the community. The development phase (also known as the growth phase) is where the economic, sociological, cultural, and ecological impacts become an issue. This development phase is commonly associated with considerable advertising and promotional efforts aimed at attracting tourists and at maintaining a balance with available resources. Therefore, the development stage is representative of a rapid increase in both sales and profits and is a time when the developer focuses on market share via market penetration strategies. By this stage, the timeshare developer is leveraging sophisticated market segmentation strategies and clearly knows which channels of distribution yield the highest rate of return. In doing so, the developer is leveraging multiple channels for specific target markets. Hence, competition during this phase is very intense industrywide.

The growth stage is closely followed by the *consolidation* (alias the maturity) stage and is the natural progression of a market that has matured in terms of competition and consumer demand. In this phase, industry competition intensifies, and therefore marketing becomes the key to the timeshare developer's success. This stage is marked by defense of market share while maximizing profits; addition of product features that differentiate the developer's product from that of the competition; and stagnant or lower pricing due to competition. In addition, existing marketing channels are already refined, which means that developers begin to offer incentives to stay competitive; all promotional activities stress product and service differentiation over that of the competition.

Stagnation is the phase between maturity and decline that is characterized by very low cost of product delivery, sales have peaked and profits are beginning to level off.

The *decline* phase, the final stage in the life cycle, is strongly impacted by positive or negative outcomes of the intensive competition of the previous stage. This does not necessarily mean that the developer should now abandon the product altogether, but rather that the introduction of new strategies might be in order. These could include new versions, new distribution methods, or price reductions—in short, anything that will inject a little life into the cycle. If the issues are insurmountable, then decline follows with a concomitant drop in tourist arrivals to the area. However, if policies are enacted that sustain the balance between precious resources and tourist demands, then the probability of decline is averted. Another option during this phase is for the developer to rejuvenate his product offerings by adding uniquely different resorts or resorts with new and appealing features. Of course, some developers may decide to engage in niche marketing by catering to a very specific target market. The last viable option is to consolidate resources by liquidating remaining inventory to other industry development.

Applying Butler's Theory to the Timeshare Industry

In applying Butler's resort life-cycle theory, it can be ascertained that the timeshare industry is still entrenched in the development phase of the tourism product life cycle. This is supported by the prevalence of timeshare resorts in commonly accepted tourist destinations such as Orlando and Las Vegas. When you reflect on the proliferation of trade and academic literature that focuses on topics relating to timesharing it is easy to recognize that the advancement of timeshare resort development within the United States and Europe is in strong evidence. Such publications include *Vacation Industry Review* (produced by Interval International), *Ventures* (produced by Resort Condominium International), *Developments* (produced by American Resort Development Association), *Vacation Ownership World* (private trade publication), *The Timeshare Industry Resource Manual* (produced by the American Resort Development Association), industry reports by various consulting groups (Ex. Interval International and RCI Consulting, the *International Journal of Hospitality Management*, *Journal of Retail and Leisure Property*, *Tourism Analysis*, and the *Cornell Hotel and Restaurant Administration Quarterly*, and the *Journal of Hospitality and Tourism Research*. The topics covered in these publications include property management, owner services, legal issues, product design and proliferation, sales and marketing strategies, consumer acceptance, financial impacts, economic impacts, increased competition, and a host of ancillary topics that highlight the sustained growth of the timeshare industry.

Key Point 1.7

The indicators of number of owners, growth in resorts, sales volume increases, increased competition, and refinement of marketing strategies indicate that the timeshare industry as a whole is in the early phases of Butler's development stage.

Growth Phase—Marketing Tactic Refinement

The second means of documenting that the vacation owner-ship industry is in the development phase is attributed to the plethora of marketing and sales programs that are devoted to either "pushing" or "pulling" the prospective consumer to purchase the timeshare product. This is a logical finding because the timeshare product is still not a sought-after good. Therefore, the developer expends considerable sales and marketing resources in an effort to place the vacation owner-ship product before potential timeshare consumers. In fact, the sales and marketing costs account for 40 to 60 percent of the initial product cost. Still, the use of various sales and mar-keting distribution channels alludes to the maturation of the vacation ownership industry. Instead of relying on face-to-face personal selling as the sole means of reaching the con-sumer, the timeshare industry is actively employing advanced strategies to promote its products. For instance, Fairfield Communities entered into a cooperative marketing agreement with Taylor Made golf products to cooperatively advertise their products. This transaction has enabled Fairfield Communities and Taylor Made to reduce their indi-vidual marketing costs while increasing their exposure to a wider consuming audience. This is not an uncommon prac-tice within the industry as a whole, and in turn these activi-ties are indicative of a maturing industry. Furthermore, the sustained double-digit growth as reported by ARDA gives testament to an industry that is in the early stages of growth. These growth figures, in combination with the fact that many branded hotel companies entered the timeshare market as early as 1984 and throughout the 1990s, indicate that the mar-ket is expanding nationally and internationally, thus repre-senting the growth cycle as noted by Butler.

The sales and marketing costs account for 40 to 60 percent of the initial product cost (ARDA, 1999b). Still, the use of var-ious sales and marketing distribution channels reveals the maturation of the vacation ownership industry. Instead of relying on face-to-face personal selling as the sole means of reaching the consumer, the timeshare industry is actively employing advanced strategies to promote its products.

Growth Phase—Product Design Advances

As the industry has matured in the number of resorts and geographical locations, so has the physical design of the resort. The observation that the timeshare product has been differentiated in product type is supported by a tiered classification system proposed by McMullen and Crawford-Welch (1999). In this system, there are five levels of timeshare products available in the marketplace: luxury, up-market, quality, value, and economy. The *luxury* market provides a product in the $20,000 range per interval that is commonly found in tourist destinations, and it offers a wide array of services and amenities. The luxury timeshare product is often a penthouse style of construction with about 1,500 square feet or more of unit space. The *up-market* is priced a little lower at $15,000 to $25,000; it is also a destination resort with approximately 1,000 square feet of space for a one-room unit and 1,800 square feet for a two-bedroom unit. The *quality* level is priced at $9,000 to $17,000 and is located in a destination area, with an average square footage of 800 for a one-room unit or 1,400 for a two-bedroom unit. The *value* level is often considered a regional resort/facility that is priced in the $7,000 to $10,000 range. The one-bedroom unit in this type of facility has about 800 square feet of space, whereas the two-bedroom unit has 1,000 square feet of unit space. The *economy* level also is found in regional markets, is priced from $5,000 to $8,000, has 600 square feet for a studio unit, and is approximately 900 square feet for a one-bedroom unit (McMullen and Crawford-Welch, 1999; Upchurch, 2002).

The price per weekly interval has generally increased since 1999 as reflected in the 2002 Financial Performance study conducted by ARDA. This national study found that the weighted average price of a timeshare week sold in 2001 was $15,571, which is an increase of 7 percent over figures reported in 2000 (ARDA, 2002a and b). In the 2004 Financial Performance Study of the Timeshare Industry conducted by PriceWaterHouseCoopers on behalf of the American Resort Development Association, the price for a week interval ranged from $13,950 to $15,055 with the weighted average being $14,652 (ARDA, 2004a). This latter study from an aggregate perspective indicates that the price per week remains relatively stable for the last couple of years, with the differentiating factor being that total sales increased by 11.2 percent in 2002 from 2001. This finding indicates that consumer acceptance is continuing to increase from a worldwide perspective.

Growth Phase—Sustained Acceptance of Timeshare Product

The American Resort Development Association (ARDA) is a not-for-profit professional trade association representing the vacation ownership and resort development industries. Established in 1969 and based in Washington, D.C., ARDA is the only international trade association that represents all facets of the vacation ownership resort industry. It has reported double-digit growth in the industry over the past twenty years, 6.7 million owners worldwide, and significant economic impacts as indicated by sales volume noted in Figure 1.3. All of these indicators signify that the acceptance of the vacation ownership product is on the rise. The assumption is that all the aforementioned factors have contributed to the stature and acceptance of this industry as a whole (ARDA, 2003). Clearly, an industry that has sustained

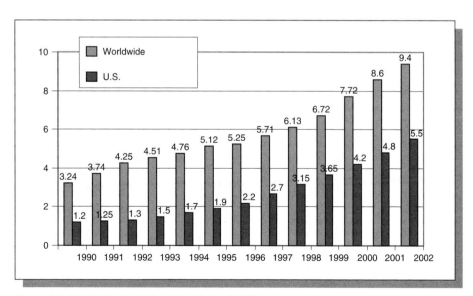

Figure 1.3 Worldwide and U.S. sales volume (in billions)

double-digit growth over the past twenty years in combination with an 80 to 90 percent owner satisfaction rating is very admirable indeed.

Growth Phase—Sustained Industry Volume and Growth

In support of this sustained growth, Figure 1.4 reported in an industry publication titled *Vacation Ownership World*, shows sustained vibrancy of the vacation ownership industry. Interestingly, the timesharing industry reported its first member of the $500-million-a-year club—the Marriott Vacation Club International (MVCI)—in 1999. MVCI amassed $540 million in sales in that year, followed by sales of $900 million in 2002 and $1,050 billion in 2003. This is phenomenal growth by one single developer. Yet, MVCI is just one developer in this global timeshare market. To gain a better understanding of the industry's overall magnitude, we should note that in 2003 thirty-four timeshare developers reported $20 million or more in timeshare or fractional sales (*Vacation Ownership*, 2004: 8–9).

The impact of branding, whether by corporate expansion or acquisition, accounts for rapid consumer acceptance. It is estimated that 60 to 70 percent of the general public gains a

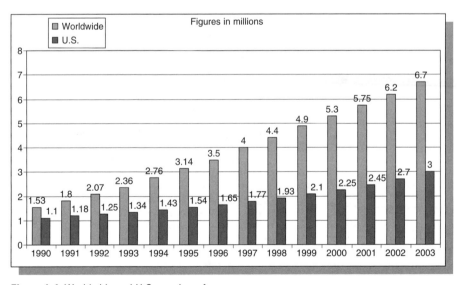

Figure 1.4 Worldwide and U.S. number of owners

measure of comfort when purchasing products from recognized names (*Vacation Ownership World,* 2000). Additional advantages of branding are the association of quality with name recognition, exploitation of database lists, branch networks, and reservation systems. It is clear that the brands are making a major impact in the timeshare industry. In fact, the top ten companies in vacation ownership, in terms of sales volume, are either associated with brands or are rapidly attempting to establish a brand. It is not a foregone conclusion that timesharing will draw the attention of additional "traditional" lodging corporations owing to its profitability and attractive client base.

Reflective Practice

Read current trade publications for information that would confirm that the timeshare industry is in the development phase of Butler's model. You should seek out performance metrics as described in this chapter, expansion into existing or new markets, product proliferation, and marketing programs that indicate further refinement of existing market segments.

Conclusion

The timeshare resort industry has evolved since the 1970s in sheer number of owners, number of resorts, increased sales volume, design and layout, and national and international locations. Few hospitality and tourism industries can boast sustained double-digit percentage growth in a period when worldwide economic conditions have moved up and down. Perhaps more importantly, this same time period saw the entrance of Disney, Hilton, Hyatt, Marriott, Starwood, and Wyndham into the business of selling timeshare intervals. Representing a radical departure from what these hotel companies did as their main strategic business unit, their industry move was therefore considered risky. Conversely, the brands have brought their philosophy of quality control and their strong ethical code to the timeshare industry, which has almost elevated the credibility of the timeshare product in the eyes of the general public.

The application of Butler's resort life-cycle model is particularly appropriate for the timeshare industry given the theory's ability to predict the stage in which an industry is in at any given point in time. Basically, Butler's model provides a rubric by which a developer can analyze its current position in the marketplace and, if needed, adjust the company's product offerings, promotional strategies, pricing tactics, deployment of human resources, and geographical dispersion of resorts.

In closing, today's timeshare product is an intriguing vacation accommodation alternative as compared to the traditional vacation resort, offering the consumer the option of owning (or at least experiencing for a lengthy amount of time via a right-to-use agreement) a private resort environment that is designed to fulfill a lifetime of dream vacations. Given the sustained development patterns being reported (ARDA, 1999a and b, ARDA, 2003; Pryce, 1999; Interval International, 2001), it is clear that consumer interest is on the rise.

Timeshare Resort Development and Financing

After studying this chapter you should be able to:

- understand the developer's role in developing timeshare resorts.

- analyze the external factors that impact resort development.

- evaluate project feasibility considerations.

- critically discuss project design considerations.

Introduction

Chapter 1 drew attention to the dramatic growth of the timeshare industry over the past thirty years within the United States and across the globe. The primary message was that the timeshare industry's growth has been pushed into the market in almost every instance, given the radically different nature of the timeshare product as having similarities with full home ownership while boasting recreational services commonly offered by traditional destination resorts. The Urban Land Institute and the American Hotel and Motel Association have reported a rich body of literature on resort development through textbooks, manuscripts, and articles. There is a paucity of development literature, however, on timeshare resorts; however, the Urban Land Institute has produced a timeshare development textbook as well as ancillary material covering the basic resort development process. As such, the theoretical foundation concerning factors influencing resort development has been tested and proven time and time again by various condominium, hotel, resort, and timeshare developers, with the end being that the same basic models of resort development are identical in principle to that of timeshare resort development. The principles that underlie these sources are outlined in this chapter, which discusses site selection, land value issues, competitor characteristics, geographical market characteristics, consumer demand characteristics, and project financing strategies. However, before dealing with these proven components of resort development, a general discussion of who the major timeshare developers are in the marketplace and the general design trends is in order.

When one thinks about the lodging industry, the names of branded hotels such as Disney, De Vere, Hilton, Hyatt, Marriott, Starwood, and Wyndham and many more hotel companies immediately come to mind. This is because these hotels have long served the general public and have developed effective marketing programs designed to cater to the business, leisure, association, government, and other consumer segments in national and international locations.

The concept of lodging and quality service, having a history dating back to biblical and early Roman times, is ingrained in the minds of consumers. In contrast, the timeshare resort product has only existed in the United States since the 1970s and is relatively unknown by the general public. Since the 1970s, the timeshare industry has gone through a variety of changes ranging from industry maturation to product advancements (Upchurch, 2002).

Relative to the evolution of the timeshare industry in the United States, the timeshare industry originated from the efforts of independent timeshare developers that operated from one to sometimes less than six projects at a time that were typically regional in scope. The face of the industry changed rapidly in 1984 with Marriott's purchase of American Resorts. It was not too long thereafter that other lodging companies followed suit. In fact, Hilton, Disney in 1994, Hyatt, and Starwood entered the timeshare marketplace in the 1990s, with Wyndham following in 2002. The importance of their entrance into this market is related to the perception of legitimacy and quality that these organizations brought to the market. In other words, consumers assumed that this industry must be legitimate if these tried and true lodging brands were getting into the picture. In light of this discussion, the reader might be given the impression that the timeshare industry is exclusively dominated by the lodging brands. While this industry gained great momentum after these lodging giants entered the market, far more independent timeshare developers than branded companies currently sell timeshare intervals.

Timeshare Resort Product Evolution

In referencing product changes since the 1970s, the timeshare resort product has evolved from conversion of hotel properties, condominiums, and apartments, with the smaller percentage being purpose-built timeshare resorts. The current trend is to build each timeshare as a purpose-built facility that offers the consumer the ultimate in space and luxury (e.g., a two-bedroom unit with approximately 1,350 square feet of space). However, the push for uniqueness in property design is not the only change that has evolved. Another change that came in the late 1990s was the construction of mixed-use timeshare resorts, fractional timeshare resorts, and private residence clubs. The mixed-use timeshare resorts combine characteristics of a traditional resort with those of a timeshare resort, meaning that part of the facility is operated as a traditional resort along with its full amenities and services, while a separate portion is operated under an ownership mode (alias timeshare).

Fractional timeshare resorts came into existence to satisfy pent-up consumer demand for an upscale product that could offer the potential owner more than one week of time. It is not unusual to find a fractional timeshare that offers increments in three-week, four-week, ten-week, or twelve-week segments. Who buys a fractional ownership? Fractional ownership interests appeal to an upscale consumer who can afford a whole ownership condominium, but prefers a fractional interest for a portion of the cost. It is not unusual to find fractional interests priced in the $200,000 to $300,000 range for a six-week interval, which makes the purchase of a fractional ownership interest a high-involvement decision. The most recent entrant into the timeshare product line is a concept known as private residence clubs. Private residence clubs entered the market post–2000 in reaction to an unmet need for a higher-end fractional ownership product that rivaled services and amenities typically offered by private equity country clubs. These facilities are typically associated with larger square footage units, golf courses and pro shop services, dining facilities, spas, and other recreational services (Suchman, 1999; Upchurch, 2002).

The timeshare industry is part of the real estate industry inasmuch as this product is being sold as a deeded interest (or as a leasehold), with the end result being that an interested consumer leaves the sales floor owning a week at a generously decorated timeshare resort. It is important to note this connection with the real estate industry because real estate is integrally related to the national and local economies (McMahan, 1989). Granted this relationship is not totally transparent, but there are logical connections between economic conditions and the development of timeshare resorts. Perhaps the most obvious connection between the economy and the development of a timeshare resort is the association between supply and demand within the context of a strong market. Still, the development of a timeshare resort is not based solely on supply and demand characteristics. Other concerns, such as land availability, supply patterns, labor, materials, and sufficient capital, are to be pondered long before any kind of physical construction begins.

The Role of the Timeshare Resort Developer

The timeshare developer plans, designs, and constructs a planned resort community that offers consumers an ownership experience, via a deed or some derivative of a right-to-use agreement, at an exclusive resort that is ornamented with what is commonly referred to as condominium-style accommodations (Crotts and Ragatz, 2002; Rezak, 2002). To offer such lavish resort accommodations and to provide consumers with a lifetime of vacation memories through the use of their timeshare interval, a timeshare developer must be able to satisfy the following areas of specialization:

- *Sufficient knowledge of real estate law, timeshare product registration statutes, and other regulatory state and federal requirements.* This requisite knowledge ranges from registering the product with the appropriate regulatory bodies (e.g, state board of regulation, land management, etc.) up to and including sales and marketing laws concerning consumer protection laws and interstate commerce.

- *Sufficient organizational structure to support the unique functional aspects of timesharing.* At a minimum, the timeshare developer should have qualified experts in the skill areas of timeshare (a) sales, (b) marketing, (c) telesales and telemarketing, (d) owner services, (e) human resources, (f) legal and regulatory compliance, (g) contract law/consumer contracting, and (h) resort property management.

- *Sufficient knowledge of financial management.* Knowledge in this skill area encompasses investment strategies for project development and long-term solvency of the timeshare developer. This includes financial strategies concerning consumer receivables, hypothecation, and securitization. This skill area is perhaps the most critical because there must be sufficient capital and cash flow to sustain the high debt structure associated with development for at least five years.

- *Sufficient knowledge of consumer accounting.* This skill area is directed toward accounting for receipt of consumer loans, review and advisement of reserves, capital expenditures, and operational budgets as assigned to the developer's timeshare resorts (either under developer or home owner control). In the latter case, the developer is serving as the property management entity.

- *Sufficient knowledge of home owner association management.* After a specified point of sellout, many states require that the home owners are given the right to develop a home owners association. It is this association's legal right to oversee the operation and upkeep of the timeshare resort. In this regard, the developer needs to be prepared to train the home owners association's board of directors in their fiduciary responsibilities as mandated by the state.

- *Sufficient knowledge of resort property management.* After the resort project is turned over to the home owners association, the timeshare developer typically offers property management services to the home owners association. These oversight services range from housekeeping, maintenance, registration (owner check-in/check-out), finance and accounting, and landscaping (Suchman, 1999; McMahan, 1989).

For a timeshare developer to be successful, these skills areas must be incorporated into the strategic plan of the organization. Once these skills areas are incorporated into the organization's fabric, it is crucial for each functional department or division to understand the role that each plays in the development process. Why is this? The most direct answer is that the timeshare resort development process requires the integration and coordination of these skills areas so that the timeshare product can be brought to market effectively and efficiently. This is very important to note for three reasons; first, the current regulatory environment requires considerable attention relative to proper registration and statute compliance; second, the timeshare product is not a sought-after product, which means that sales and marketing efforts are a priority from the outset of the project; and third, all these skills areas converge at the point of consumption, which means that the consumer is provided with a quality product that is legitimate and need-fulfilling (Upchurch, 2002).

Key Point 2.1

The development of timeshare resorts requires knowledge of real estate law, internal human resource development, financial management, consumer financing, association management, and resort property management.

Resort Development—Proven Models

A favorite saying in the lodging industry is that all developers must master three important factors concerning site selection: (1) location, (2) location, and (3) location. Other factors of course influence the resort build-out process, but locating a resort property in a very accessible and highly trafficked area can overcome other shortcomings. This is perhaps why many timeshare developments are located in destination markets such as Vail, Colorado; Orlando, Florida; Las Vegas, Nevada; Branson, Missouri; and Pigeon Forge, Tennessee. Because these are destination markets, other draws bring volumes of vacation travelers to the area, which makes a point-intercept location strategy a logical choice. Still this is one of but many location strategies that have worked well for various timeshare developers (Barrett and Blair, 1988).

The Destination Factor

The markets mentioned earlier (Vail, Orlando, Las Vegas, Branson, and Pigeon Forge) are all located in tourist destinations noted for their leisure, recreation, cultural, historical, educational, gaming, or some other form of drawing power.

31

Therefore, the destination location strategy of being located near the primary tourist draw makes a timeshare resort very appealing to consumers owing to their proximity to the local attraction. A related benefit to the timeshare developer is that the surrounding area will typically offer a wide variety of retailing, restaurants, and staple providers that are of value to the timeshare owner. In addition, these markets typically offer access to a sizable labor market that is already training in the skill sets needed by the timeshare operation.

The Proximity Factor

A necessary part of constructing a timeshare resort, as with hotels and resorts, is access to electricity, gas, sewer, telephone, and water supplies. If these utilities already exist in the area and connection permission can be acquired from the appropriate municipality, then another major factor of site selection is satisfied. In most cases, the timeshare developer will have to present the economic benefits of building the timeshare resort to the building commission. This is especially important to note because many municipalities control growth through the building permit process. The type of information that the timeshare developer should present to the building commission includes projected property taxes, number of jobs and level of jobs created (line level, supervisory, and managerial), environmental impacts, and estimated expenditures within the local economy.

Other aspects under this particular strategy include access to police and fire protection services. If the timeshare resort is not easily accessible or is located in such a way that response time is limited, then it will be more difficult to sell a prospect on the concept of ownership.

Key Point 2.2

Key determinants of a resort's location encompass access to a sufficient number of consumers that fit the intended purchaser profile, proximity to points of interest, resort accessibility, environmental impact concerns, price per parcel, feasibility considerations, competitor characteristics, demand factors, pricing metrics, economic considerations, and regulatory issues.

The Accessibility Factor

The physical location of the resort must accommodate a variety of on-campus and off-campus access issues (meaning on- or offsite). Of first importance is how readily accessible the resort is to main thoroughfares so that resort owners can easily get to retail establishments, entertainment sources, restaurants, and other areas of interest by means of personal vehicles or public transportation. Not only should the resort location have ease of access to off-campus services, but it should also afford the resort owners an element of safe entrance and exit from the resort facilities. In brief, an entryway or exit that leads onto a highly congested roadway is less than favorable to most resort owners because of safety and privacy issues.

Reflective Practice

Develop a rubric that measures the accessibility of a resort and the attractiveness of the resort's proximity to area tourist destinations. Once you have this rubric developed you are to visit a local timeshare resort and apply your instrument. After you have conducted your analysis, you are to discuss your findings in class.

From an on-campus perspective, the physical site should offer enough space to support ease of access to physical features of interest to the resort owners. A good example of this would be enough space for a private walkway to the beach, tennis courts, golf course, or other planned recreational services. Another on-campus issue of importance to resort owners is that sufficient parking space is available for their personal automobile(s), that parking is secure, and that it is conveniently located to their unit/villa.

The Environmental Factor

Developers consider environmental impacts from a couple of different angles (see Table 2.1). The first area of concern is that the timeshare resort does not cause a negative impact on surrounding businesses or residential areas. For example,

---

Site Selection Considerations

Are the physical considerations of the parcel suitable for the timeshare resort development?

Is the site accessible to major roadways and other modes of transportation?

Are there tourist draws in the area that can bring a sufficient supply of prospects?

Does the parcel have utility access? Or will this have to be established?

How seasonal is the immediate tourist market? Is there an off-season?

What timeshare resorts are in the immediate area?

Can the developer's estimated return on investment be made for the amount invested?

Will the parcel offer privacy and safety to the owners?

Table 2.1 Site Selection Considerations for Timeshare Development

excessive water runoff that would cause erosion would be less than a positive outcome for surrounding or potential business and residential areas. A second and more pressing concern occurs when the timeshare development disturbs the natural habitat of protected animals or rare flora or fauna that are indigenous to the area. Granted this should not occur given the permit to build approval process, but the timeshare developer still has an obligation to ensure that such actions do not occur. A third concern arises when the timeshare development disrupts the local residents' daily routines or enjoyment of the natural environment. For instance, if the development blocks residents' view of a mountain range, lake, or some other natural scenery, there is likely to be a negative backlash from the community. Any such adverse situation will strain community relations and may make the resort owners feel less than welcome.

There are, of course, many site considerations involved in the process of selecting a parcel of land other than those previously mentioned, some of which are mentioned in Table 2.1. As alluded to earlier the physical placement of the resort is tied to accessibility as well as the drawing power of immediate tourist attractions, presence of retail outlets, entertainment and other sought after products and services. Aligning with this "drawing power" of the immediate locale is the tourist appeal to these products and services. In essence, the greater this association, the greater is the flow of tourists that are drawn to leisure and recreational services as offered at timeshare resorts. Due to this relationship it is no surprise to find a high concentration of timeshare resorts in tourist destinations. Once this level of demand is determined, the timeshare developer turns his or her attention toward analyzing the quanitity and quality of other timeshare resort developments in the area, both current and proposed, availability of land and the price of such, access to utilities for the development of the resort, and a watchful eye toward the privacy of safety of those that will eventually purchase at this resort.

The Land Value Factor

The value of the land has a direct connection with the demand for the parcel of land. This is definitely true for timeshare developments because the markets are often considered primary parcels owing to their proximity to tourist attractions and other leisure and recreational attractions. Simply because land is available, this does not mean that the timeshare developer will leap at the chance to purchase primary land. Rather, the timeshare developer has to consider return on investment relative to the asking price of the land. In other words, the higher the projected yield, the greater is the estimated real estate value of the land that is being purchased, which mandates that the astute timeshare resort developer calculate return on investment for purchase of the land, preparation of the land, and construction of the facility. Simply stated, if the asking price exceeds the developer's projections of revenue and cash flow, then an alternative location will be sought or, in some cases, the project will not come to fruition.

The Feasibility Factor

As alluded to earlier, the building of a timeshare resort is a capital-intensive proposition that mandates that the timeshare developer generate an accurate assessment of project yield based on current and projected market conditions. This is not as easy as it might sound given two factors: first, the general public is slowly warming up to the concept of timesharing, and second, the sales and marketing costs alone amount to approximately 40 to 60 percent of a resort project's overall costs. This observation means that the time-share product is "pushed" out to the marketplace in an effort to stimulate demand, which logically places a high level of importance on determining each project's feasibility as accurately as possible from the outset. Therefore, in estimating demand the timeshare developer considers (a) industry reports concerning development patterns and consumer interest, (b) estimates of local tourist demand, (c) an assessment of market saturation, (d) consumer pricing sensitivity, (e) projected economic conditions and travel patterns, (f) a benchmark of other timeshare developments in the area, (g) a review of regulations that surround the timeshare development, (h) a profile of tourist attractions, events, convention centers, and hotel business patterns, and (i) an assessment of labor patterns in the area.

Case Study 2.1

Bob was a recent graduate from a university program that focused on time-share resort development, so he was ready to share his knowledge with his new timeshare employer. His first position was in project feasibility of this upstart timeshare operator. Because this company was new, Bob had free rein in designing a process to determine market conditions and project feasibility. His first decision was to set a strategy meeting with those who worked in the project feasibility department. The first assignment that he gave his staff was to gather information on the financial impact of the industry to the region, to determine the economic impact of the industry on the region, to investigate how present competitors were performing in the area, and to assess owner satisfaction information within the region.

The Benchmark Factor

Whether the developer is an entrant into the market or a seasoned operator, regional and national studies that profile the industry are of tremendous value. The type of information that is generated from industry reports covers the whole gamut of issues related to development and operations.

Overall, these reports can be categorized as financial impact studies, economic impact studies, owner satisfaction surveys, and state of the industry studies, each of which has its own merit to the developer.

Reports classified as *financial impact studies* focus on financial ratios that indicate operational effectiveness for the developer. Typical ratios reported include sales volume, consumer loan down payment, length of consumer loan, percentage of down-payment, aging of receivables (current, 30–60–90), percent and amount of development loans (includes hypothecation, securitization, and sales of receivables), percent and amount allocated to the resort construction process, and percent and amount allocated to running the resort. This information is very useful for timeshare developers when projecting expected revenues and expenditures associated with the resort development process. This information is also useful for publicly traded companies when public releases are made concerning the financial viability and solvency of the industry. From a perspective of advancing timeshare resort development, this kind of report can rapidly attract new entrants into the market. This type of outcome is good for two reasons. First, the entrance of other developers or additional site construction perpetuates the vibrancy of the timeshare product. Second, the increase in product growth offers consumers access to a wider array of products in destinations of their choice.

Reports classified as *economic impact studies* concentrate on the contribution of timeshare development to local, regional, state, and national economies. Statistics collected from these reports include annual sales volume, taxes collected, number employed, and other direct and indirect financial contributions to the economy. This type of report is useful for the timeshare developer in making a case to the city planners concerning the economic benefits of building a timeshare resort in the area.

Key Point 2.3

A main part of the resort's development feasibility analysis hinges on benchmarking the state of the industry and efficiencies of rival competitors.

Owner satisfaction surveys are conducted by consultant firms (e.g., Ragatz and Associates, Yeaswich, Pepperdine, and Brown, PriceWaterHouseCoopers, and other firms), by the two primary exchange companies of Resort Condominiums International (RCI) and Interval International (II), and by timeshare developers. The reports that can be purchased in the public domain are very beneficial to existing and entering timeshare resort developers owing to the content found in these reports. Such information encompasses general consumer satisfaction with products and services, appeal of marketing packages, and consumption of ancillary products (e.g., cruise line exchanges). Of particular value are consumer profiles concerning satisfaction with particular services, expressed desire for services not yet provided, and points of concern that impact the owners' decision to maintain their current consumption level, their interest in purchasing additional time from the same or other timeshare developers, and loyalty factors. This type of consumer information is very valuable in positioning a particular resort within the marketplace.

To date, the *state of the industry reports* have been sanctioned and produced by the American Resort Development Association. Dependent on funding, these state of the industry reports are intended to be an annual review of where the industry stands on factors of: number of resorts, number of units, sales volume, average price per week, number of weeks owned, average maintenance fees, number of owners, purchase motivations, product satisfaction, and consumer demographic and psychographic profile.

The type of information is helpful to the developer because it provides a historical view of the growth, penetration, and acceptance of the timeshare product within geographic regions, states, and host countries. Therefore, an existing or entering developer can take this information and refine his marketing approach, tailor his sales programs to the appropriate markets, and pursue development of resorts in popular geographic locations or plan to enter burgeoning markets.

Perhaps the most important piece of information collected from a state of the industry report involves why consumers buy the timeshare product. Once these factors are ascertained, the timeshare resort project is designed in such a manner as to match or exceed consumer demands. The focus on determining *why* the consumer may or may not buy the timeshare product is extremely important given the high ratio of investment in the sales and marketing process. By doing so, the developer is able to streamline her sales and marketing process so that efficiencies are gained.

The Demand Factor

In an effort to determine the attraction factor for the projected resort's destination, the developer engages in a review of tourist demand information that is readily available from local tourist bureaus, conventional and visitor bureaus, and chamber of commerce offices. The information sought includes volume of tourists (regional, national, and international), seasonality of tourist demand, number of resorts in the area (timeshare and nontimeshare), demographic profile of tourist, and capacity, flow, and design of the roadways and airport in handling present and future traffic volume. This information is collected for two reasons: (1) the developer wants to make sure there is sufficient tour flow in the area, and (2) the consumers who come to this area match an economic and product usage profile as established for the timeshare resort project.

The market for a timeshare development is greatly different from a hotel product and a primary housing market. The consumer of a hotel product is seeking a nonownership temporary lodging experience for leisure, vacation, or business purposes, and the level of frequency of visitation is driven either by accrued personal vacation time (for leisure purposes) and by company demand for business purposes.

Reflective Practice

Contact your local tourist bureau, chamber of commerce, or visitor bureau to determine the demographic of area tourists, annual volume of tourists, available hotel rooms and occupancy rate, available timeshare units in the area, and occupancy level. In your analysis, discuss if the tourist profile appears to match the timeshare consumer market and if growth in timeshare sales is possible based on your analysis.

How does the timeshare consumer differ from the hotel and the primary housing market? The consumer of a primary residence clearly has invested in her primary residence as a means of maintaining and increasing her personal equity, which means that the purchase of the primary residence is an investment strategy. In contrast, timeshare caters to a consumer who seeks a second home that is largely for leisure and vacation purposes and has little if any connection to the conduct of business or for personal investment purposes. Furthermore, the timeshare consumer purchases an interval at a timeshare resort of choice almost exclusively for long-term vacationing. Given this analysis, it is safe to say that a timeshare purchase fits on the spectrum of frequency of usage as greater than that of the hotel guest (on the typical annual stay profile) but less than full home ownership. The general assumption of this view is that because they stay longer than the typical hotel guest the economic contribution to the local economy is conceptually greater. Therefore, the astute timeshare developer would gather information concerning average number of meals eaten out, average number of dollars spent on meals, entertainment, attractions, and related expenditure patterns that would in turn be presented to the local building commission as evidence of economic benefits associated with construction of the planned timeshare resort.

Part of the market saturation process will entail a review of existing timeshare operations in the immediate market area that cater to the "same" consumer that the proposed development is targeting. The initial step in this process is to review building permits for existing timeshare developments to gauge the total units, units sold, units available, mix of units (lockoff, one-room villa, two-bedroom villa, three-bedroom villa, etc.), unit amenities offered, recreational services, type of common ground areas, salesforce characteristics (e.g., pay scale of sales personnel, commissions paid, closing ratios), market program success (both onsite and offsite programs), pricing points per unit type, owner demographic and lifestyle characteristics, and a qualitative assessment of the internal strengths (e.g., management experience) and external weaknesses (e.g., lack of brand-name recognition) associated with each timeshare development. This analysis of the competition would not be complete without reviewing existing timeshare rental programs. In cases where a timeshare resort offers a rental program, the developer should gather information on the viability of the resort's rental program in terms of units rented, fees paid, and conversion of rental guests into owners.

The Price Factor

Another factor centers on the disposable income of the proposed timeshare consumer. Generally, households that demand private, upscale secondary housing will generally pay for the luxury, quality, and convenience that a timeshare resort offers within destinations of interest. This is assuredly the case as reported in various industry reports that rank quality of accommodations and services offered as one of the top ten reasons for buying a timeshare (ARDA, 2004b). Two assumptions are being made here: first, there are various demands on the average household's income, and second, not everyone can afford a whole-ownership interest (i.e., fifty-two weeks out of a year). This second point is exactly why a timeshare is appealing to the price-sensitive household. In essence, this means that the developer has to determine the pricing point of the targeted consumer so that sales and marketing efforts will prove to be fruitful. In determining this demand for a timeshare interval, the developer will collect information on family size, employment, household income, disposable income, degree of interest in purchasing a timeshare interval, and pricing sensitivity.

The Economic Factor

Timeshare developers also have to look at the relationship of the national economy to the local economies. Why? This is because fluctuations in the national economy influence stability or instability in local real estate markets. The general association is that demand for real estate is influenced by population growth and shifts in population demographics, which is coupled with employment opportunities and increasing household income. Does this general relationship

false and deceptive sales and marketing activities. In this regard the act of many states requiring sales personnel to be licensed real estate professionals is one step toward overseeing the sales process via a state controlled real estate certification process. At the federal level the reach of the federal government is largely focused on protecting the consumer by applying existing federal laws that range from truth-in-lending, equal opportunity, fair credit reporting, and investment restrictions via legislation designed to protect consumer investments (e.g., Real Estate Settlement Procedures Act and Securities Acts).

The Labor Factor

The need to assess labor problems is directly linked to the construction and preopening operations of the timeshare resort. With regard to construction, the availability of qualified labor in the area is a valuable resource that cannot be overlooked. Some developers may choose to bring in their own construction crew. A word of caution is necessary because the local unions might not allow this type of activity. If this is the case, then the developer must be aware of union regulations and abide by them without fail.

When it comes to the pre-opening phase of the timeshare resort, the developer will hire qualified salespeople from the local community to begin selling timeshare intervals. This can present a dilemma to a timeshare developer because some states require timeshare salespeople to hold a real estate broker's license. If this is the case, the pool of skilled sales representatives might be more restrictive than expected. Furthermore, more extensive training might need to occur if the hired individuals are without timeshare sales experience. This is often the case with new salespeople coming from the automobile, real estate housing, and land sales industries. This is just one example of a labor issue that confronts the developer because the daily operation of a timeshare resort has many other semiskilled and unskilled labor needs. The point is that labor issues do not simply disappear after the resort is built because the developer often retains the property management contract or keeps the title to the underlying real estate and therefore the entire resort operation.

The Immediate Market Condition Factor

The bottom line in choosing a location is that the capacity to absorb timeshare developments has been strong. To acquire this information requires the developer to be diligent in collecting information on existing and planned timeshare resorts for the area in question.

Based on industry estimates of consumer demand for timeshare housing in the market area, the next step is to forecast tour flow and interest in the exact destination and then estimate the resort's tour flow that will be generated via the developer's marketing programs. This information in turn generates yield rates for each marketing program, which in turn assists the developer in projecting sales tour flow volume per day, week, month, quarter, and year. Once this information is determined, it is much easier to estimate the level of market penetration that the resort will garner against other timeshare resorts in the area, if any.

In analyzing the competitive set, the timeshare developer will collect information on the number of timeshare resorts, unit configuration (lockoff, one-bedroom, two-bedroom, three-bedroom), type of recreational services offered, number of units sold (by type), how long the resort has been in operation, whether or not the resort is branded, whether the resort offers a rental program, available resort amenities, proximity to local attractions, ease of access, price points per unit type, sales structure (independent contractor or not), compensation packages (management and nonmanagement), benefit programs, estimates of sales productivity (daily, weekly, monthly, quarterly, and annual), knowledge set of senior management, marketing program structure and marketing program success ratios (if available), tour flow (show rate and no-show rate), prospect profile, and owner profile.

An additional area that is of extreme importance to timeshare resort owners is resort security. As a result of revolving ownership, there will be a high level of families going in and out of the resort on a weekly cycle, which means that it can be difficult to distinguish who is an owner, who is visiting, and who does not belong on the premises. It is therefore in the developer's best interest to evaluate the security systems of other timeshare resorts to determine the type of precautions to implement at the planned resort.

The Capital Factor

As noted earlier, the timeshare industry had a difficult time receiving funding during the 1980s and the 1990s due to image problems (in the 1980s) and a real estate depression (in the 1990s). From the 1990s onward, the real estate market improved, and timeshare developers successfully took their product to the market. The net result was that the number of projects, sales volume, and owners increased both nationally and internationally (Pryce, 2002).

For any project to come to fruition, an appropriate amount of capital must be acquired for the different development phases. If this is not done, the project is in danger of being underfunded and as a result is destined for failure. If failure occurs, the developer's credibility is challenged and the financial industry as a whole reacts by becoming cautious about lending money to a timeshare development. In general, if a project fails, the financial institution has to engage in a foreclosure process, which is good for neither the developer nor the lender. Therefore, it is of prime importance for the developer to have sufficient capital at-hand so that land acquisition, land preparation, and resort construction can occur per schedule (Urban Land Institute, 1987).

As noted earlier, timeshare resorts were built in phases in response to demand patterns and cost reasons. The purchase of a suitable site is based on a price that reflects opportunities for a significant return on investment and for future building of additional timeshare units. The initial pricing of the land can indeed limit future expansion if the pricing exerts a negative influence on available funds for the construction of additional buildings. On the other side of the spectrum, the developer does not want to purchase too much land at the outset just in case the market goes soft, which would mean that the developer would carry the cost of the undeveloped land. In other words, the developer constructs a pro forma analysis that maximizes income and minimizes expenditure estimates for the proposed project. Specifically, the pro forma includes an income statement (sales estimates), capital costs, operating expenses, and return on investment for the life of the project.

The first step in constructing a pro forma analysis is to estimate the development costs associated with the project. Costs associated with the primary site include excavation, foundation footings, parking facilities, common areas, retailing facilities, maintenance facilities, clubhouse facilities, sales center facilities, housekeeping facilities, security facilities, loading bays and docks, and superstructure associated with construction of the villas and recreational facilities such as the golf course, tennis courts, squash courts, and riding trails. Additional costs might be those associated with the demolition of existing structures on the land that cannot be used or those associated with converting existing units that were on the site upon purchase that can be used within the existing resort design. The key goal is to acquire an estimate of the required equity needed to complete this phase of the project (Blicher, 1999).

The second step is to estimate the operating costs associated with the development phase of the project. These costs extend for the life of the project (perhaps five to seven years) before the resort is turned over to the home owners association. This, of course, assumes that the developer is planning to release the rights to the underlying real estate to the home owners association at the designated level of project sellout as determined by state statute. In the case of right-to-use developments (versus deeded estate), the developer will retain control of the underlying real estate and all taxation related to the same. Under this type of real estate transaction, the estimates of operational costs extend past the development phase and into the ongoing operation of the resort. Operational expenses that need to be estimated by the developer include services concerning sales agents, administrative overhead, owner relations, legal counsel, finance and accounting, marketing, telemarketing, and office supplies among many other personnel and nonpersonnel functions. These operating expenses must be evaluated accurately because faulty estimates can lead to missed vendor or mortgage payments that might result in strained relations or eventual loss of property. A critical part of estimating operational expenses is the rationale behind assumptions for each expense item. If, for instance, each sales representative is expected to close three out of ten tours at an average of $20,000 sales each, the sales manager onsite must be very proactive in ensuring that this average is attained. Nonetheless, constant monitoring and reevaluation of the underlying assumptions are instrumental to developer success and especially so in very competitive markets. Perhaps the bottom line is that the best assumptions are based on local market data and cost estimates, and where present, these sources generally serve as a guide for an appropriate ratio of expenses as a percentage of sales volume (Blicher, 1999).

The last piece of the pro forma process takes in the broader picture of determining the level of cash flow appropriate for the planned project. Once the developer has determined sales estimates, expense estimates, and acquired information concerning the project's interest on loans taken out for project purposes, and loan terms, the process of estimating net cash flow, return on equity, and amount of equity to be invested can be determined. For the sake of this cash flow analysis, the typical loan extends for seven years at an interest rate of 10 percent and produces a return on equity in year three of the project. The reader should note that there is a negative cash flow for the first two years of the project and that the developer does not bring a return on cash equity until year six of operation. This estimated cash flow statement indicates that there is little margin for error in the early years, but if the assumptions are followed, the developer reaps a very healthy 32 percent cash return on equity by year seven. Therefore, from a macro perspective the construction of a cash flow projection offers a good estimate of whether or not the resort project makes sense for the developer to engage company resources at the outset of the planning phase (Suchman, 1999; Blicher, 1999).

Key Point 2.4

A pro forma is a financial project of project feasibility that focuses on sufficient cash flow for the planned resort project.

Why is a discussion of market demand, sales (revenue) estimates, expenditure projections, and a cash flow estimate important to the developer? The estimation of market demand, sales and expenditure estimates, and cash flow projections, though a critical element in resort project planning, does not provide the whole picture concerning the financial success of the proposed resort. What must still be addressed is the availability of affordable financing that can support the magnitude of the timeshare resort project. If affordable funding is not available, then it makes very little difference if the operational and cash flow indicators are outstanding.

Funding the Resort Project

The availability of capital lending agencies for the timeshare industry has gained strong interest since the mid- to late 1990s, partly as a result of the general growth of the economy and sustained financial performance by leading timeshare developers. Certainly, the developer has to have a solid reputation within the industry for producing quality developments completed on time and the developer's management structure has to have extensive experience in timeshare resort development. While not the only factors that a lender reviews, these are good qualitative indicators of development success.

Until the late 1990s, very few lenders were willing or understood the nature of timeshare real estate. Needless to say, the general trend of lending capital to a developer for a single-building, 50-room villa expanded to projects that proposed multiple-building developments that numbered up to 1,500 villas within a single site. Clearly, then, lenders were amenable to financing large and complex timeshare resort projects, and they were not overly concerned about the risks associated with such expansive developments. This trend is alive and well today. One can therefore conclude that time-sharing lending has "come of age." If you listen closely to developers talk about their resort developments, you will quickly realize that timeshare development is all about financing. The process of seeking out project funding encompasses determining front-end expenses necessary to get the product from the concept to the development phase, and finally to the point-of-sale, at which time the developer offers an internal loan to consumers who need assistance in financing their timeshare purchase.

Preopening Loan Models

Construction and development loans have to be structured properly so that acquisition and project development can occur as previously described. Construction loans are required to purchase the land and to prepare it for development, whereas development loans take over where the construction loans end so that the development of the physical structures can be accomplished.

The pursuit of construction and development loans is a mainstay of timeshare resort development, and if these principles are not followed, the project never gets off the ground owing to inadequate funding. In order to avoid this type of situation, the developer is challenged to conduct a financial analysis in an effort to determine how much external financing is needed to complete the project. Naturally, during this phase the developer desires to seek out a lending agency that offers the lowest interest rates possible and provides a time-frame that allows the developer to maintain a sufficient cash flow. In doing so, the developer will often seek out a loan for construction that is separate from the development phase. When done in this manner (called multisource funding), the developer is projecting the equity and terms of the construction, and development loans will assure a maximum return on the borrowed capital. Ultimately, the decision to take out a single-source loan covering the process of construction to development, of course, depends on market volatility and other elements of risk. From the financial institution's perspective the developer's risk is determined by reviewing financial market conditions, the developer's ability to provide equity in the project, the availability of other equity sources, the nature of the planned project (e.g., number of units, recreational outlets, phasing, and scope of common areas), the type of usage (deeded, mixed use, right-to-use, etc.), existing relationships with the financial lender or other financial lenders (i.e., financial record), and the developer's management expertise.

Reflective Practice

Interview in person or via phone a lending agency that provides loans to timeshare developers. Your charge is to determine the factors that this organization uses to determine loan risk.

Working-Capital Funding Sources

Various sources of funding are available to the timeshare developer ranging from commercial banks, sale of receivables, hypothecation, Wall Street investment strategies involving securitization, and lending institutions that focus on timeshare real estate transactions. Commercial banks provide funding for short-term to intermediate loans ranging from five to seven years for the primary purpose of constructing and developing the planned resort as noted previously. On the other hand, the proven investment strategies of sales of receivables (consumer notes or consumer end loans), hypothecation, and securitization require professional training in very high-end investment strategies as noted below.

Financial Investment Model: Sale of Consumer End-loans

At the point that the developer engages his or her sales division, the developer is pressed to be vigilant in his or her cash flow estimates in order to sufficiently fund the timeshare sales division. This is a very important consideration because costs associated with sales, marketing, and administrative efforts can range from 40 to 60 percent of the product cost at the point-of-sale. This rather high percentage means that controlling cash flow is critical at the beginning stages of the resort's life.

In the active sales phase, the developer incurs costs associated with providing mortgages to consumers at the point of purchase. This process of providing mortgages to the timeshare consumer is commonly known as end-loan financing and is another source of revenue for the developer that is very distinctive to the timeshare industry. Therefore, it is of the utmost importance to the developer to control the flow of dollars from acquisition up to and including selling the project out because there is very little margin for error in the use of available funds. In fact, certain assumptions apply to the financing of these consumer end-loans that, if not understood, can lead to developer failure in reaching an estimated breakeven point per sale. For example, for an interval price of $10,000 with a consumer downpayment of $1,000 with an assumed advance rate of 90 percent based on the interval sales price (advanced by the lender to the developer), the developer will be left with $100 cash remaining from the sale. The reason for this is that approximately 30 percent mortgage release payments are required of the developer, in addition to approximately 60 percent operating expenses associated with the process of marketing and selling the timeshare product. These costs have the net effect of compressing developer gross yield during the first two to three years of being on the market.

A strategic business center for the timeshare developer is offering purchasers the option of financing their purchase onsite via a credit arrangement. The timeshare developer allows buyers to pay for their purchases through monthly payments made over a number of years rather than in full when the contract is signed. Under this model, selling on credit creates a receivable on the business's balance sheet and earnings on the business's income statement. Selling on credit does not, however, provide an immediate cash flow. Businesses need cash flow to pay their own bills in terms of mortgage, payroll, utility bills, contractors, and other operational expense items; therefore, it is desirable for the timeshare developer to sell receivables in order to raise cash.

If a business chooses to sell its receivables to create cash flow, it will need to make a decision as to whom to sell the receivables. A financier who specializes in the purchase of receivables is traditionally called a factor, and the sale is referred to as "factoring the receivables." The factor expects to earn a return on the money paid for the receivables, so the amount paid is less than the amount that will be collected from the customer. The longer the factor expects to wait before collecting the receivables, the less it will pay for them.

Creditworthiness of the note pool also influences the lending process and especially so when customers fail to pay what they owe (default on their obligation). In order to protect against possible defaults, a business may decide to sell its receivables "with recourse," meaning that it promises to repay the lender if any of its customers default. In this case, the lender will not care about the credit quality of the receivables; instead, it will concentrate on the financial condition of the developer that is selling the receivables. If the developer's business is in lackluster condition, the lender will pay less for the receivables sold with recourse because there is the risk that the developer will not be able to make good on its promises. Conversely, when a developer decides to sell its receivables "without recourse," the lender will adjust the amount paid for them to reflect the risk that some of the notes may not be collected. How much of a discount will depend on the lender's analysis of the credit quality of the developer's financial status in combination with the project quality of the consumer notes.

Key Point 2.5

Sales of receivables, hypothecation, and securitization are investment strategies that supply capital to maintain existing operations and to fund the build-out of additional residential units and common areas.

Financial Investment Model: Hypothecation

Hypothecation refers to the process of pledging an asset as collateral (security) for a loan. The most common usage is the phrase "to hypothecate a mortgage," which occurs when a borrower assigns rights to a piece of real estate (such as a hotel and the land on which it stands) or other asset (such as accounts receivable and inventory) to a lender. This asset, called the collateral, is pledged as security for a loan in addition to the promissory note (obligation to repay) that is signed by the borrower. If an asset is hypothecated, the loan is secured. If no collateral is pledged, the loan is unsecured.

In the event of a default (failure to repay) by the borrower on a secured loan, the lender has the right to seize the hypothecated asset (the collateral) and sell it, using the proceeds to repay the loan. In contrast, in the case of a default on an unsecured loan, the lender must take the borrower to court to force repayment. This may result in the borrower filing for bankruptcy protection, in which event the lender will have to wait for the bankruptcy court to determine how the remaining assets of the borrower will be divided among all of the unsecured creditors.

A single asset may be hypothecated to more than one loan. In this case, the first loan has a senior claim (first lien). The other loans have subordinated or junior claims (second lien, third lien, etc.). In the event of a default, the collateral is sold and the most senior loan gets repaid first. Subordinated claims get repaid in order and only if any proceeds remain. Once the proceeds from the collateral have been dispersed, any "secured" lenders who have not been repaid in full must make a legal claim as an unsecured creditor. For this reason, subordinated claims provide less default protection for a lender (Gilkeson, 2005).

Financial Investment Model: Securitization

Securitization is a process in which a number of financial assets, typically end-loans (alias consumer loans) of some specific type, are sold to an external legal entity (known as a special-purpose vehicle) that focuses on investing funds in the capital market. This external entity then sells new securities to investors based on the assets it holds in trust. The group of loans owned by the entity is called the asset pool. The payments made to investors in these new securities come from the earnings of the loans in the pool. The securities created during a securitization are called Asset-Backed Securities (ABS). The most common form of ABS are those created from one to four family residential (home) mortgages; these are called Mortgage-Backed Securities or MBS. Other ABS are created from timeshare receivables, commercial real estate loans, home equity loans, automobile loans, student loans, and credit card receivables.

For lenders, the advantage of securitization is that it allows originators of loans (such as timeshare resort owners and other lenders) to sell assets that, individually, would be very illiquid (difficult to sell for an amount close to their underlying value). This allows the lender to specialize in originations, reusing the same capital over and over again as new loans are originated, sold for securitization, the proceeds of the sale used to originate a new group of loans, and so on. For example, a timeshare resort developer may be very good at developing a new resort, marketing it to potential buyers, evaluating the buyer's credit, and creating a receivable (loan) by which the buyer agrees to make monthly payments over a number of years. The developer, however, may not wish to have its capital tied up until the buyer makes the required payments. Securitization allows the developer to sell these receivables, take the profit from the project, and reinvest its capital back into a new resort.

Investors prefer to buy ABS rather than individual loans for two reasons. First, each ABS share represents parts of each individual loan in the pool, so the ABS investor is well diversified. If the investor instead bought individual loans, he or she would have to take care to build a well-diversified portfolio. Second, most ABS provide added default protection for investors. This may come from a third-party insurer who agrees to make good on any defaults by the borrowers in the pool. Or the protection may come from overcollateralization, which occurs when the value of the individual loans in the pool is greater than the value of the ABS that are issued. It is also possible for a lender to sell loans to the pool with recourse. Selling "with recourse" means that the original lender is liable if too many of the borrowers default. If the investor bought individual loans rather than ABS, he or she would have to evaluate the credit risk of each individual loan, which is an expensive and time-consuming task.

Conclusion

The process of building a timeshare resort follows similar principles associated with real estate development processes as practiced by traditional destination resorts and other similar real estate development projects. This process requires due diligence on the developer's part for two reasons: (1) the financial success of the operation, and (2) consumer satisfaction with the products and services offered. This implies that from project conception up until the time at which the last villa is sold the timeshare developer is acutely aware of the level of financial return that each phase of the resort project must yield. This observation explains why so much pressure is placed on marketing and sales staff to hit or surpass daily sales targets. However, to get to the point of engaging the sales and marketing division, the developer must ensure that the project offers those characteristics that have proven linkages to resort project success.

The core components concerning knowledge of real estate law, expertise in site development, expertise in sales, marketing, telemarketing, owner services, sufficient human resources in all functional areas of constructing and operating a resort, knowledge of financial investment strategies, expertise in consumer loans and accounting procedures, and knowledge of home owner association management are vital to preopening and daily operation of a timeshare resort. In terms of considering a particular site for development, the developer must be aware of local, regional, and national economic conditions because there is a relationship between the economy and labor-related issues, consumer disposal income, and lending patterns. The underlying connection is that a weak economy does not easily equate to project success. The regulatory environment exerts an influence on development and ongoing operation concerns to the degree that a simple miscue could be very costly to the operator in terms of fines. In addition, it goes without saying that the availability of professionally trained personnel that understand timeshare sales, marketing, accounting, financial, and property mangaement functions are in relatively short supply due to the evidence of few training institutions or academic progams that focus on timeshare curriculum issues. The net result is that timeshare developers are limited to a small pool of "veterans" to develop and manage their timeshare resorts. The immediate market is intertwined with the attractiveness of the surrounding parks, entertainment, and other services that are appealing to the timeshare owner, which in turn is related to the presence of competition and the quality of the competition in the immediate market area.

The overriding message in this chapter concerns working capital and is extremely important when it comes to a project's success. Working capital is needed to acquire the land, develop the land, develop the resort, and then maintain future development. Project financing, in turn, is integrally related to site access, proximity to tourist destination or other areas of major interest, initial cost of the land, and price that the market will bear for the timeshare experience. The primary methods of generating sufficient capital to sustain resort growth are through the sales of receivables, hypothecation, and securitization. All three are based on loans that consumers have entered into with the developer to finance their purchase. To practice any of these financial strategies, the timeshare developer has to have a very sound understanding of lending, risk assessment, and financing a large amount of receivables to maintain growth.

CHAPTER **3**

Real Estate Development

Learning Objectives

After studying this chapter you should be able to:

- understand the general history of the lodging industry relating to the proliferation of the time-share real estate market.

- understand regulatory laws in the planning and development of timeshare resorts.

- apply input-output models for resort development purposes.

- critically discuss the multiplier effect in the resort development process.

Introduction

As noted throughout this text, the timeshare real estate industry continues to grow at an unprecedented rate and as such contributes significantly to regional and national economies (ARDA, 2004a and b). These national and global reports as sanctioned by the American Resort Development Association (ARDA) are important for a variety of reasons, especially as regards an understanding of the consumer's increasing desire to own private land. This is an important consideration because the United States has a long history of private ownership of land and material goods, which is touted to be the people's inalienable right (McMahon, 1989). This pursuit of ownership in combination with prestige and pursuit of a lifestyle which is designed to reward the consumer for a life of hard work has fostered the timeshare industry's tremendous growth.

The sheer magnitude of the real estate industry and all the activity it generates is impressive. The larger real estate industry, which is one of the most lucrative in the world, consists of many different sectors from real estate development to real estate investment. Associated with the growth of a real estate market are natural product extensions, changes in design and growth in differing markets as influenced by consumer demand, which in turn are associated with regulatory issues that protect the interest of the community, the developer, and the consumer, with the outcome being a significant contribution to the local economy. To this end, the timeshare segment of this broader real estate market is a significant contributor as well.

For the purposes of this chapter, timeshare real estate development is concerned with those conditions that help determine supply and demand for a given project. This chapter focuses on a review of proven concepts that determine a timeshare resort's level of profitability and therefore financial success in the marketplace. The concepts examined encompass demographic characteristics of the intended target market within the destination, specific site considerations, and lifestyle characteristics of the target market. In almost every instance, timeshare resorts are located in tourist destinations, which implies that the typical consumer is attracted to area attractions, entertainment, and events. Because of this focus on a similar demographic (the vacationer), some would say that the timeshare industry is an outgrowth of the accommodation industry. Because of this similarity, we present a brief history of the accommodation history.

History of the Accommodation Market

The relationship between the traveling public and the major modes of transportation within the context of traditional lodging accommodations and timeshare resorts is important, given the consumer demand for business and pleasure travel. For instance, it is not by happenstance that the City Hotel in New York opened its doors to the public for business and leisure purposes in 1794: this opening was associated with the transportation advances and roadway improvements of this period. The City Hotel was just one example of full-service lodging accommodations that appeared at this time.

It was also not by chance that hotels during the 1800s were built along rail lines throughout the country. This general trend was radically altered in the 1950s and 1960s following improvements in the United States' intrastate and interstate highway system. Experts generally conclude that tourism sprang to life during this period because of the convenience of highway travel and a strong economy. It was during this period that consumer demand strongly influenced real estate developments. For instance, the hotel market expanded its product lines ranging from economy (budget) motels to luxury hotels in major cities and in recreational destinations. From the 1970s onward, and with relatively few exceptions, the lodging industry continued to grow by expanding product lines to encompass full-service hotels, economy units, all-suite hotels, resorts, spa resorts, boutique hotels, and more.

Associated with this proliferation of the lodging market was the desire by real estate developers to offer a product that was neither full home ownership nor a rental

easier to estimate the consumption patterns of timeshare products and services of timeshare product available in the marketplace.

Reflective Practice

Review an article on the current and projected demographic patterns and discuss how these will impact the types of product and services offered by timeshare resorts.

Reviewing the broader demographic is one element of identifying specific consumer segments that use the timeshare product. For example, owners could be divided into varying age groupings that define career and vacation patterns per household and by geographical region. In general, the predominant timeshare owner is in the 35–44 and 45–65 age brackets (Carn, Rabianski, Racster, and Seldin, 1988). From a marketing perspective, this means that a project director would want to make sure that this type of demographic was readily available within the area in which the resort was proposed. The second group of demographic characteristics concerns the consumer's economic characteristics, with the most common being household income. Although different timeshare developers have differing demographics, the key point is to know how the resort will be positioned in the marketplace and then to price the product accordingly based on the chosen household income target. Each income grouping has differing disposable income levels, which in turn impacts how much the consumer can afford to spend on a villa. The developer will estimate the total volume of sales per household income grouping (e.g., 35,000 to 45,000; 46,000 to 55,000; 56,000 to 75,000; 76,000 to 100,000); product offerings can vary between these classifications. Roughly put, this means that those with a lower disposal income level will seek out a product that has a lower price point and lower frequency of usage (such as a biennial package), whereas those who can afford a higher priced package will want a multiple-week package (such as a fractional resort product) or an upscale higher priced product.

Key Point 3.2

In tourist destinations, timeshare resorts cater to a national and an international vacationer demographic. However, these demographics are different from their pricing points.

The Zoning Factor

Starting in the 1970s, the proliferation of timeshare real estate development brought to the foreground the regulatory role of municipalities, and regional and state entities in regards to private and public project developments. In particular, local zoning directives as imposed by municipalities began to prescribe how privately owned land could be used as noted in guidelines established by local governmental bodies. It became commonplace for developers to face zoning ordinances that specified type of development (e.g., single-home housing, multiple-family housing, etc.) that could be built on the land, height of physical structures, location of physical structures, density of the residential population, amount of required open spaces on the parcel, and exact area of the parcel that could be occupied. Even though it might not be readily apparent, the primary goal of municipal ordinances then and now ensures that land usage is complementary and does not lead to violations of the public health, safety and welfare.

The most common form of zoning classifies land usage into the distinct categories of residential (R), industrial (I), and recreational or commercial activities (RC). In general, a C-1 (commercial zone) classification allows for commercial enterprises that sell product or services to the general public; businesses that are manufacturing based are classified as industrial enterprises; and residential enterprises generally refer to parcels that are for the purpose of creating family dwellings. It is when one considers developments such as timeshare resorts that the classification combines classification in these operations that are both commercial and recreation based. This is why municipalities classify timeshare resorts as recreation/commercial (RC), seeing that this

Option A = Cluster Development Option (refer to section 19.09.040)

Option B = Lot Reduction Option (refer to section 19.09.050, and to individual zones)

Option C = Lot Development Option (refer to section 19.09.060)

Option D = Small Lot Subdivision Option (refer to section 19.09.090, and to individual zones)

Option E = Mobile Home Subdivision Option (refer to section 19.35.060 and 19.37.060)

Option F = Mobile Home Park Option (refer to section 19.35.060)

Source: http://www.pimaxpress.com/Planning/plan4c.htm

Table 3.1 Abbreviated List of Zoning Classifications, Principal Uses, and Development Standards in the United States

classification consists of recreational services and family dwelling components. Tables 3.1 and 3.2 are examples of how exhaustive zoning ordinances can be for a given municipality. As the tables show, zoning classifications are not identical between municipalities; however, they do have a common denominator: they all uphold public health, safety, and welfare.

Key Point 3.3

The primary purpose of zoning laws is to ensure that land usage is supportive of public health, safety and welfare.

In the United States, attention at the state level to the health, safety, and welfare of citizens is not accidental; to the contrary, this emphasis is a direct outcome of the United States Standard Zoning Enabling Act of 1926. This federal act explicitly gave each state the power to "promote health, safety, morals, or the general welfare" of its citizens by allowing zoning ordinances at the city, town, and county levels. Furthermore, this act required that in all cities, townships, and counties any such ordinances must be in concert with each municipality's comprehensive plan. The term *comprehensive plan* basically means that a master plan must

Residential

Zoning Classification	Principal Uses	Minimum Lot Area SqFt/ Width Ft		Minimum Area perunit SqFt	Minimum Yards Front Side Rear Linear Feet	Building Height / Stories	Other
CR-1 Single Residence	Single-family residences	36,000	100	36,000	30 10 40	34/2	Options A&B
CR-4 Mixed Dwelling Type	Single-family & multi-family residences; duplexes	7,000 (5 acre min. site Option D)	None	SF: 7,000 MF: 3,500 (Option D: SF: 3,500 average)	Site Setbacks: 20 10 10 Setbacks on individual lots not on edge of site: zero-lot-line placement of buildings is permitted, subject to P.C. Bldg. Code	34**	Options C&D

Business

Zone	Principal Uses	Minimum Lot Area/SqFt Width Ft	Minimum Area perunit SqFt	Minimum Yards Front Side Rear Linear Feet	Building Height/ Stories	Other
MR Major Resort	Major resort	Minimum 20 acre site area. One guest room per 4,356 square foot site area		50 50 50 (from the edge of site)	34	Maximum site cover: 33%

Table 3.2 Zoning Classifications by Functional Type

(Continued)

Zone	Principal Uses	Minimum Lot Area/SqFt Width Ft	Minimum Area per unit SqFt	Minimum Yards Front Side Rear Linear Feet.	Building Height/Stories	Other
CB-1 Local Business	Retail business	Residential: 10,000 Non-res.: None	Res.: 60	Residential: 1,000 Non-res.: None	20 7 25* (residential) 20 None 25* (non-residential	Res.: 34** Non-res.: 39	Option C
CB-2 General Business	CB-1 uses; wholesale; storage of equipment and household goods; bars	Residential: 7,000 Non-res.: None	Res.: 60	Residential: 1,000 Non-res.: None	20 7 25* (residential) 15 None 10 (non-residential)	39	Option C

Table 3.2 (*Continued*)

be on file that clearly specifies a "single, unified general physical design for the community, and it attempts to clarify the relationship between the physical development policies and social and economic goals" of the community (O'Mara, 1978, p. 69).

Reflective Practice

Determine what the zoning ordinances are in your locale and how these might apply to a timeshare resort project.

The zoning classifications (or groups) may occur in various combinations as appropriate to the municipality. For example, a timeshare complex might be segregated into separate zones for multiple-family residences on one acre, onsite hotel, and a high-rise condominium complex. This example could become more complex by the inclusion of commercial operations such as small stores, theaters, and restaurants.

The Resort Site Factor

First and foremost, the decision to build a resort at a specified geographical area and on a selected site is founded on a preliminary analysis of consumer demand for the product, direct competition in the area, economic feasibility associated with the project, economic trends within the country and region, and costs associated with the preconstruction and construction of the resort project. Once these items satisfy the developer's specified metrics, the design process follows.

According to McMahan (1989), site location in the property development realm is akin to success, even if the "development is poorly planned or its management inept" (p. 113). In fact, the old adage that the most important element of project success is location, location, and location has been proven countless times in the accommodation industry. It was not uncommon for roadside motels during the 1950s and 1960s to leverage this concept by building units at major intersections along the interstate system following the retailing principle of point-intercept. While this principle is true to a large degree when it comes to locating timeshare resorts, two additional concepts play a critical part in the site selection process. These concepts are intrinsic location value and relative location value (McMahan, 1989).

Intrinsic value in the context of many timeshare resort locations is inherent, given the tourist draw to the region as the direct result of major theme parks, attractions, entertainment, recreational, or cultural activities. For instance, the Orlando market has intrinsic drawing power owing to Disney's Magic Kingdom, Epcot, Animal Kingdom, and MGM Studios, Cirque du Soleil, Universal Studios Islands of Adventure and Universal Studios, Anheuser Busch's SeaWorld and Discovery Cove, and an assortment of other attractions, such as Gatorland. These tourist operations bring millions of visitors to the Orlando market annually. The primary message is that developers will factor in the drawing power of the local and regional attractions, events, parks, and entertainment in an effort to derive an estimate of demand for their timeshare products as part of their feasibility process.

Relative location value is the more formidable of the two location metrics in that it deals with the physical characteristics of the immediate plot of land relative to the physical attractiveness of immediate parcels of land as sought by timeshare owners. Therefore, from the developer's perspective the proximity of the timeshare resort to beachfront, retail stores, theme parks, movie theaters, and similar items of appeal is of utmost importance during the project planning phase. For timeshare resorts that are located in tourist destinations, these external "draws" are very appealing to the vacation- and recreation-minded consumer who is drawn to the area on a repetitive basis. Hence, owning a week or more in a conveniently located timeshare resort that offers superior accommodations and square footage relative to traditional hotels is an added advantage of timeshare ownership. First and foremost, the decision to build a resort at a specified geographical area and on a selected site is founded on a preliminary analysis of consumer demand for the product, direct competition in the area, economic feasibility associated with the project, economic trends within the country and region, and costs associated with the preconstruction and construction of the resort project. These basic concepts and more are contained in Table 3.3.

Category	Purpose	Data source
Roadway Analysis - number and location - planned improvement - # of lanes, widths, speed zones, carrying capacity - traffic volume by direction - points of congestion - physical road condition - mass transit availability	To determine the carrying capacity to surrounding area	a. Local traffic count studies b. Municipal roadway plans c. Thoroughfare planning documents d. Traffic engineering studies
Location Analysis - time, distance, and route to attractions, entertainment, restaurants, and other points of interest - number and location of site's access points & congestion at these points - distance to buildings - safety of parking facilities - analysis of competitors' location	To determine the resort site's level of convenience and accessibility to points of interest	a. field observations b. actual measurement of driving time at various times of the day and week
Visibility Analysis - viewpoints at different elevations - obstruction of views - density of traffic flow - signage (number, location, size of competing signage)	To determine conditions that affect the resort site's visual appeal to the owners	a. field observations b. site maps, topographical and land-use maps that concern grades and elevations of the property

(*Continued*)

Category	Purpose	Data source
Physical Features & Design Features - shape of site - size of lot, street frontage, etcetera - building features (location, configuration, architectural features) - soil conditions - vegetation - drainage - geologic conditions - topography - types and range of building usage - number of parking spaces - safety of parking - length and width of parking spaces - vehicular flow - pedestrian flow - parking standards (handicap space)	To determine onsite features that affect the site's ability to perform desired resort functions	a. field observations b. site engineering studies c. planning, design, and cost estimate studies d. architectural planning standards e. industry standards
Other site characteristics - availability of services (electricity, natural gas, communications, water, sanitary sewer, drainage, solid waste treatment) - police and fire protection	To determine the level of support infrastructure that affect the resort's ability to perform necessary functions	
Regulatory characteristics - zoning - building and occupancy codes - environment regulations and environmental regulations - licensing - right of way and easements	To determine the type and range of local, state and guidelines that influence the resorts development	a. review of local municipal zoning and ordinance documents

Source: Carn, Rabianski, Racster, and Seldin (1988). Real Estate Market Analysis.

Table 3.3 Site Development Factors

Key Point 3.4

A major part of determining the viability of a resort is dedicated to site selection. The chief factors that concern site selection are roadway analysis, location characteristics, visibility considerations, design concerns, utility and safety considerations, and regulatory issues.

Another aspect of relative location value centers on how easy it is for the timeshare owner to get to and from the resort during her stay. From an owner's perspective there are multiple issues associated with the resort's location. First, costs are associated with transportation to and from the resort even when it is the vacationer's own vehicle. The average time spent in the vehicle is also often important to the vacationer who generally has only limited time on vacation and therefore time is a premium. Second, the resort's parking should be readily accessible and conveniently located near the vacationer's unit, and the parking lot should be secure. Third, the developer must consider whether the existing roadways are congested and if they are, should inquire whether the city has plans to improve the roads in the near future. As noted previously, timeshare owners consider their vacation time a premium, and being stuck in high-volume traffic or roadways under construction is simply not appealing and can certainly lead to dissatisfaction.

As indicated in Table 3.3, the physical location of the resort is not one-dimensional. Parcel conditions include impediments to visibility, elevation of the property, setback distance from major roadways and other facilities, number, height, and type of signage in the area that might obstruct property views, physical property boundaries and available acreage, topography of the parcel, natural vegetation, availability of lakes and other bodies of water, drainage capacity, and geologic conditions that are conducive to construction of the estimated buildings. In short, finding prime real estate is not as easy as it sounds because physical deficiencies that could drastically impact the types of buildings and recreational venues might be placed on the land. Moreover, when it comes to timeshare resorts, the variety of retail space, entertainment space, unit types, and recreational space is extremely important to the vacationer.

Reflective Practice

Invite a timeshare project feasibility or project director into your class to discuss the elements of site selection. You should attempt to put the concepts in order of priority and sequence.

Another element that exerts a functional influence on site development is that of access to public utilities. Since most timeshare developments are built in phases, the designer must give consideration to the availability of utility services such as water, electricity, gas, telephone, cable/satellite, and trash removal for the sales center, club house/registration area, and the first phase of timeshare units, as well as future construction of other timeshare units as according the master plan. Not only does there have to be sufficient handling capacity for present and future growth, but the purchased utilities must be designed in a manner that offers the maximum efficiency. This latter point is important from the perspective of the home owners' association because once the home owners' board of directors takes control of the resort operation, they do not need to be overly concerned with exorbitant utility costs. Any unexpected costs are generally passed onto the timeshare owners through an increase in their annual maintenance fees. This, of course, could result in a situation that owners will not accept without adequate justification.

Fourth, the various regulatory characteristics that need to be considered during the design process exert an influence on immediate project viability and ultimate long-range project success. For instance, ensuring that the parcel is zoned appropriately is a necessary prerequisite to the remaining development phases. After the initial zoning requirements are satisfied, the developer continues onward with a review of construction code restrictions, material standards, environmental restrictions, and occupancy code restrictions. In addition, a review of existing property easements and deed restrictions that might restrict property usage is a prerequisite before construction can begin.

The last and extremely significant aspect of the preconstruction phase concerns the conduct of an in-depth analysis of the competition. This process encompasses a thorough review of financial and structural factors, specific site characteristics, and relative location characteristics of the proposed resort location in relationship to the competition, area attractions, entertainment, cultural and historical sites, and the like. During the project's feasibility phase, the developer projects sales volume by marketing channel, by geographic site, and by region. These projections are often based on the historical performance of similar timeshare resorts that the developer already operates. If this information is not available, then the developer resorts to industry-based norms. From the developer's perspective, two major questions need to be answered during the feasibility study. First is the issue of whether prime real estate is available, and if it is not, whether a secondary site will be appealing and therefore profitable. The second concern is whether the site in question is priced at a level that makes the project viable from an economic perspective. This second concern is critical and is one that the developer gives strong consideration to when estimating the project's financial success.

The Lifestyle Factor

The timeshare developer must be ever vigilant to monitor changing consumer trends that specifically relate to real estate and vacation patterns. This sounds like an odd comparison, but when you look at the timeshare industry from its fundamental components, the truth is that developers are in the practice of purchasing land and developing this land into pristine resort accommodations that include luxurious villas, recreational areas, retail outlets, entertainment vistas, and educational events that appeal to changing consumer vacation and lifestyle patterns. The operative term is *changing* because demographics and therefore lifestyle patterns do alter over time and therefore can drastically impact the type of amenities and services that the developer must provide at a *future* time. Of course, projected trends can be ignored, but this might be a costly mistake that leads to loss of market share, unused inventory, and potential financial problems for the developer. Worse, it might end in an inferior product for those consumers who have purchased a product that will not meet their changing lifestyle needs. Therefore, the main premise of this chapter is that the astute timeshare resort developer will monitor certain demographic and lifestyle projections.

Key Point 3.5

Timeshare developers must be vigilant in monitoring changing consumer trends so as to design resorts that meet and exceed evolving consumer lifestyles.

Second-Home Market Trends

One especially significant real estate pattern that has a direct relationship to high-end timeshare and fractional products is the second-home market. The reader should understand that the second-home market is not necessarily considered a competitive product for high-end timeshare or fractional products. The reason for this difference relates more to financial investment structures and tax laws that favor second-home scenarios as opposed to high-end timeshares and fractional products. In short, high-end timeshares and fractional purchases are not generally considered an "investment," nor are they subjected to the same tax laws. As such, the consumer profile appears to be similar in terms of demographics, but the consumer's reason for purchase can differ dramatically. With that fundamental difference understood, the primary reason for tracking the second-home market resides in understanding the underlying economic and lifestyle trends that correspond with this highly affluent and mobile market. Why? Because this consumer market is similar in principle to the demographic and lifestyle profile of those timeshare consumers reported in industry reports (ARDA, 2003; Ragatz, 2003a; Upchurch, 2004).

Directly following the conclusion of World War II, the concept of second-home ownership came into vogue with rising household incomes and a world economy that began to rebound from the recent global strife. Not only did the economic condition improve for investment in the vacation and leisure market but various tax laws favored the deduction of second-home ownership under certain rental conditions. This basically meant that the upper-middle class could enjoy the benefits of owning a vacation home while deducting those periods in which the vacation home was rented out to others that aspired to vacationing in luxury without the burden of full ownership. As you can tell by this brief definition, second-home ownership within this context has similarities to timesharing because of this less than full ownership status. In addition, this idea flourished to the degree that vacation homes sprang up in highly sought after tourist destinations such as Hilton Head, South Carolina; Vail, Colorado; Orlando, Florida; and many other promising locations (McMahan, 1989). Basically, this means that the appeal of owning a vacation home existed long before timesharing was introduced in the United States. This phenomenon proves that owning a vacation home, in a way, seeded the path for the introduction of timesharing within the United States. The ultimate question is whether this trend toward owning a vacation home, either in the form of full ownership or a fraction thereof, will be sustained in the future.

Peter Francese, in *American Demographics* (2001) proposed that the second-home market is projected to explode over the upcoming decades in the United States. The main impetus of the projected growth in this market has been the changes in tax laws that now favor investment in a second home. Francese continues to develop the justification for this projected growth based on consumer needs for vacation homes in the Sunbelt and tourist destinations, the need for summer getaways to cooler locations, the desire of city dwellers just to get away from the hustle and bustle of city life, or perhaps a compelling usage to get back to nature. Regardless of the reason, demand is swelling for accommodation needs that are not being met by the primary domicile. In this report Francese observed that "U.S. Bureau of Census projected that household size is at an all-time low, while household income is at an all-time high . . . one-third of households have children whose active schedules tend to limit the use of a second home." (Francese, 2001, p. 26) This report goes on to note that 30 million households are made up of married couples with no children, who are twice as likely to purchase a second home versus their married with children counterparts. Furthermore, the consumer group that is rising the fastest is the 55–64 age group, which historically has been the group most inclined to purchase a second home. The *American Demographics* report estimates that this market accounts for an additional 1 million second-home purchases. Again, in reflecting on other industry reports, this 55–64 group is also a major purchaser of timeshare and fractional products. From another perspective, households with an annual household income of over $75,000 will account for approximately 2.4 million households seeking a vacation home purchase. This trend is a perfect match with the household income patterns reported in various timeshare industry reports as well (ARDA, 2003; Ragatz and Associates, 2003; Upchurch, 2003).

Where might these consumers prefer their vacation home to be located? This *American Demographics* report indicates that these leisure- and recreation-minded individuals will be seeking accommodations in secluded areas, historical areas, beachfront locations, lakeshores, and riverfronts, all of which fit primary timeshare locations.

If these projections concerning second-home purchases relative to vacation home needs are accurate, it is also likely that the timeshare and fractional market will flourish from this projected demographic and lifestyle trend.

The Multiplier Effect Factor

According to the World Bank (2000), the service sector has exceeded the manufacturing of goods and the most important production activity to the degree that the service sector accounted for 60 percent of the world's gross domestic product. The tourism industry as a whole grew at about 2.2 percent, with the hotel and restaurant industry subset being leaders in this sustained growth pattern (Smeral, 2003). Thus, the tourism industry is a major contributor to the world economy, and the timeshare industry is just one element of a grander scheme. Although the timeshare industry has fewer resorts than does the hotel industry, the sustained double-digit growth pattern noted by the

American Resort Development Association (ARDA, 1999a and b; ARDA, 2003) provides compelling evidence that the timeshare industry is also a significant contributor to the economy.

With regard to understanding the scope of the timeshare industry, it is important to reflect not only on the historical development of the industry (see Chapters 1 and 4) but also on the sustained real estate development patterns from an international perspective. When doing so, the resultant composite review of existing literature from the United States, Europe, Asia, the Pacific Rim, Latin America, and Africa points to specific trends that can result in strategic marketing and development decisions for the timeshare industry as a whole from a multinational perspective. The following section addresses these multinational development issues by incorporating academic research concerning real estate development from these countries (Gibb and Hoslei, 2003).

Key Point 3.6

Timeshare developers can make very convincing arguments to city planners when economic and financial impact reports are based on the multiplier effect. The multiplier effect takes into consideration the direct and indirect benefits associated with the resort development in terms of its contribution to the community.

Gibb and Hoslei (2003) assert that property development, of which timeshare resort properties are a subset, contributes significantly to the economic and urban development of communities. It is easy to understand that the construction of timeshare resorts generates economic returns in the form of real estate taxes, which in turn are allocated to the betterment of roadways and improvement in community services (e.g., police, fire, utilities). The construction of timeshare resorts also contributes to community development in the construction phase by hiring local contractors and subcontractors that commonly use local laborers. This impact on the community continues after the resort is operational by hiring community members for line-level as well as management positions. Moreover, an additional economic return to the community is accrued from the presence of employees, owners, exchanges, and renters. This additional economic return is known as the multiplier effect.

The Multiplier Effect

The multiplier effect is important for developers to understand because this concept relates critically to the resort's economic contributions to the local community and other governmental bodies. For the timeshare product, the multiplier effect refers to the *direct* output indicators of total sales, taxes, and other indices of economic benefit that accrues from owner, exchanger, or renter of the resort's facilities. *Indirect* benefits also accrue when the owner, exchanger, or renter expends his disposal income in the local economy by consuming restaurant, entertainment, cultural, and other services in the local community. The third element of the multiplier effect is known as the *induced* effect, which is the economic impact contributed by resort employees within the local community via their spending patterns. One of the more complex pieces of a multiplier model is the concept of leakage. Leakage occurs when monies that are intended to be spent in the local community "leak" out to outside sources such as goods or services that are imported from another geographical region. Even with this challenge, calculating the multiplier effect is an onerous task, though not impossible. Fletcher (1989) and Frechtling (1994) presented and reviewed advanced statistical models that are capable of measuring the multiplier effect within tourism settings.

Reflective Practice

Research the multiplier effect topic and give a report on how various hospitality and tourism industries use this technique.

The magnitude of information that the Regional-Input-Output Modeling System (RIMS II) process can yield is evidenced by the following report generated by the United States Bureau of Economic Analysis (BEA), as cited from the BEA's 2004 report.

> Direct tourism-related employment grew by 7,300 employees (seasonally adjusted at annual rates) in the second quarter 2004, the most recent quarter for which data are available. For the second consecutive quarter, the largest gains in tourism employment occurred in the food services and drinking places industry, which added 3,000 jobs, and the recreation and entertainment industry, which added 2,100 jobs. The traveler accommodations and air transportation industries each contributed an additional 700 new jobs. In the first quarter of 2004, direct tourism employment grew 2.0 percent (revised).

> BEA's estimates of tourism-related sales include figures for both "direct" and "indirect" sales. Direct tourism-related sales comprise all output consumed directly by visitors (e.g., traveler accommodations, passenger air transportation, souvenirs); indirect tourism-related sales comprise all output used as inputs in the process of producing direct tourism-related output (e.g., toiletries for hotel guests, the various ingredients used to make the meals served airline passengers, and the plastic used to produce souvenir key chains). Indirect sales were estimated using commodity-by-commodity total requirements coefficients from BEA's annual input-output accounts. Bureau of Economic Analysis (2005).

Before continuing onward, a discussion on the history of RIMS II and how it works is in order. In the 1970s, the Bureau of Economic Analysis (BEA) developed a method for estimating regional "input-output" multipliers that became known as RIMS (Regional Industrial Multiplier System). In the 1980s, the original input-output model was enhanced by the addition of other input-output indicators and became known as RIMS II (Regional Input-Output Modeling System), resulting in a handbook published for those interested in applying RIMS II. In 1992, the BEA produced a second edition of the RIMS II handbook, basing this model's multipliers on more recent data and improved methodology. The most recent revision of the handbook, 1997, offered details on the multipliers, data sources, and methods for estimating the input-output measures.

For each respective industry, an input-output table shows the industrial distribution of inputs purchased and outputs sold. Each industry table is derived from the BEA's proven input and outputs for various industries, and in addition each economic region is classified by industrial structure and trading patterns. The strength of RIMS II is that multipliers can be estimated for any region composed of one or more counties and for any industry, or group of industries, that is classified in the national input-output table as developed by the BEA. The outcome is that RIMS multipliers serve as a cost-effective way for analysts to estimate the economic impacts of changes in a regional economy. To effectively use the multipliers for impact analysis, one must provide geographically and industrially detailed information on the initial changes in output, earnings, or employment that are associated with the project or program under study. The multipliers are then used to estimate the total impact of the metric under consideration on regional output, earnings, and employment.

The RIMS II model is derived through a three-step process. In the first step, the national I-O table that is produced by the Bureau of Economic Analysis is specific to each region by using six-digit North American Industrial Classification System (NAICS) location quotients (LQs). The reader should understand that each location quotient is based on estimates of personal income data (by place of residence) for service industries and that BEA's wage-and-salary data (by place of work) are used to calculate location quotients in nonservice industries.

The Importance of NAICS

In February 1999, Canada, Mexico, and the United States launched a joint initiative to develop a comprehensive demand-oriented product classification system that complements the new supply-oriented industry classification system introduced in 1997. This relatively new industry classification system is known as the North American Industry Classification System (NAICS) and is intended to replace the Standard Industrial Classification system (http://www.census.gov/epcd/www/naics.html).

The long-term objective of this multicountry initiative is to develop a market-oriented classification system for products that (1) is not industry-of-origin based but can be linked to the NAICS industry structure, (2) is consistent across the three NAICS countries, and (3) promotes improvements in the identification and classification of service products across international classification systems. Relative to service products, this system classifies real estate products and accommodation services under this new system.

In the second phase of the development process, the national input-output table is designed to be region-specific. The table information is adjusted to reflect regional earnings leakages resulting from individuals working in the region but residing outside the region. In addition, this information is modified to account for regional consumption leakages stemming from personal taxes and savings.

In the final phase of development, a mathematical model is used to estimate the multipliers. The net result is that the input-output model is capable of measuring output, earnings, and employment multipliers, which can be used to trace the impacts of changes in final demand on directly and indirectly affected industries. The net result is that this regional input-output (I-O) multiplier model is a useful tool for conducting regional economic impact analysis (http://www.bea.doc.gov/bea/regional/rims/brfdesc.cfm).

The primary message for the timeshare developer is that monitoring and documenting inputs and outputs associated with timeshare development is beneficial to the operator, the consumer, and city planners. For example, if wage and benefit information is available to the developer, the ability to influence city planners is greatly enhanced by being able to present this information in an effort to obtain proper zoning and approval of a project based on financial and economic impact pieces of information that is collected through this process. This type of information is helpful to consumers because it helps support the credibility of the timeshare industry as a whole in the eyes of the local community and the region. For instance, if the developer can attribute local economic growth in terms of employment, increased expenditures within local trades, and increased monies going into local tax coffers, then it is fairly easy to prove that the developer has financial worth and status to the community as a whole.

Perhaps a more accurate and concise picture of financial or economic impact is the annual percentage change in the real value-added indicator for the hospitality and tourism industries and the real estate-based industries as noted in Table 3.4. Upon reflection, you see that the terrorism activities that occurred in 2001 negatively impacted the sustained growth of both markets. The real estate market witnessed a 1.2 percent drop in real value, while the arts, entertainment, accommodations, and restaurant market went down by 1.8. Again the reader should be aware of other timeshare industry figures reported by industry organizations because the financial indicators collected by these entities attest to the sustained growth in the industry as noted by their direct outputs. This reflection indicates that the timeshare industry is a major contributor to "sustained" economic growth in local, regional, and national markets.

Note: BEA data, including gross domestic product, personal income, the balance of payments, foreign direct investment, the input-output accounts, and economic data for states, local areas, and industries are available at http://www.bea.gov.

Regardless of the specific type of input-output multiplier model used, the primary message is that the measurement and collection of this type of financial and economic impact information via an input-output model is extremely beneficial to the advancement of timeshare real estate industry.

	1995–2000	2001	2002	2003
Arts, entertainment, accommodations, restaurants	3.7	−0.7	1.8	1.9
Real estate, rental, leasing	4.4	3.9	1.4	3.2

Table 3.4 Annual Percentage Change in Real Value Added by Industry

Applying Input-Output Models

To date no such timeshare-specific study exists that has deployed the RIMS II methodology or a similar approach to gauge the direct and indirect impacts of the timeshare industry. Conduct of a study of this magnitude could lead to greater understanding of the industry's direct and indirect impact on local, regional, and national economies. This in turn could raise the level of awareness of the industry that would exert an influence on investors and consumers alike.

A timeshare resort study using the multiplier model would take into consideration owner, exchanger, and renter expenditures on local transportation, entertainment, food, and beverage services, and other related goods and services in the local community, based on surveys conducted at the resort by management or a consultant team. The next phase would estimate the resort's total economic contribution in terms of taxes and other fees paid to the local and state economies, employee and management earnings, and employee and management consumption of local goods and services. As mentioned above, leakage would have to be considered as entered in this model for a true reflection of the economic influence of the direct, indirect, and induced elements. To date there has not been a study that employs a proven and valid multiplier effect model concerning the economic impact of the timeshare industry. Instead, the industry has focused on descriptive indicators of financial impact in combination with hypothetical estimations of the industry's impact on local and national economies.

Within a broader context of the real estate and tourism industries, the relative impact of the timesharing has not been measured using reliable and valid instrumentation such as RIMS II. When such a study is finally conducted, and it will be, consumers, legislators, the media, and other concerned stakeholders will take note of the impacts that a given timeshare resort exerts on the immediate local and broader communities. This is an especially important consideration because timesharing is closely related to tourism in many international locations. It is even more important to reflect on this observation because tourism services are intricately related to national income and employment.

An assumption can be made that once market saturation has been achieved with regard to basic needs and durable goods, a growing and aging consumer demographic will have more money left to spend on leisure and tourism services, as well as on product-based goods and services such as vacation home products.

This increased consumer demand for vacation home products will lead to a positive impact in terms of employment because of the increased demand for labor. In turn, the consumer's increased income elasticity in combination with increased consumer demand for vacation home products will drive pricing of these products upward. Obviously, this simple relationship between an increase in household disposable income, demand for vacation accommodation products, and the resultant price elasticity given here cannot offer a complete picture of all aspects of timeshare development, but it can provide an additional perspective for analyzing the growth of timeshare real estate. For a more complete view, it is necessary to consider the contributions of international trade and economic theories and the globalization of timeshare real estate development. In addition, sociodemographic changes, improvements in transport, technologies, political understanding of timesharing, and increased clarity in timeshare laws all have a substantial impact on timeshare real estate development. Overall, the general expectation is that the direct and indirect growth of the timeshare industry has a positive impact on the tourism market and the real estate market.

Case Study 3.1

The project development staff of the Culhaven timeshare company is located in the mountain region of the western United States and as such has typically built resorts in ski destination areas. However, their growth has been very lucrative so that they are now considering developing beachfront resorts in South Carolina and Orlando. The development team is currently debating how the resort development process will be different in these beach destination areas.

Conclusion

The interrelationship between a relatively sustained real estate development trend within tourist and urban destinations, an increasing consumer desire to engage in rest and relaxation activities, a general increase in average household income, and continual improvements in individuals' discretionary income levels has resulted in a sustained interest in owning vacation ownership products (timeshare or fractional) in the United States and abroad. This trend most assuredly indicates that consumer interest in the timeshare product is increasing and that this is very likely to remain a sustained pattern. From the developer's perspective, this means that the resort design process is becoming a much more challenging process than that of the past. Land prices will continue to become premium owing to the shrinking availability of premium locations, competition will continue to increase in terms of product availability, and the range of onsite resort products and services will continue to increase in quality. For the consumer, this may mean that increased competition within the development arena will put more timeshare products on the market, which in essence will lead to a greater proliferation of product types and perhaps a moderating effect on pricing.

The developer must practice due diligence in analyzing supply and demand characteristics for the area in question. Expertise with one type of resort in a different type of geographical location does not always equate to success in a different market. Therefore, location and site selection factors require the application of a very methodical approach to ascertaining whether sufficient demand is present and the market share can be obtained. Acting with due diligence in reviewing access to the site, proximity of the site to area draws, entrance and exit patterns, visibility of the site, scenic viewpoints, property configuration and design issues, topographical concerns, access to utilities, and adequate police and fire protection are major concerns that have to be determined in advance of land acquisition. The collection of this information does not entirely complete the decision to build because regulatory issues such as zoning, right of way, environmental protection, noise ordinance and other municipal rules must be considered as well. And even when this information is obtained, the picture is not totally complete because the developer must collect information on the availability and access to the intended consumer demographic and recreational preferences because these impact feasibility and project design considerations.

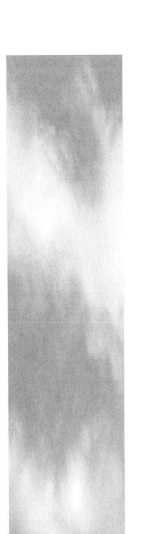

CHAPTER 4

Timeshare Markets and Consumer Behavior

Learning Objectives

After studying this chapter you should be able to:

- contrast and compare different techniques for segmenting timeshare customers.

- analyze current timeshare customer profiles.

- critically evaluate models for understanding customer behavior.

- explain the variety of motives for timeshare ownership.

Introduction

It is important to understand timeshare consumers and the motives of people who buy into timeshare because the efforts of firms in the timeshare business can be better focused. Specifically, this chapter makes the distinction between customers and consumers because those who make the decision to purchase timeshares are consuming experiences rather than making one off-purchase decision. The whole timeshare experience involves continuity in the relationship, which differentiates it from a hotel stay. Even those who use their timeshare to trade in to different locations have an ongoing relationship with the operating company.

This chapter explores a number of models for describing the characteristics of timeshare customers, using their demographic characteristics and occasionality. These models are useful because they show that timeshare ownership is not evenly spread across the population and that the motives for making a timeshare purchase vary. Without doubt, perceptions of timeshare held by potential consumers are an important factor for timeshare operators. The negative publicity generated by unscrupulous operators, using high-pressure selling techniques, has created an unfortunate image even for the bigger resort operators (ARDA, 2002a). Consumer learning and the development of consumer attitudes can be employed to shape future markets and strategies for consumer firms.

Customer behavior studies help explain how customers make purchase decisions and give a better understanding of the key influencers in the decision-making process. Since many new customers have prior knowledge of unscrupulous trade practices and widely reported scandals in the news media, sales approaches must be sensitive to customer preconceptions and fears. Companies wishing to sell timeshare space must first adopt sales strategies that provide the most fruitful potential responses, and second, adopt strategies that are in tune with consumer purchase needs. Before consumer behavior is explored it is necessary to set the scene by exploring current trends in timeshare ownership.

National and International Market Expansion

The American Resort Development Association's *State of the Industry* for 2003 reports that the growth of the timeshare industry has been relatively stable since its inception. The report indicates that there were 5,425 timeshare resorts in January 2003, with 1,590 located within the United States. For the United States, the previous composite figures calculated in 1997 accounted for 1,204 resorts, which equates to an annual increase of approximately 4.7 percent. In contrast, the last known figures (1994) concerning international market growth uncovered an approximate growth rate of 3 percent. With regard to fractional resorts, a major difference exists between the United States and the international market in that of the 138 reported, 123 fractional resorts were located within the United States' borders. This indicates that the concept of owning four or more weeks (which is a rough definition of a fractional interest) is gaining rapid acceptance within the United States compared to international ownership.

Relative to the timeshare industry's lodging counterpart, the typical timeshare resort does not have as many units per site. Acquisition, construction, development costs, and the intensive process of pushing the timeshare product into the marketplace mandate that timeshare resorts are built in phases. Thus, timeshare resorts are commonly built in phases whereby each successive unit is brought online once the previous phase has passed a preestablished return-on-investment level *and* consumer demand (based on tour flow) is at a sufficient level to support the next phase. Although there are a few exceptions, the average size of a timeshare resort in the United States is approximately eighty-three units while this number decreases to sixty units within the international marketplace.

In the United States, the heaviest market concentration of timeshare resorts is in the Sunbelt region and/or tourist destinations. Florida commands the majority of the resorts with 366, California is next with 125, followed by South Carolina with 119, Colorado 75, Hawaii 73, North Carolina 59, Nevada 56, Missouri 49, Texas 49, and Arizona 46. The remaining resorts that total to the 1,590 U.S. resorts are spread out

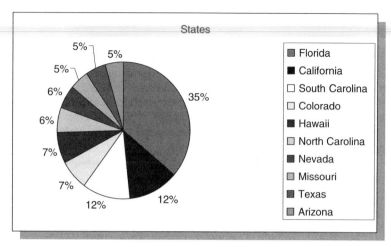

Figure 4.1 Resort Distribution In the U.S.Timeshare Market

among northeastern, midwestern, and western states (see Figure 4.1).

The dispersion of worldwide resorts displayed in Table 4.1 represents nine geographically distinct areas of the world, with over ninety countries represented in total. This listing of participating countries is strong testament to the fact that timesharing is not the exclusive province of the United States and in Europe as one is often led to believe. This is yet another indicator that timeshare resorts fulfill a variety of vacation needs for millions of consumers worldwide.

U.S. versus Worldwide Sales Performance

Another sign of industry maturation is linked to sales performance indicators for timeshare resorts that are classified as being in the "selling" mode. The first known attempt to collect and report sales figures for timeshare resorts occurred in 1990 and has been consistently reported each year up to the present.

The U.S. profile indicates that $1.2 billion in timeshare sales was generated in 1990, with steady increases up to $5.5 billion in 2002. These figures are remarkable given various downturns in the economy during this same period. Even more

Asia	Africa
China, India, Indonesia, Korea, Malaysia, Japan, Singapore, Sri Lanka, Taiwan, Pakistan, Philippines, Thailand	Egypt, Gambia, Kenya, Morocco, Reunion, Senegal, South Africa, Tunisia, Zimbabwe
Australia/Oceania	**Europe**
Australia, Cook Islands, Fiji Islands, French Polynesia, New Zealand, New Caledonia	Iceland, Norway, Sweden, Finland, United Kingdom, Denmark, Ireland, Germany, Belgium, France, Poland, Czech Republic, Switzerland, Austria, Hungary, Andorra, Italy, Spain, Portugal, Malta, Greece, Turkey, Cyprus
Caribbean	**Central America**
Antigua, Aruba, Bahamas, Barbados, Belize, Cayman Islands, Dominican Republic, Grenada, Guadeloupe, Jamaica, Martinique, Neth Antils, Saint Croix, Saint Lucia, Saint Kitts and Nevis, Saint Maarten, Saint Vincent, Virgin Islands	Belize, Costa Rica, Guatemala, Panama
Middle East	**North America**
Israel, Jordan, Lebanon, Syria, United Arab Emirates	Alaska, Bermuda, Canada, Mexico, United States of America
South America	
Argentina, Bolivia, Brazil, Chile, Colombia, Ecuador, Paraguay, Peru, Uruguay, Venezuela	

Table 4.1 National Locations of Timeshare Resorts Worldwide

compelling is the growth in the international timeshare market from $3.24 billion in 1990 up to $9.4 billion in combined developer sales. This equates to a $2.04 billion gross difference (U.S. versus worldwide) in sales in 1990, while there was a $3.9 billion gross difference in 2002 between the United States versus worldwide timeshare developer performance. Clearly, timesharing has come of age in the international marketplace (see Figure 4.2).

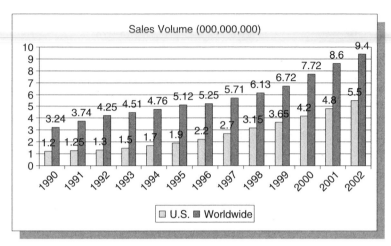

Figure 4.2 International and U.S. timeshare sales volumes

Another gauge of acceptance of the timeshare product is the growth in ownership base within the United States and in the international marketplace. Figure 4.3 shows very little difference in the number of timeshare weeks owned (traditional weeks or the equivalent in points) between the U.S. and international markets in 1990. Yet, over time, the growth of interest

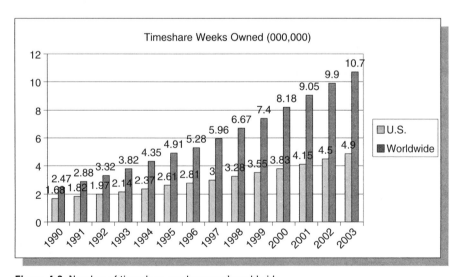

Figure 4.3 Number of timeshare weeks owned worldwide

in timesharing in the global market (10.7 million) has rapidly increased over that in the United States (4.9 million).

From an aggregate perspective, the growth in both markets sends a very strong message that the "push" marketing strategies employed by timeshare developers is having a sustained growth effect.

Key Point 4.1

Since its inception, the timeshare industry has gradually gained in worldwide expansion, number of resorts, number of owners, and sales volume, which is a trend that indicates increased market acceptance.

Timeshare Market Segmentation

Much marketing effort can be wasted by attracting interest from people who for one reason or another are unsuitable potential customers. Either they have insufficient funds to make the purchase, they have unstable employment prospects, or they are just not at a time of life when timeshare is the right purchase for them. Lead generation, either by agents or in-house, is a potentially costly business because industry conversion rates average about 1 in 10 (ARDA, 2002b). These costs are further compounded if leads result in sales that are subsequently rescinded when customers change their minds and decide not to go ahead with the purchase.

Before going on to outline some ways of segmenting customers and current timeshare customer profiles, it is valuable to pause for a moment and think about the nature of timeshare service offers. Many debates have been held about the marketing of services and the extent of the differences with marketing products. Marketing has been largely concerned with ensuring that *the marketing mix* is appropriate—that is, ensuring that the product, place, price, and promotion are consistent with each other and focused on an identified *market segment* of customers. The 4Ps have been added to in the case of services because of the elements of services listed earlier. Table 4.2 lists the marketing mix for services, which now include people, processes, and premises in addition (Lashley, 2000).

Product	In timeshare the nature of the actual accommodation units in the form of the apartment or lodge constitutes the core element of the product that is being purchased by the customer. This might also include the supplementary product in the additional facilities in the resort – leisure facilities, golf courses, restaurants, bars, that make up the setting in which the accommodation is located.
Price	This will include the overall pricing strategy – this communicates something about the product – high price = good quality, low prices = value for money. The timeshare price consists of a number of elements – the purchase of the time in the unit, the additional service charges, and additional prices of leisure facilities, meals in restaurants, green fees, etc.
Place	It is often stated that most hospitality and tourism, including timeshare, marketing consists of location, location, location. Even though many timeshare owners use the services of exchange companies, there are many whose purchase is solely linked to a key location. Even those who make regular exchanges are identifying with a location type and hence the geographical position of time resorts is a key element of the offer to customers.
Promotion	The messages and media for telling customers about the brand and developing their understanding of what to expect is also an important consideration. Firstly, this is useful for focusing on media likely to be used by the key market segments of customers. Secondly, the public relations image of timeshare, and of the specific operator shape preconceptions held by customers.
People	The interaction of various personnel with customers is also part of the offer to customers and shapes their evaluation of the resort operator. This starts with initial contacts and sales personnel and goes on through on-going relationships in their regular visits to the resort. Traditionally this dimension of the marketing mix has been the least well managed, though many firms now see the people dimension of the mix as core to developing competitive advantage.
Processes	How customers are dealt with by the company, the documentation, the professionalism and tome of communications and the business dimension of the relationship also contribute to the total customer experience. The availability of flexibility arrangements for changing weeks within the primary resort or the ease with which it is possible to exchange the arrangement with another similar resort are also important features of the timeshare marketing mix.
Premises	The overall décor, property configuration in the form of bedrooms, in-suite facilities, living space, quality of fixtures and fittings have to be consistent with the brand. In addition to timeshare accommodation, the overall resorts premises contribute to the total customer experience and are thereby an element of the marketing mix presented by the operator to the customer.

Table 4.2 The Timeshare Services Marketing Mix

Key Point 4.2

The marketing mix identifies the different elements of benefits supplied to customers when they buy a service. The service marketing mix includes seven elements: product, price, place, promotion, people, processes, and premises.

The issues discussed in Table 4.2 are discussed more fully in Chapter 5 and in Chapter 12, but the table reminds us of the need to focus the timeshare marketing mix on the specific needs of the target market segment or segments of customers. Table 4.2 provides an overview of some of the key techniques for segmenting the potential population so as to identify clusters of customers with characteristics in common. Two key approaches are detailed in this chapter. The first is a fairly traditional approach that identifies variations in customer *demographic characteristics*—socioeconomic group–age–family life-cycle position. The appendix to this chapter provides an example of some of the segments that combine these various demographic factors. These are also discussed in Chapter 12 because several of these groups may provide future marketing opportunities. The second approach is to segment customers via *occasionality*, that is, the occasions for which customers use the business. Occasionality focuses not so much on the nature of the customers but on the reasons they are buying a timeshare property. These reasons shape their perceptions of the benefits of timeshare and their evaluation of the success of their purchase.

Segmenting customers via demographics is a fairly traditional way of segmenting customers. Some of the models developed involve using combinations of these dimensions. The categories suggested highlight some of the key elements, though there are many variations to the detailed categories suggested. Socioeconomic groupings combine a number of dimensions that include income but are chiefly concerned with occupational categories. These categories tend to also reflect job status, educational background, skill levels, employment conditions, and social class of the group. The six-category grouping is just one of a number of different segmentation devices; other researchers advocate as many as eight or twelve categories. The key point is that timeshare ownership is not generally spread across all socioeconomic groups. Rather, it tends to be concentrated in the higher socioeconomic groups, reflecting higher income levels.

Life-cycle position tends to reflect the stages in a typical, though somewhat traditional, life. Traditionally, individuals reach adulthood and experience a period of bachelorhood prior to marriage, then they start a family, and ultimately experience retirement. Life-cycle segmentation recognizes these traditional stages in a typical life and reflects the different interests and needs in these stages of life. Again, there are a number of systems for identifying these positions. Some allow for the fact that in many Western societies traditional families are no longer the dominant model. For example, increased divorce rates have increased the number of single-parent families and families comprised of second marriages. Also, increased rates of female employment have significantly added to the number of double-income households. In many markets, DINKIES (double income no kids) are a significant market segment because these households typically have high levels of disposable income and few restrictions on their time. Timeshare ownership tends to be concentrated in groups with high disposable income and can be seen to cluster in *Full Nest* and *Empty Nest* categories (Palmer, 2001).

Gender categories are important where the market tends to be gender specific, as it is in cosmetics, for example. Even where the market includes both, the message aimed at men and at women will be varied so as to reflect different perceptions, images, and language appropriate to each. Although most timeshare purchasers are mixed-gender couples, either with dependent children or without, there are potential markets in the gay community. In these cases, resorts may find a market niche with the gay male or gay female sector.

Understanding gender variations is also important in the timeshare sector because of the effect of gender differences on the way the sexes perceive the timeshare product, and the involvement of each in the decision-making process. Are different messages likely to have a different resonance with the two parties? For example, are there differences in the perception of the timeshare purchase as an investment, or as a venue for leisure activities, or as a home from home? As we shall see later, decision making within the family may be complex, and different partners may have different roles and influence in the process. Among *Full Nest* purchasers, children may exert a major influence on the purchase decision even though they themselves do not make the decision and do not pay for the actual purchase.

Geographical segmentation systems vary, but most systems divide geographical locations by zip code (post code) areas. These identify housing types, forms, or tenure and thereby indicate income levels and socioeconomic groupings. For example, areas that contain high levels of multi-let accommodations or public housing or trailer parks are unlikely to yield many potential timeshare customers. Timeshare operators can use these geographical location systems to direct postal promotional material and introductory offers at locations where there are the most potential customers. Thus owner-occupied, suburban locations including properties with higher purchase prices are more likely to yield more fruitful responses.

Other forms of categorization relate to individual and family lifestyle choices. People have varying interests in nature and the environment, health consciousness, materialism, and hedonism. Timeshare operators can identify different messages aimed at different groups. Thus, some resorts will appeal to those who like nature and the environment, and are health conscious, while other resorts will be much more attractive to pleasure seekers and the theme of an ongoing party. In other cases, timeshare owners may well see the purchase as an investment. In each case the type of persons, how they see the world, their values, attitudes, and beliefs will differ from those of other groups. As a consequence, the nature of the resort that attracts them, and the messages provided about the resort, will need to be consistent and targeted at the specific group.

Markets may be segmented by personality and behavioral characteristics in several ways. The most obvious includes issues related to extravert/introvert dimensions and stability/instability. These factors will influence the type of resort that individuals select and the message most likely to resonate with them. For example, extroverts will look for resorts and images that suggest other people, crowds, and typically perhaps parties and fun. The more introverted person will be interested in solitude and resorts that suggest outdoor solitary pursuits.

Key Point 4.3

Demographic segmentation describes customers or potential customers according to their population characteristics—socioeconomic group, life-cycle position, gender, geographical location, lifestyle, and personality.

See Table 4.2 for some examples of ways of segmenting customers so as to better understand timeshare customers in general and the specific market being attracted to a particular resort. Systematic marketing management aims to ensure that the marketing mix is consistent with the needs of a market segment or segments.

Case Study 4.1

De Vere Resort—Slaley Hall, Northumberland, United Kingdom

Slaley Hall is one of the De Vere Group's three locations with timeshare developments associated with hotel properties. Currently, the resort has sixty-five timeshare units built in the form of lodges with accommodations ranging from a single bedroom through three bedrooms. Some of the larger lodges can sleep up to eight people. The resort is set on 1,000 acres of the Northumbrian countryside and contains two high-quality golf courses, as well as leisure club facilities and other recreational facilities located in the hotel. The 4 star hotel includes an à la carte restaurant and cocktail bar, as well as budget bar and dining facilities.

Although some owners are young married couples without children and under the age of 35 who could be described as DINKIES, most are 40 years of age plus and have families with children. Most are professionals and senior managers as typified by socioeconomic groups A and B. The younger families have dependent children, though the majority have older children and are primarily at the Empty Nest stage. But even in these cases, children and their families accompany them on holiday. Many customers live within a two- or three-hour drive of the resort. Given the strong local sense of regional location felt by many people born in the area but now living elsewhere, many customers could be described as "ex-pats." That is, customers who have an emotional link to the area and visiting the resort can be seen as "going home."

Golf and walking opportunities, together with the resort's location near many beautiful spots along the Northumbrian coast and Hadrian's Wall provide many opportunities for visitor entertainment. In addition, resort managers provide a program of additional family entertainment. All free of charge to resort owners, the program includes pony trekking, quad bikes, golf lessons, clay pigeon shooting, general knowledge quizzes, and nature trails. These entertainments are greatly valued by owners with older dependent children.

Key Point 4.4

Clearly defined market segmentation assists the timeshare developer in identifying potential customers and the package of property and leisure facilities that best meet potential customer needs. In addition, marketing and sales activities are more effective because they are more focused on the most lucrative potential customer base.

Timeshare Ownership

The American Resort Association reports that timeshare owners tend to be within a specific age band and to have a higher than average income. The largest owner age group is within the 35- and 55-year-old band, and almost 80 percent have an income over $50,000 (ARDA, 2002a). Also, 64 percent have a college degree and 31 percent have a postgraduate degree, demonstrating a profile that suggests a more professional set of owners. Certainly, timeshare owners are more likely to be from professional and managerial socioeconomic groups—see A and B in Table 4.2. In addition, 85 percent of U.S. timeshare owners are married with children, confirming the Full Nest category in various stages. The European timeshare owner typically has no children at home and most likely is at an Empty Nest stage (TRI Consulting, 2001). This picture is further supported by the age of timeshare owners in Europe. The greatest proportion of new owners are between 40 and 60 years of age (TRI Consulting, 2001: 52), and this age group makes up 40 to 50 percent of all owners. While the majority of owners can be described as middle-aged, married, and from the higher socioeconomic groups, ARDA (2002a) suggests that there are significant ownership segments among single-person households and retirees.

Timeshare ownership tends to be concentrated in certain countries. Although the 4 million timeshare owners originate from all continents and most countries across the globe, 48 percent of all owners are based in the United States and 31 percent live in Europe. Of these European owners, 30 percent are resident in the United Kingdom and 20 percent are German citizens (TRI Consulting, 2001). Timeshare ownership is therefore not evenly spread; over six of every ten timeshare owners come from just three countries—the United States, the United Kingdom, and Germany.

With the exception of resorts aimed specifically at single and retiree owners, resort operators typically prefer to make sales presentations to couples because they find that in most households both parties have inputs into the decision-making process. In most cases they would also put lower and upper limits on age profiles so as to target potential purchasers who are most likely able to make a purchase. Similarly, they will look for employment stability and creditworthiness. ARDA (2002b) reports that in some cases, U.S. resort operators are reluctant to sell to non-U.S. citizens because of potential problems caused by exchange rate fluctuations.

Timeshare developers use these profiles as a way of focusing the resort at particular target segments. In some cases, the specific segment allows the resort operator to gain an exclusive position with a particular segment—for example, retirees, gays, or younger single-person households. Whatever the profile, resort operators are looking for sales prospects that match the segmentation categories identified as the target market. Marketing strategies are aimed at promotional activities that generate potential sales contacts that are most likely to create the best conversions.

As the market matures (ARDA, 2002b), the market is becoming increasingly segmented. Some developers are building larger and more luxurious units as a way of appealing to higher income earners with more disposable income and a requirement for luxury accommodation. Also, they are looking at packaging sales with access to time periods longer than traditional weeks. In some cases, people can opt for fractional interests of twelfths, tenths, fifths, and quarter shares. At the other end of the market, resort operators are looking for ways to access more price-sensitive markets. Some reduce the length of the right to use the property to ten or twenty years so as to appeal to younger people or older purchasers unwilling to make a contract covering thirty or forty years. European operators have introduced *canal boat* timeshare arrangements whereby the sale is no longer a fixed property but a waterborne mobile home (TRI Consulting, 2001). In other cases, purchasers can opt for biennial usage whereby the purchaser buys the right to use the property every other year. *Holiday packs*, favored by some European operators, fall somewhere between a package holiday and timeshare by offering arrangements that do not extend beyond three years (TRI Consulting, 2001).

Occasionality in Timeshare Markets

In addition to the market segmentation technique based on customer demographic profiles, many leisure retailers now segment customers according to the occasions for which they use the leisure service. The same customer may make use of a restaurant for several eat-out occasions—for example to *refuel* while working or shopping; because they *can't be bothered to* cook and they eat out as a replacement; to celebrate a *special occasion* to mark a birthday or anniversary; or for a *family meal out* (Lashley and Lincoln, 2002). On each of these occasions the customer has different motives and different expectations of the meal. These expectations also shape the customer's evaluation of the success of the visit, and operators need to understand the customers' *critical success factors* important for the customer's visit. In some cases, customers' critical success factors for one occasion are in conflict with those of customers visiting for other occasions. For example, those visiting restaurants for a family outing occasion may have needs that conflict with those who are visiting for a special meal occasion.

Timeshare operators need to be aware of occasionality dimensions among customers in order to better target promotional messages and to ensure that the profiles of resort guests/owners are compatible. The following presents a few examples of occasions that might apply to timeshare purchase decisions.

Home from Home Occasions

Some customers buy into a timeshare because they have a need for a sense of permanence and belonging in a specific location. They are most likely to visit the resort and their unit regularly at the time of the week purchased. The home from home customers are concerned chiefly with having a base that is perceived as their space and their "second home." Familiarity and getting to know the area in which the resort is located are important considerations. Research by Sweeney (2003) confirms that respondents like the familiarity that comes with owning a timeshare. One respondent said, "*You get to know the pictures on the walls, and you know where the corkscrew is.*" Another stated, "*It's very relaxing to arrive in a place you know.*" A third said, "*Yeah, I know exactly what's happening, and I know all the shops and where the markets are.*" Two of the respondents also referred to timeshare as having your own country cottage for a week, "*It's like having a country cottage, with a private swimming pool a hundred yards away, except it's only yours for a week,*" and "*So it's really like having your own country cottage for a limited period.*" The provision of detailed information packs that provide customers with information about the area, things to see and do, places of interest, and a local's insider knowledge are likely to be important critical success factors to customers who have made their resort purchase for this reason. Critical success factors will be concerned largely with relationships with staff at the resort and other resort owners. Social functions and opportunities to meet other guests are therefore also important critical success factors. Being recognized by resort staff and being treated as a valued customer, even a friend, by resort personnel are also critical to success. These customers are less likely to swap their week(s) for other locations or weeks, and they might find visitors in the same resort who are "swappers" a contradictory occasion. In these circumstances, a changing cohort of fellow resort users does not allow them to develop friendships that are an important aspect of their occasion.

Swapper Occasions

In direct contrast to the home from home occasion, some timeshare owners buy into a property never really intending to stay there. For them, the purchase is more akin to club membership that gives access to vacations in similar properties around the globe. Their property represents a currency through which they can purchase regular holidays with a greater sense of security. To some extent, they know what they are buying into because they have seen the quality of the purchase in their own resort. In other cases, timeshare owners may want to go to their standard location and will want to exchange their week(s) for others in other resorts. Sweeney (2003) provides insights into these occasions. One respondent owns a timeshare in the Costa del Sol as well as Scotland: *"The Spanish one we've tended to use every second year, and we've exchanged it as well"* (R2, p2: 63–64). Another respondent owns a timeshare in Madeira: *"Well we have been to Madeira twice now, and probably won't go back, so the exchange is the whole basis of it."* Critical success factors include transparency and equivalence. All involved in the exchange process want to ensure that potential exchanges are clearly identified and that the process allows for consideration of the relative value of the week being given up by the owner and the value of the property selected to exchange into.

In most cases, resort operators are affiliated with one other major international resort exchange company. These are Interval International and Resort Condominiums International, both of which operate out of the United States, though both have global resort profiles. Collectively, they include almost 6,000 resorts and have 4 million members internationally. In addition, some companies operate their own internal exchange processes whereby swappers can move to other resorts operated by the same company. Where an operator is also a hotel operator, there are some companies making exchanges from timeshare to hotel properties. The flexibility offered by these exchange systems has been a major factor in expanding the timeshare market because they have opened up opportunities for more traditional tourist visits to those who do not want to be tied to a specific site every year. *Points clubs*, whereby the consumer buys into a scheme, rather than a specific property, allow this type of customer to have access to multiple destinations (TRI Consulting, 2001). Points clubs are a natural and logical extension of the "swappers" need.

Activity Occasions

Here the timeshare purchase is linked to some particular activity that is attractive to specific market segments. The activity might be associated with golf, whereby customers want to have access to a good quality golf course. The opportunity to use the course at times convenient to the owner and at a reasonable charge are critical success factors. Other activities might relate to walk holiday activities, cultural and sporting activities, as in skiing or sailing or surfing activities. In all cases, access to the activity information, timetables, and links to these activities, even if they are outside of the resorts, are critical success factors. Family holiday occasions can be contradictory occasions because they may involve guests and packages of services to guests that are not compatible with those who are interested chiefly in activity vacations.

Family Holiday Occasions

The timeshare purchase is concerned with providing a venue for family holidays. The timeshare property contains attractions for all the family. Often the week or weeks purchased are consistent with school holidays—in some cases for the main holiday and in other cases associated with a second or third holiday. Critical success factors relate to the extent to which the property and the resort match the needs of all family members. Given the long-term nature of the timeshare relationship, it is likely that the venue will need to develop activities to match the various stages of the *Full Nest* outlined in Table 4.2. In addition, because of the likelihood that family members may span several generations and allow for owners to age into the *Empty Nest* phase, the resort has to be able to offer flexible facilities and adapt to the changed needs of owners and their families.

These critical success factors describe clusters of motives for choosing a particular timeshare property. Clearly, owners may make choices with more than one occasion in mind; so the home from home occasion and the family occasion are completely compatible. This occasionality model is useful, however, because first it suggests that the reasons for purchasing a timeshare property vary and that each decision to purchase involves some expectations of the benefits of the purchase and the factors critical to success. Second, the occasionality model suggests that motives and needs can vary, even for the same purchaser, and that resort operators need to be aware of these changing needs. Sweeney's (2003) research with timeshare owners confirms these varied and mixed expectations and needs.

Other Critical Success Factors

As indicated earlier, the location of the resort in proximity to attractions is one of the key critical success factors. Like all tourism venues, timeshare resorts have to be located in association with some desirable destination. Over 60 percent of European timeshare properties are located at beachside settings; the remaining locations are found in countryside, mountain, lakeside, and ski settings. A very small number are located in urban locations (ARDA, 2002a). That said, not all resorts are located in high-volume tourist destinations; many service a regional demand—that is, with a three-hour drive to the resort. In some cases, people will travel even further afield to these regional resorts because they are associated with that particular region. People born and brought up in a particular area who now live elsewhere will buy a timeshare property as a means of reconnecting with their roots.

Ease of access is another critical success factor. The resort must typically be located close to major communications networks, airports, train system, and road network. Given that a one-week timeslot is the most common ownership package, traveling time needs to be kept to a minimum because of the relative impact on total time available. In addition, time spent during the vacation period traveling to the attractions associated with the destination needs to be considered. Ease of access and travel around the resort are also factors that will be critical to resort owners, exchangers, and renters.

Key Point 4.5

The motives for buying a timeshare arrangement vary and may change over time as family and personal circumstances change. An awareness of the customer occasion is important for both selling activities and for the development of service flexibility so as to meet changing customer needs more effectively.

Consumer Decision Making

The models outlined in this section frequently assume a rational and formal process to decision making that is typically displayed as a flow diagram. As we shall see, these models can be criticized for these very reasons, but they are useful in attempting to describe the process and influences. Figure 4.4 reproduces one of the generic models related to consumer decision making. The model based on the seminal work of Engel, Kollat, and Blackwell (EKB) is said to be a descriptive rather than a predictive model (Williams, 2002). However, it was developed to consider the purchase of high-risk purchases and as such is applicable to timeshare decision making.

The EKB model commences with a recognition of a need and motivation. *Stage 1: Motivation and Need* suggests that the decision process first requires this recognition of need and desire to do something about it. Later, Engel, Blackwell, and Miniard (1995) recognized that a range of individual and environmental influences was likely to affect recognition of need and the willingness to do something about it. Individual

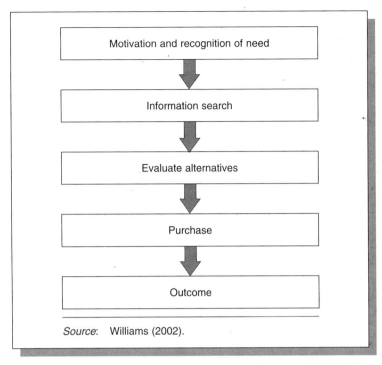

Figure 4.4 Basic Engel, Kollat, and Blackwell Model of Consumer Decision Making

influences starting with consumers' knowledge of the time-share product, their motivation, attitudes, beliefs and values, lifestyle and demographics, and the like, impact on recognition of a need to explore timeshare. Similarly, environmental influences such as culture, social class, family and friends, and shared views about timeshare impact on the evaluation of the need. The knowledge dimension, at both an individual and an environmental level, is particularly relevant to timeshare sales. High-profile cases of unethical behavior by timeshare sales teams and resort operators shape knowledge and understanding of what is on offer and the sale process. It is possible, for example, that the need of some potential owners, for what they identify as a regular "home from home" will not be translated into a need for timeshare because it is not seen as a legitimate option. Undoubtedly, the negative image of timeshare creates a backdrop against which perceptions of the need for a timeshare purchase are shaped.

The search for information relating to the possible purchase takes place in *Stage 2: Information Search*. Sources of information may include the mass media, family and friends, sales personnel, and the Internet. Typically, a purchase decision such as timeshare, incorporating a substantial purchase price and long-term commitment, will involve a substantial search process in Stage 2. In theory, the search process increases as the potential risk increases. To some extent, the growing brand presence in the timeshare field simplifies and reduces the perceived risks involved in the purchase. Thus, brand knowledge enables a shorted and more focused search because the brand presents a source of information and represents a set of expectations about the nature of the firm and its repute as an ethical trader. The increasing number of timeshare owners who purchase additional weeks with a resort operator with whom they have a relationship are in effect reducing the need to engage fully in the search stage of the purchase.

Once information has been gathered, the EKB model suggests that the potential purchaser evaluates the alternatives. Hence in *Stage 3: Alternative Evaluation*, the potential choices available are considered and related to the criteria and values, attitudes, and beliefs held by the potential purchaser. These will vary, even within the same decision maker, and will depend on the consumer occasion involved. Hence, evaluation of the potential purchase of the "home from home" is more likely to consider different factors than those considered for swapper occasions. Again, the model suggests that this process is likely to be longer and more elaborate for higher risk purchases.

Stage 4: Consumption and Outcomes involves processes that evaluate the outcomes of the experiences. Has the consumption experience exceeded, matched, or not met expectations? The timeshare purchase typically involves a long-term relationship including many visits over the time of the tenure. The same process may be involved, and customers will evaluate the success of their decision as a result of each visit. Research on service providers in general shows that loyal and satisfied customers have real business value. They are more likely to tell others when they have a good experience, and these positive messages are more readily believed by family and friends. Loyal customers generate new business because they encourage others to buy. In addition, existing customers are cheaper sources of new sales than are the new customers. Research shows that a sale generated from a new customer can cost fourteen times more than a sale generated from an existing customer (Carper, 1992; Leach, 1995).

Key Point 4.6

Attempts to provide a rational model of consumer decision-making behavior suggest that consumers got through a number of stages—motivation and need, education and search, alternative evaluation, consumption and outcomes.

This model is normative in that it represents an uncritical view of decision making. It assumes that purchasers are operating in a perfect market, where rationale-based optimum decisions are made in equal power relationships with supplier firms. Williams (2002), however, raises some questions about all these assumptions. Markets are rarely perfect, buyers seldom have all the information available, and many make decisions irrationally. A frequent criticism of timeshare sales operation is that they have put customers under undue and unfair pressure to make a purchase decision. This is why most regulatory authorities now insist on a cooling-off period when the customer has the right to break the agreement.

This model has also been criticized within the context of hospitality services because it does not allow for the emotional dimensions that are an important part of hospitality services (Teare, 1995). These emotional dimensions are present in the initial decision to buy the timeshare property, and they are also a feature of subsequent visits to the property. Teare (1995) developed a general model for hospitality services that might be used as a model for describing idealized decision-making processes. However, this model represents a schematic of how the process might be imagined rather than a model that can assist in predicting consumer behavior. Bareham (1995: 13) sums up some of the criticisms when he states that "most models can be criticised as providing no more than a description of a range of influencing variables. There is a danger that the mere drawing of boxes and arrows, which shows links between variables, may imply causal relationships which do not exist."

Other research traditions focus on the consumer as an individual and consider cognitive influences on consumer behavior. Consumer motivation, perception, personality, learning, memory, and meaning provide insights into the way consumers think and thereby provide insights into decision-making processes (Wilkie, 1994). Through the study of motivation, it may be possible to better understand why consumers make timeshare purchases, or through the study of perception, how information from the outside world is translated internally to provide meaning. Why, for example, do some consumers have positive views about timeshare, while others hold negative ones? How does personality influence consumer behavior and how do individuals learn about the things they know as consumers?

Although a number of definitions have been given for the complex notion of motivation (Williams, 2002), simply put, it concerns why people do what they do. Psychologists broadly refer to identification of needs and drives and behaviors directed toward goals that satisfy them. Timeshare consumers are attempting to satisfy needs though their decision to purchase. Using Maslow's (1954) hierarchy, the purchase may involve satisfaction of *status* or *esteem needs* because the purchase reflects a desirable consumer durable. It may involve satisfaction of *belonging needs* because the timeshare represents a permanent place to which to return. This may be of particular importance for *home from home* occasions. The sense of place might also involve the satisfaction of *self-actualization needs*, particularly where the location represents a symbol of a valued lifestyle, say involving nature and environmentalism. Herzberg's (1966) explanations of human motivation can be helpful in understanding timeshare consumer behavior through the notion that satisfaction, at its highest level is likely to involve emotional and intangible dimensions, as well as their evaluation of the physical facilities. If these physical facilities are not up to customer expectations, customers will be dissatisfied, whereas facilities better than expected will not create satisfaction. Their treatment by sales and after-sales staff, as well as during visits to resorts, is most likely to create satisfaction.

Learning theory considers the processes of how individuals change their knowledge, feelings, attitudes, and beliefs about the world as a result of experience. Two broad learning theories have been used in commercial settings. *Behaviorism* is concerned with stimulating consumer actions, not so much through rational and cognitive thought but through the association of desirable images with behavior. Timeshare operators who conduct advertising campaigns that feature images of happy families taking sunshine holidays linked to timeshare properties are attempting to use *classic conditioning* techniques. That is, they stimulate a decision to buy through an association with desirable images. In contrast, *operant conditioning* techniques aim to stimulate repeat behavior through the use of sample weekends or sample visits to the property. This strand of behaviorist theory suggests that people can be conditioned into repeating behaviors through various forms of the free offer whereby they learn to repeat the behavior to which they have been introduced. In both cases, behaviorists are concerned not with internal thought processes, but with the behavioral outcomes—timeshare use and purchase.

The *cognitive* school of learning theory focuses on learning as knowledge through memory and concepts. While this approach might incorporate learning from trial and error, learning is also based on generalizing principles and the application of memory. The fact that many people *know* that the timeshare business is unethical is a result of learning. In this case, however, people are using some knowledge of bad practice to generalize over the whole provision. They are making prejudgments about all timeshare organizations on the basis of the knowledge of a few. Timeshare operators have to work to overcome this knowledge and to create new knowledge of the industry. Memory is a key concept in learning because it aids retrieval of learning when it is needed.

Here the use of repetition as a way of cementing knowledge of an event, or imaging so as to establish pictorial reference, or using personal example all help to establish a piece of knowledge or emotional impression in the individual. Thus, the shared knowledge about timeshare has been learned not so much through personal experience and knowledge, but through repeated negative stories in the news media. Branded operators are often able to work from a new knowledge base. That is, the customers know the brand and the integrity of the company, and they use this knowledge to inform judgments about the timeshare offer. Knowledge of the brand, often linked to a hotel brand such as Marriott, Hilton, or De Vere, has been an important factor in the growth of timeshare because brand knowledge overcomes negative images.

The personality differences between consumers is an area of interest in the study of consumer behavior. Statt (1997: 63) describes personality as "the sum total of all the factors that make up an individual human being both individual and human; the thinking, feeling and behaving that all human beings have in common, and the characteristic pattern of these elements that make every human being unique. . . . stresses the important role that unconscious processes that may be hidden from the individual but are partly perceptible to other people." The development of this pattern of behaving in the world comes as a result of inherited and environmental experiences that are compounded through life's experiences, but that also often contain unexpressed feelings that inform decisions and choices. As a consequence, merely asking consumers what they want or need does not always reveal actual purchase patterns. Psychographic techniques have been developed to reflect personality differences that identify patterns of needs; these patterns can be used to identify products and services or messages about them that match these personality patterns.

Associated with these personality differences are *self-concepts* that are developed through each individual's lifetime as he or she experiences life and interactions with other people. In each case, the self-concept involves behaviors associated with the roles that individuals play: father, husband, wife, mother, executive, lecturer, student. In addition, self-concepts define consumption patterns. Purchases and patterns of consumption help demonstrate this concept of the self to both the individual and others. Hence, the leather jacket and jeans worn by the "biker" are as much a symbol of the self as are the business suit and briefcase. In both cases, clothes and artifacts are serving as badges of and symbols about the individual. Obviously, these self-concepts influence purchase patterns beyond clothes, food eaten, drinks consumed, motor vehicles, and types of homes, and most purchases can be explained as extensions of or expressions of this self-image.

Timeshare ownership can be viewed in a similar light. Those who are purchasing timeshares for "home from home" occasions are expressing different dimensions of self-image than those who purchase for swapper occasions. In both cases, timeshare ownership may well signify a self-image perception of status and success. The timeshare represents a symbolic second home. On the other hand, home from home occasion consumers have self-concepts that include permanence and stability, whereas the swappers may well have self-images that include excitement and variety: "we are not boring, we go to lots of interesting places." While these comments are somewhat speculative, self-concept theory probably has the most to offer timeshare resort operators. Previous research suggests that self-concept research displays the most consistent results and offers the greatest promise to business organizations (Foxhall, 1992).

The consumer's perception of the world is another area of study that provides insights for timeshare operators. Put simply, perception is the process whereby messages received by the senses—sight, hearing, smell, and touch, are interpreted and given meaning by individuals. Most importantly, prior experience and prejudgments are influential in the way these messages are perceived. As mentioned earlier, timeshare has been dogged by prejudgments made by potential purchases because of the way certain high-profile cases have been treated in the mass media. These prejudgments create an influential set of expectations that operators need to address. Perception is also influential in evaluating the success of the purchase; the quality of fitting in the unit, the quality of the resort, and the updating and refurbishment of these facilities are all factors that help consumers evaluate their purchase. Brand perceptions are also an important consideration because the brand establishes a set of perceived messages that influence customer expectations. Along with other service sector events, timeshare brands help consumers resolve potential risks in the purchase.

Finally, consumers are either explicit or implicit members of groups. Individuals belong to two types of groups. They are members of small groups where all members are known to each other, such as the family and work groups. Individuals are also members of larger groups in which not all members are known to each other, but which give individuals a sense of self—for example, profession, nation, football club. In both cases, group membership influences individual behavior by establishing norms of behavior to which the individual conforms. Even where these norms are not formally expressed, individuals will often conform to these norms as a way of identifying with one group and by implication not identifying with others. *Reference groups* are expressed as a group of people who influence an individual's behavior (Williams, 2002). For timeshare operators, reference groups provide a useful means of overcoming some of the negative images of the timeshare offer. By associating timeshare with more successful people, others see timeshare as a must-have consumer durable. It becomes a necessary signifier of status and position and a symbol of membership of the aspirational group.

Key Point 4.7

Marketeers need to understand consumers as individuals through consideration of variations in motives—learning and memory—personality and groups to whom they reference group affiliations.

Conclusion

Timeshare markets are segmented because not all of the population is in a position to make the timeshare purchase. Differences in income, employment stability, and career, as well as differences in family circumstances, mean that the timeshare offer is not of interest to everyone. Research on current timeshare ownership suggests that owners tend to be middle aged, belong to families with or without dependent children, have higher than average incomes, and are more likely to have a higher education than the population as a whole. In these circumstances, resort developers and operators must understand the various techniques for segmenting the potential market so as to better target marketing efforts and generate potential sales leads.

In addition, the timeshare market itself is not homogeneous. Clearly, different motives exist for buying into timeshare, and these motives create different expectations as to how the timeshare product should be offered and organized. These expectations develop critical success factors by which customers evaluate the timeshare experience. An understanding of the critical success factors associated with different occasions is crucial for the delivery of timeshare experiences that are in line with customer perceptions and needs. The notion of occassionality also questions the extent that timeshare resorts can appeal to all timeshare customers in the same way. Different expectations and critical success factors may mean that some customer groups are in contradiction to others. That is, their mutual expectations are at odds with each other.

Finally, consumer behavior in general and decisions to buy into timeshare occasions in particular can be better understood through considerations of the individual differences and factors influencing their behavior. Models of consumer behavior are useful because they describe how the consumer should approach decision making for purchases but are often criticized because they are not adequate predictors of actual consumer behavior. Studies of personality differences, consumer learning and memory, perceptual differences, and reference group affiliations help to provide some insight into the personal and environmental factors that influence consumer decisions. Certainly, an informed understanding of these influences will help timeshare resort operators to focus on the factors that will have the greatest resonance with identified clusters of customers or potential customers.

Appendix

Cohorts Defintions

Source: http://cohorts.com/index.html

Married Couples

Cohort Segment Name		Description	Median Age	Median Income
	Alex & Judith	**Affluent Empty-Nesters** Dual-income, older couples who use their high discretionary incomes to enjoy all aspects of the good life.	61	$143,000
	Jeffrey & Ellen	**Affluent Couples with Kids** Urban families who, despite having children at home, have sufficient financial resources to own the latest high-tech products and to lead very active recreational and cultural lifestyles.	43	$141,000
	Barry & Kathleen	**Affluent Professional Couples** Educated, dual-income, childless couples who have connoisseur tastes and are focused on their careers, staying fit and investing.	46	$133,000
	Stan & Carole	**Upscale Middle-Aged Couples** Unburdened by children, these creditworthy, dual-income couples divide their time between the great outdoors and domestic hobbies.	49	$74,000

Cohort Segment Name	Description	Median Age	Median Income
Brett & Tracey	**Hyperactive Newlyweds** Young, dual-income, childless couples whose energies are channeled into active sports, outdoor activities, careers, and their home lives.	31	$65,000
Danny & Vickie	**Teen-Dominated Families** Middle-aged, middle-income families whose teen-dominated households keep busy with outdoor activities, computers and video games.	42	$57,000
Burt & Marilyn	**Mature Couples** Comfortable, close-to-retirement homeowners who are active investors and who engage in charitable activities, travel, politics and their grandchildren.	66	$57,000
Todd & Wendy	**Back-to-School Families** Families with midrange incomes, preadolescent kids, pets, and lots of video, computer, and outdoor activities to keep them occupied.	38	$55,000
Chad & Tammie	**Young Families** Up-and-coming young families who curtail their lifestyles expenses through less-costly outdoors activities and working around the house.	32	$53,000
Frank & Shirley	**Older Couples Raising Kids** Conservative grandparents and older parents raising kids, whose home-oriented lifestyles include pets, home workshop, gardening, and sweepstakes.	60	$48,000

(Continued)

Cohort Segment Name		Description	Median Age	Median Income
	Ronnie & Debbie	**Working-Class Couples** Moderate-income couples with traditional interests including fishing, hunting, automotive work, and crafts.	47	$38,000
	Eric & Rachel	**Young Married Starters** Young, childless renters whose lifestyle patterns include outdoor activities like camping, fishing, and running, as well as automotive work and video games.	28	$21,000
	Elwood & Willamae	**Modest-Income Grandparents** Retired couples with modest incomes who dote on their grandchildren and engage primarily in domestic pursuits.	72	$20,000

Single Females

Cohort Segment Name		Description	Median Age	Median Income
	Elizabeth	**Savvy Career Women** Affluent, working women with sophisticated tastes, very active lifestyles, and good investing habits.	41	$173,000
	Virginia	**Upscale Mature Women** Older women approaching or enjoying retirement, who travel and have upscale interests, including charitable causes and investments.	59	$72,000
	Allison	**Educated Working Women** Childless, professional women building their careers, developing sophisticated tastes and staying fit.	33	$52,000

Cohort Segment Name		Description	Median Age	Median Income
	Andrea	**Single Moms with Careers** Successful, professional single mothers who balance their careers with the demands of raising their children.	39	$50,000
	Bernice	**Active Grandmothers** Home-oriented women who enjoy handicrafts, indoor gardening, and their grandchildren.	61	$35,000
	Penny	**Working-Class Women** Childless female office workers who are concerned with their appearance; enjoy music, pets, and handicrafts; and add intrigue to their lives with the prospect of winning the big sweepstakes.	43	$18,000
	Denise	**Single Moms on a Budget** Single mothers with modest incomes who indulge their kids with video games, movies, and music, and who try to find a little time for themselves.	36	$18,000
	Megan	**Fit & Stylish Students** Young, fashion-conscious, career-minded female students who enjoy music, aerobic sports, and the latest in high tech.	26	$17,000
	Minnie	**Fixed-Income Grandmothers** Older single women who spend lots of time on their grandchildren, handicrafts, and religious reading.	73	$11,000

Single Males

Cohort Segment Name		Description	Median Age	Median Income
	Jonathan	**Elite Single Men** High-powered, career-driven men with sophisticated tastes, extensive investments, and the means to travel the world.	42	$172,000
	Sean	**Affluent Guys** Affluent, health- and fitness-minded men with investments and upscale interests.	43	$96,000
	Harry	**Well-to-Do Gentlemen** Mature men who are savvy about their investments, travel, and politics.	58	$49,000
	Ryan	**Energetic Young Guys** Young, physically active men with strong career drives and upscale interests, including electronics and technology.	33	$47,000
	Randy	**Single Dads** Single fathers who enjoy outdoor activities, their home workshops, and electronic entertainment with their kids.	37	$42,000
	Jerry	**Working-Class Guys** Blue-collar men who spend their free time in the garage or outdoors.	46	$19,000

Cohort Segment Name		Description	Median Age	Median Income
	Jason	**Male Students and Grads** Physically active, technologically inclined young men finishing school or embarking on their first job.	26	$17,000
	Elmer	**Sedentary Men** Aging, sedentary men with fixed incomes and few interests beyond their grandchildren and their gardens.	73	$17,000

Households That Defy Classification	
Omegas	Omegas are people who are impossible to classify distinctly. They may be married or single, home owners or renters, 18 to 65 years old, have incomes that range from very low to six figures, and enjoy numerous and diverse interests.

CHAPTER 5

Relationship Marketing, Selling, and Beyond

Learning Objectives

After studying this chapter you should be able to:

- critically discuss the value of relationship marketing in timeshare resorts.
- evaluate sales and contact generation techniques.
- critically analyze the link between selling tactics and customer loyalty.
- identify and evaluate long-range techniques for maintaining customer loyalty.

Introduction

Those who are buying timeshare weeks are typically entering into a long-term relationship with resort operators, either directly or indirectly. Some owners are buying into a particular location and the familiarity of place that the permanence of the site represents to the "home from home" customers discussed in Chapter 4. In other cases, the relationship with the resort into which they have bought is less permanent because they are swappers. In even these cases, however, the relationship between the resort operator and the customer needs to be worked. The base resort is losing revenue from onsite purchases when customers go elsewhere. In addition, existing customers are a more low-cost source of additional sales. Resorts that receive large numbers of visitors or swappers from other resorts have a vested interest in enticing them back. Developing a successful and valued relationship with customers is important for resort operators, regardless of the way the customers use the resort.

Timeshare operators need to adopt approaches to customers that are founded on the principles of relationship marketing. Such an approach starts with the generation of prospective customers through all the stages of the presentation, the closing deal, and previsit contacts, and throughout each and every visit. All contacts need to reinforce and build on the long-term relationship between organization and client. Although sound ethical practice as discussed in Chapter 10 suggests that this is the way to do business, there are more immediate business benefits to building the relationship. Satisfied and happy customers are much more likely to purchase additional time periods, and perhaps more importantly, they become in effect champions for the business with family and friends.

This chapter explores some of the issues specific to customer and organizational contacts. It deals with issues that have relevance to those discussed in Chapters 4 and 8 because relationship marketing has to consider issues relevant to consumer behavior and to customer perceptions of service quality, as well as expectations of service delivery.

Relationship Marketing and Customer Loyalty

Timeshare by its very nature involves a longer term relationship than many transaction-based customer–supplier interactions. Obviously, there is an initial transaction at the point-of-sale, but the fact that owners are buying the right to use a property within a resort on a regular basis means that the relationship is ongoing and that relationship marketing has much to offer the resort operator in building customer loyalty. Even when owners are swapping their property ownership rights so as to stay in other resorts, the base resort should still be developing customer loyalty through relationship marketing so that owners have a sense of home or belonging.

Like many other management terms, *relationship marketing* sounds straightforward enough but in fact embraces a number of meanings (Palmer, 2001). Some define the term as any contact between customers and firms regardless of their commitment to each other, while others are more focused on building a lifetime relationship with the customer involving issues such as commitment, interdependence, and trust (Gummeson, 1999). This last-named perspective seems to offer the most fruitful approach to timeshare operators.

Some writers perceive relationship marketing as involving three levels of approaches (Berry, 1995). On a *tactical level*, relationship marketing is limited to sales promotion techniques, which are often associated with information technology but are concerned with creating incentives to visit the business or to purchase. These schemes rely largely on economic benefits to customers and do not generate loyalty beyond the scheme. An example is hotel-discounted rates to customers through "loyalty schemes" or "club card holders." On a more *strategic level*, relationship marketing is said to be a process whereby customers are tied into a relationship with supplier firms through legal, economic, technological, geographical, and time bonds (Palmer, 2001). Classic timeshare relationships are based on this relationship approach. Prior to the extension of exchange schemes, owners were buying into semipermanent relations with resort operators. As in other cases, this can lead to a form of customer detention rather than retention where emotional bonds have not been established. Without a more symmetrical relationship, customers are often in a disadvantaged position in relationship to the firm because of "inequalities of knowledge, power, and resources, rather than mutual trust and empathy" (Palmer, 2001: 114). To a large extent, these relationships are best developed on the basis of the ethical considerations to be discussed in Chapter 10. The most successful schemes build long-term customer relationships through mutual rewards and cooperation designed to achieve genuinely beneficial mutual goals.

Relationship marketing at a more *philosophical level* requires a change in marketing focus. Marketing shifts the focus from customer groups, their perceived needs, and products or services supplied to them via selling opportunities to customer emotions and emotional needs in the service context. This entails using employees to meet the needs of customers better than competitors do.

Figure 5.1 provides a comparison of more traditional approaches to marketing with the relationship marketing approach. Timeshare resort operators have strong opportunities to build relationships over the long term by focusing on customer retention and resort repeats by tracking customers and their buying patterns, as well as developing strong customer commitment through a multilayered approach to quality customer experiences across the resort.

Traditional Transaction-Oriented Marketing	Relationship Marketing
Focus on single sale	Focus on customer retention
Short-term orientation	Long-term orientation
Sales to anonymous buyers	Tracking identifiable buyers
Salesperson is the main interface between buyer and seller	Multiple levels of relationship between buyer and seller
Limited customer commitment	High customer commitment
Quality is the responsibility of service operations departments	Quality is the responsibility of all

Source: Palmer (2001).

Figure 5.1 Components of Transactional and Relational Exchange Compared

This focus is highly consistent with points made about customer needs here and in Chapter 7, and later in Chapter 12. A constant theme in these chapters is that hospitality, including timeshare, involves more than a mere service encounter. Acts of hospitality in the way guests are hosted by management and staff are likely to build a loyal customer base whereby such relationships are based on genuine acts of "hospitableness" (Telfer, 2000). In particular, an awareness of the emotions of hospitality (Lashley, Morison, and Randall, 2004) helps develop customer feelings of welcome, personal worth, safety, and comfort. By returning to some traditional definitions of hospitality and ensuring they are used to inform service practice, customers can be converted into friends and thereby loyal customers.

Thus, it is perhaps an error to assume that all customers are looking for such long-term relationships, and so it is important to consider different buyer motives and to adopt strategies that are more responsive to specific customer needs. The experience of major food retailers suggests that it is possible to produce thousands of different promotional messages, each shaped by the details of customers' individual purchase records. Sensitive and well-thought-through strategies do build loyal customers, providing they genuinely focus on customer needs. Increasingly sophisticated customers quickly pick up on attempts to view them as a captive audience who can be sold other products from the company's portfolio.

Key Point 5.1

Timeshare resort operators have opportunities to build a loyal customer base through the use of relationship marketing techniques.

Benefits of Customer Relationship Marketing

One of the most widely recognized benefits of customer relationship marketing relates to the relative costs of losing and replacing existing customers. Owners who decide to sell their property interest and have to be replaced cause extra costs to the resort operator. Similarly, resort owners who transfer out to another resort represent lost revenue to the resort operator, particularly if no income exchange fills the gap. Owners or visitors who decide not to use resort facilities during their visit also represent lost custom and revenue. Service organization costs are considerably increased if new customers have to be constantly generated. Figures vary, but the cost can be anything from six to fourteen times more to gain sales from new customers than from existing customers. Current timeshare owners are an important source of additional sales.

The European timeshare sector experience shows that approximately 17 percent are "no-shows" while almost 50 percent of owners exchange from their base resort (TRI Consulting, 2001: 40). Approximately 30 percent of resort owners occupy the property during the purchased week(s), while almost 60 percent of unsold property resort weeks remain unoccupied at any one time. These figures show that the sector has considerable room to improve occupancy levels. Improving the relationship with timeshare owners can make a significant contribution to filling in the gaps by reducing the number of no-shows and by increasing the volume of ownership occupations.

In addition, relationship marketing can help target more profitable customers in promotional activities. Not all customers are equally valuable, as we have seen; some are more likely to transfer than others, and timeshare operators need to focus on those who are most likely to return to the resort or use the resort regularly. In other cases, resort customers can be assessed according to their average spending while in the resort. Those who are most likely to dine in the resort's restaurants or to use other facilities produce more revenue than those who limit their disposable income spent while at the resort, or who spend away from the resort.

Higher customer retention rates mean ultimately an improving market share as fewer lost customers together with new customers, adds to the total of customers available. Sales to existing customers are more efficient because sales messages are focused on the specific needs of each customer. Less time is needed to establish relationships, and the timeshare sector is important because existing users have fewer anxieties, bonds of trust already exist, and interpersonal relationships are well established. A cycle of success is created, resulting in improved pay for sales staff and improved morale. This leads to improved quality of service, more employee and customer motivation, and thus improved sales.

Key Point 5.2

Relationship marketing benefits the organization because loyal customers are a lower cost source of additional sales, personal recommendation, and greater profitability.

Building the Relationship

Building relationships with timeshare customers involves four dimensions: the physical product presented by the accommodation and the resort in general; employees who are effective in building relationships with customers; the right mix of customers; and the measure of service experiences so as to make improvements.

Products

The quality of design, fittings, and maintenance shape customer perceptions of the physical aspects of the resort. Although many resort developers will target the design and fit at specific groups, some customers have been disappointed by the failure of resort operators to maintain the property to original standards. In some cases, firms have failed to allocate sufficient funds to ensure maintenance and refits. As a result, the resort and units develop a shabby appearance that leads to negative feelings about the relationship. In addition, customers' expectations are not static. As they experience upgrades in the quality of the equipment and facilities in their own homes, their expectations of what constitutes a high quality fit changes over time.

In addition, customer needs in terms of the facilities, equipment, and support may vary according to age and family life-cycle position. As children grow or mature into adults, timeshare facilities may need to adapt to meet these changes. Good relationship building requires the resort operator to be aware of these changes in circumstances for each customer.

Employees

Every contact with the customer should build on and develop the relationship. This is beyond the responsibility of the marketing department. Customer contact from reception, through maintenance, to billing and administration, has to reinforce and build the developing relationship with the customer. Gronroos (1994) suggests that employees need to be "part-time marketeers." Others suggest that each employee should be regarded as *the* service provider; in other words, it is contacts with people that fundamentally impact on the relationship with the organization. Bearing in mind the emotional dimensions present in most service encounters and the specific emotions associated with hospitality services, we see that employee emotional performance is fundamental to building the loyal customer.

This book makes the link between employment practices and the development of desirable customer experiences and thereby loyal customers in Chapters 4, 7, and 8. The careful recruitment of employees who have the correct emotional profile, skills, and employment stability is an important first step. But training, performance appraisal, rewards, management styles, and levels of empowerment, together with career structures and prospects, all need to be consistent with the objectives of building relationships and developing long-term customer loyalty.

The way employees are motivated, inspired, and organized needs to be consistent with the need to build relationships. Participative forms of empowerment (Lashley, 2001) appear to offer an important model because they encourage employees to do whatever it takes to ensure customer satisfaction. The employees are empowered with the authority to make decisions, allocate resources, adjust procedures, and rectify service errors as they see fit for the customer. This approach to managing recognizes that customer needs and wants vary and that rigid standards and procedures are frequently counterproductive because they either produce inflexibility or limit personal initiative. Empowering individuals or work groups to make a range of decisions that managers or supervisors might make in a traditional organization requires careful planning, a long-term cultural commitment to customer satisfaction, and a trust-oriented culture—features not readily found in organizations in the sector.

Customers

A number of issues relate to customers in timeshare resort operations. First, fellow customers are themselves part of the customer experience. Often the attraction of buying into the semipermanence of a timeshare property is related to the idea of fellow owners being "people like us." Relationship marketing and the building of a loyal customer base need are based on selecting customer profiles, life-cycle position, and other demographics. Similarly, the number of swappers within a mix of "home from home" buyers needs careful consideration because in the latter case neighbors and regular owners on holiday at the same time reinforce the experiences of familiarity and belonging.

Customer profiles in terms of spending patterns are another aspect of the relationship marketing strategy. For example, sales analysis offers opportunities to provide guest services in an unprompted manner. Noting that a guest usually buys the same newspaper or drinks a particular wine or likes a specific seat in the restaurant can all help the guest to feel important and valued. Furthermore, guest sales analysis can help to determine the value of customers to the business as a whole (Rust and Oliver, 1994). Based on this analysis, it is possible to calculate a potential "lifetime value of a customer." This information may also be used to stimulate visits by the more valuable customers. For example, by attempting to minimize the number of no-shows among this high-value group, the resort operator can help maximize income.

Measurement

Measurement can be used to control the process, assess volumes and flows, and provide feedback on the effectiveness of various initiatives and actions. It is important, however, that these measures incorporate measures from both parties' perspectives. Stakeholder analysis of success is important because it allows the organization to account for success in ways that are sensitive to customer needs. Typically, a balanced scorecard approach adopts a range of measures that include "tangible" and "hard" measures as well as "intangible" and "soft" measures. These might include customer satisfaction surveys, customer complaint analysis, staff satisfaction, and staff retention measures together with some of the sales and economic data referred to earlier. These measures need to explore issues beyond those adopted by current accounting procedures and practice. In fact, an overreliance on accounting measures is incompatible with the development of the sort of long-term relationships being advocated here.

Key Point 5.3

Relationship marketing in the timeshare involves four dimensions. The physical product presented by the accommodation and the resort in general; employees who are effective in building relationships with customers; the right mix of customers; and the measure of service experiences so as to monitor and make improvements.

Rust and Oliver, 1994; Rust and Oliver et al. (1994: 387) report experiences from the U.S. retail sector which show three factors important in establishing strong relationships with individual customers, which might be helpful for resort operators,

1. *Keep it local.* A relationship implies contact between specific individuals—employees and customers. Benchmark practice suggests that resort managers should have responsibility for developing relationships rather than the company as a whole. This squares with the interpersonal and emotional dimensions of the relationship.

2. *The program should include tangible and intangible benefits.* Tangible benefits might involve price discounts and priority promotions that are available only to loyal customers.

Intangible benefits might involve priority attention, access to popular seating positions in the restaurant, or priority check out/in.

3. *Good communication is essential.* Frequent communication with loyal customers reinforcing their special relationship is important. Best practice suggests that this might include six to eight contacts per year, including announcements, promotions, and surveys.

Building customer loyalty requires more than just repetitious behavior. Customers who frequently visit a resort or service within the resort may be doing so because only limited choice is available and they may use the facility because there is no alternative. In effect, they may be quite dissatisfied with what they get and would happily switch if they were given the chance. In other cases, repeat purchases are more a by-product of customer inertia rather than genuine satisfaction and long-term loyalty. Customers who are loyal through inertia will behave differently than those who have strong emotional ties to it. Figure 5.2 identifies a model showing a number of stages and degrees of loyalty. Loyal customers are ultimately those who have a strong emotional bond with the organization and who act as advocates of the business to family, friends, and others with whom they have contact.

Customer loyalty depends on two dimensions: a positive attitude to the product, brand, or service provider and high

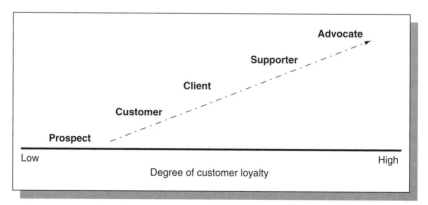

Figure 5.2 Levels of Customer Loyalty

repeat behavior. They state that the absence of both shows low loyalty, whereas the absence of a positive attitude with high repeats is "spurious" loyalty. Satisfaction with the services provided by a resort operator is a prerequisite of building loyal customers. Without customer satisfaction it is impossible to build positive attitudes.

Many loyalty schemes for hotels have been described as failures because they have been little more than sales promotion schemes, offering just price incentives to "disloyal brand switchers" (Palmer, 2001). It has been common practice to tie customers into loyalty schemes by offering frequent user discounts or special benefits such as room upgrades to frequent customers or frequent fliers in airlines. The problem with these schemes is that they may produce short-run sales increases, though often at discounted prices, but with little long-term gain because customers can be easily seduced by competitors who improve on the offer or replace it when the offer runs out.

Key Point 5.4

Timeshare loyalty schemes will develop the strongest relationships by developing a sense of mutual trust, personal commitment, and emotional bonds that are genuinely felt.

Timeshare Sales and Selling

If timeshare resort operators are to build long-term customer loyalty among resort owners in particular, the relationship should start to develop right from initial contact, in the prospect stage. As Chapter 10 will suggest, the unethical practices employed by some unscrupulous operators in the past are not only morally wrong but also bad business because they destroy opportunities to develop a long-term profitable relationship with customers.

One important difficulty faced by timeshare operators is that resort sales involve the selling of a property to people who live elsewhere, sometimes within reasonable driving distance but frequently thousands of miles away. This need to bring the timeshare customer to the resort, rather than bringing the product on sale to the market, has been a major influence producing the poor practice employed by some practitioners in the past. Since "prospects" had to be converted to sales while they were in the resort, people were sometimes subjected to intimidatory selling tactics and made to sign deals that they later regretted. The fact that much of the legislation in place internationally is designed to allow a cooling-off period is a response to these sales pressures, which is itself an outcome of the nature of timeshare property location. The ethical timeshare operator wishing to build a loyal customer base needs to be aware of these pressures so as to ensure that each prospective customer is treated as though he were to become a long-term loyal customer.

Generating Prospects

Prospects typically tour in pairs as partners, and it is important to remember the two parties and their concerns. Traditional approaches often used to see the male in a typical heterosexual relationship as the prime decision maker. In more contemporary relationships, both parties are often party to the decision, and there is a need to be concerned with the needs of each and to be sensitive to developing the loyal customer with each party. The two parties may vary in their understanding and concerns about making a purchase. The salesperson therefore must be aware of the prospects' potential fears and allay them during the selling process. To some extent, the degree of comfort or discomfort felt by the prospects will be determined by the methods resort operators use to get prospects to the selling meeting in the first place.

Timeshare Europe's (TRI Consulting, 2001) research suggests that a shift has taken place in generating prospects from the vacation-destination, street-based contact canvassers to a more organized benefit-driven approach. It was felt that the approach that dominated the industry in the late 1980s and early 1990s was largely responsible for some of the more negative publicity and image problems at the time. Off-Premises-Contacts (OPCs), as these initial contacts with prospects are termed, are now more likely to be generated through mini-breaks or short vacations. Usually, these are offered to prospects at a reduced rate or free, subject to an obligatory visit to a sales presentation. Usually, these mini-breaks are offered through direct mail or telemarketing approaches. Where the resort is owned by a hotel chain, hotel guests are targeted as prospects and are offered the chance of a "free" or reduced rate break. In these cases the resort and the hotel unit work in synergy with mutual benefit to both. In other cases, resort operators allow prospects temporary resort ownership and a reduced time frame at a reduced rate. These "trial memberships" or "exit" programs allow the prospect to sample the resort before making a longer term commitment. All these approaches provide a sound basis for developing customer loyalty with the prospective owner. They also provide an unthreatening, mutually advantageous basis for the relationship which can be built on with those who decide to buy. Even where a prospect has decided not to take up the offer, these initial contacts need to be properly conducted because some people will be buyers in the future.

TRI consulting's report on the European Timeshare sector (2001: 93) reported the following range of tactics for generating prospects for a resort.

- **Drive-to programs** typically occur at offsite sales locations or where prospects are invited to attend an onsite sales presentation at a resort location that is within a two-hour drive of the prospect's home.

- **Direct mail** is a marketing exercise in which promotional literature is distributed by mail to a listing of prospects obtained by the developer or marketing company.

- **Telemarketing** is usually undertaken using dedicated phone-rooms with sophisticated technology where operatives will cold call prospects, offering a discounted holiday break or some other incentive.

- **Referral programs** are the least expensive marketing techniques. Names of prospective buyers are acquired from current owners in an attempt to bring them to the resort for an onsite sales presentation. Prospective buyers identified through referrals are often contacted through telemarketing efforts.

- **Mini-Vac** (sometimes called Fly-Buy) programs bring prospective buyers to the resort by offering a free or reduced-cost stay at the resort. At some time during the mini-vacation, attendance at a sales presentation is required. Mini-vacations can be offered through direct mail and telemarketing.

- **Trial membership programs** use a reduced-cost temporary membership at the resort to lure an undecided buyer to the resort. Like mini-vacations, when using the trial membership, the guest will attend a sales presentation. These types of programs can be used with an individual initially via contact through direct mail or telemarketing.

- **Two-step** means the solicitation of invitees, either by direct mail or telemarketing means, to attend an initial podium-style presentation offsite in order to determine overall interest levels, income, and demographic qualification. This is followed by an invitation to take a subsidized mini-break onsite at a resort where a sales presentation is then undertaken with what is termed a warm, qualified lead.

- **Home sits marketing programs** are often used in conjunction with offsite sales locations. Rather than the customer coming to the sales representative, the sales representative goes to the prospect's home or office. This program can be very beneficial in increasing sales by using sales representatives to generate much of their own business.

- **Affinity marketing** opportunities involve working with travel companies or with charge card vendors and have been used by a number of organizations.

- **Off-premises contact (OPC)** involves the soliciting of individuals walking past the OPC booths or locations within a resort's vicinity to visit the resort for a sales presentation. The ability to prequalify the lead in a short period of time is critical to the success of OPC programs. The OPC technique is becoming less prominent within the industry as a marketing or lead generation activity.

In view of our earlier observations on the value of existing customers as a source of sales, it is not surprising that the TRI

Consulting report (2001) suggests that many resort operators use "warm" leads and organize "warm" tours from among existing customers and leads provided by them. Again these relationships suggest satisfaction and warmth of feelings about what they are experiencing, which can be used to build the loyal customer base.

Key Point 5.5

Timeshare operators wishing to develop long-term loyal customers through relationship marketing need to carefully select methods for generating prospective owners as some approaches are more compatible with this objective than others.

Case Study 5.1

Jim and Jean are young professionals in their late 20s living in a desirable district in a major city. As yet they have no children, but they plan to start a family in the next few years.

One day Jean receives an invitation in the mail offering a free two-night holiday at Eco Lodge, a mountain resort about six hours' drive from their home. The offer also states that the resort will provide $50 toward their expenses. The only requirement is that during their stay they will attend a sales promotion session and go on a conducted tour of the resort. Also, charges will be levied if the couple makes a booking and then do not show up.

Although the letter made no mention of it, Jim and Jean knew that the offer was associated with a promotion to sell a timeshare at the resort. They decided that they did not want to buy a timeshare property but would go on the holiday anyway. It was a free break, and they thought it might be something to consider later in their lives, when the family came along.

The holiday went well, the resort was set in a beautiful location, and their apartment was impressive, though they did not change their minds. This was not the right time for a purchase. The only unhappy point came during the sales presentation. The sales representative became quite angry when it was obvious that Jim and Jean were not going to make a purchase. He said, "Look here, we have spent $300 getting you down here, you shouldn't have come if you were not going to make a purchase. It is immoral. You are taking food off my table, because I have spent time with you and earned nothing." Jean said, "That's unfair because your letter made no mention of an obligation to buy from you. We have attended the sales meeting and been on the tour, we have met our obligations." With that they left the room; the sales representative was furious.

On their way back home, Jean and Jim were still upset by their experience and decided that while they liked the resort and location, they would look elsewhere when they wanted to buy into a timeshare property. Jean said, "I don't want to be involved with anyone who would stoop to such bullying tactics."

Selling and Making the Sale

In principle, the selling process starts with the first contacts with the prospects because the various strategies to attract prospects to the sales event in effect support the sale by reducing prospect fear and stress, informing the prospect, and establishing a favorable image. The actual selling processes formally take place at the sales encounter and involve the relationship between the salesperson and the prospects. It is important that the encounter takes place in the right kind of environment. Offering a friendly and professional reception from the staff, comfortable surroundings, and a generally relaxing environment is important.

ARDA's sales pyramid (2002b: 103) suggests that there are seven fundamental stages in the sales encounter. The first stage, *greeting and prospect registration*, requires that the staff make the prospects comfortable and begin the process of reducing anxiety and threat. It is important to verify names and addresses in order to keep an accurate record of those who attend the presentation. This is particularly important when contacts have been provided by an external promotion agency. These initial contacts set the scene by establishing positive or negative impressions of the organization and the individuals concerned.

The second stage, *pre-tour activities*, involves the outline of the resort and apartments and may entail full podium presentation or personal presentation to individual prospects by each salesperson. The presentation may include multimedia, using video and film. The presentation should provide lists of benefits that the resort, facilities, and surrounding location offer. Linkages to exchange companies are also frequently an element of the presentation at this stage. However, it is more effective if the presentation can be tailored to the specific perceptions and reasons for buying that are uppermost in the prospect's mind. Chapter 4 discusses a number of motives for buying a timeshare property; the presentation is most effective if it is informed by the specific needs of each prospect.

The whole selling process needs to be concerned with *establishing rapport* between contact personnel and the prospect. The sales representative in particular needs to develop this rapport because it is the sales encounter that gives the prospect the most anxiety. The decision to purchase a timeshare is a "high involvement decision" (ARDA, 2002b: 105) because the potential cost of the purchase typically represents a significant financial commitment, and poor image and negative stories that many people may hear also add to the anxiety level. Typically, the representative uses the pre-tour stage to discover key information about current lifestyle and vacation preferences, current and future vacation needs, as well as motives for making the potential purchase. It is on the basis of this information that the salesperson decides on the best way to present the property and the resort to the prospect.

During the fourth stage, the *tour*, the prospect has the opportunity to view the quality of the accommodation that is being offered and to see the general quality, upkeep, and range of facilities that are available. As the tour allows physical inspection, it is a highly persuasive aspect of the selling process. People are much more likely to believe the evidence of their eyes than imagine what it might be like through plans, models, or even film footage. It is also important that prospects be given every assurance that what they are seeing is typical of what they will experience. The surrounding environment needs to be properly maintained, and that other guests at the resort are compatible with their needs, as suggested in Chapter 4.

Throughout the pretour and tour phases, the salesperson *continues to develop the relationship* with the prospect. While each person approaches the sale in a different manner, it is vital that the sales representative be empathetic to the prospect's needs. In many cases, different prospects need to be handled by different sales personnel. Some representatives have an easier relationship with some types of customer than others—couples with children, young married couples, older people, or people with specialist sporting interests.

The greatest test of the sales encounter comes during the sixth phase, *making the offer*. Some organizations bring in a specialist salesperson during this phase because it is assumed that the more experienced person will get more sales. While this approach has some merit, it does interfere with the attempt to build a relationship between the salesperson and prospects. In some ways it may be seen as a little threatening because prospects have been developing a relationship with the salesperson and now suddenly in come the "big guns."

The *trial close* involves getting to the final agreement. The prospect may still have some doubts about the offer, though these doubts will typically have been dealt with in the earlier stages. By now, the effective salesperson has picked up on the issues concerning the prospects and has already attempted to allay their concerns. Similarly, the sales representative should have picked up on the motives for making a purchase, or the fit with the prospect's holiday and vacation needs. Frequently, price issues are at the forefront of any discussion during this stage. To encourage an immediate decision, ARDA (2002b) suggests a number of incentives at this stage: a price drop, a discount for a cash sale, an additional discount for purchasing more than one week, or discounts linked to the developer's desire to shift certain types of property and potential reductions in repayment levels by extending the repayment period. Whatever the detail of the package agreed to, the cooling-off period in some legislative areas allows the prospect to withdraw from the deal if he or she feels uncomfortable with the agreement. It is not in the seller's interest to be overly assertive at this stage.

Key Point 5.6

A carefully planned sales encounter will reinforce the development of the long-term relationship between company and owners. Selecting sales personnel who are most empathetic with the prospective owner is an essential first step.

TRI Consulting (2001: 94) has identified some of the dominant approaches to selling timeshare weeks.

- **Primary onsite sales** presentations are made to suitably qualified leads who have been selected either by local marketing or warm tours generated through other channels.

- **Offsite** sales are made on either cold or warm tours, in purpose-designed sales centers, with all supporting materials to show off the resort(s) in question. These offsite centers can either be at established resorts within a multisite business which are selling a system product or they can be operated by independent marketing companies operating in conjunction with brokers or acting as agents for the primary developer.

- **Be-Back** strategies should be encouraged. A be-back is a potential purchaser who declines a purchase during a sales tour and says she will think about it and "be back" at another time. Over time there is potential for increased vacation ownership sales from people who have elected not to buy during the initial sales exposure. Assuming that only 15 percent of all customers who listen to a sales presentation buy, this would mean that 85 percent are nonbuyers. Many industry practitioners have achieved success with targeting and subsequently selling to the nonbuyers through specifically defined strategies. At least one major vacation ownership club has recognized that the majority of its sales come from those who buy at some time following their initial visit. To be effective, be-back strategies must be well defined and executed with proper timing and consistency.

- **Exit programs** (or trial membership) offer a vacation product at a lower price than that which is initially presented, though for a considerably shorter period of time. This lower price is usually offered when the customer cannot afford the primary product or is not willing to make a commitment to purchase during the initial visit.

- **The counselor selling** technique focuses on the customer and identifies his or her needs as opposed to the more traditional "sell the product—whatever it takes" technique. Customized training programs are available to teach the counselor technique. Use of this approach is beginning to influence a movement toward a more positive consumer image of the industry, but it is still not being adapted by all industry practitioners. Until this transition occurs, the industry image will continue to suffer.

- **Home sits** are appointments made to visit the prospects in their home at their convenience.

- **Interactive technology** materially assists in the sales process. Video and computer software plus interactive technology is being used to involve the prospect in the sales process. Although these techniques are not being used on a widespread industry basis, the future is certain to bring more opportunities to integrate modern technology to advance sales.

After-Sales Contacts

Once the sale has been confirmed and the cooling-off period passes, the relationship with the customer needs to be continued in order to build customer loyalty. The general approach to receiving and processing the reception of the owner during the visit is key to building loyalty. Ensuring that the owner is made to feel comfortable and secure is a common feature of most hospitality services, and the resort staff needs to be trained and managed in a way that will achieve this comfort level. Much of the discussion about human resource management practices in this chapter and about service quality in Chapter 8 deals with the general issues of service requirements. Some additional ways of building loyalty from customers may be used: remembering their favorite newspaper, or preferred drink, or seating in the restaurant are all examples of service additions that will help the owners feel special.

Many resorts also need to maintain contact with customers through entertainment programs at the resort. Quiz nights, various competitions, games, pony trekking, swimming competitions, and a whole host of activities may provide a program of entertainment for guests in any one week. Many resorts will compile clientele profiles depending on whether the week in question occurs during the school term or school holidays. If held during school holiday periods, the entertainment will need to be directed to the needs of younger family members; weeks in school term time are likely to require events aimed at adults.

A well-thought-through quality program of entertainment is one technique that will improve the customer's sense of value received. As owners return to a resort or try out new ones, their judgments of value will be informed by their experiences during the vacation. An organization wishing to build long-term customer relationships and customer loyalty needs to continue building the customers' sense of improving and increasing service delivery. The need to exceed customer expectations is at the heart of customer evaluations of quality and value and will work to build customer loyalty.

Key Point 5.7

The ongoing relationship needs to be developed through a range of post-sale activities that exceed customer expectations.

Conclusion

This chapter shows that timeshare resort operators have much to gain from marketing strategies that focus on using relationship marketing and building loyal customers. If any one resort manages to retain more of its owners as visitors, as well as increase the number of visitors from other resort ownership, then demand for the resort's service will increase as will fees and charges, thereby increasing profitability. Building loyal customers is also profitable because the most effective sales are made through customers who are advocates of the business. Loyal owners are more likely to bring in the most fruitful prospects because their recommendations help attract serious inquirers. Indeed, loyal and satisfied owners are a valuable source of additional sales.

Relationship marketing aimed at building customer loyalty is most effective when it is built on a clear understanding of the need to meet customers' emotional needs and to achieve customer satisfaction. The relationship builds through all contacts with the company starting with first contact with the prospect. Prospect generation has been a major source of concern in the past. Practices that involve dishonesty and trickery in order to get prospects to a sales meeting are not suitable to establishing long-term relationships. Similarly, high-pressure selling and bullying techniques do not start the relationship on a sound footing. An ethical approach that perceives first contact as important in the ultimate relationship is essential.

After-sales relationships should continue to build the relationship. Ensuring that customers continue to experience added value reinforces the linkage between the customer and the resort operator. The owners' perceived value will be increased if the services available and service quality delivery go beyond the expected. Service quality and service quality management, together with staff training and management, are important strands in developing loyal customers.

Consumer Finance

After studying this chapter you should be able to:

- discuss the economic impact of timeshare real estate.

- analyze the role and purpose of the consumer loan process and the relationship with resort development.

- appreciate the legislative framework governing the consumer purchasing process.

Introduction

The timeshare industry has advanced in quality of product offerings, services offered, entrants into the market, diversity of product offerings, and by the metrics of sales volume, number of owners, and number of available resorts (ARDA, 2004; Ragatz Associates, 2003; Interval International, 2003). From a product life-cycle perspective, these indicators show that the timeshare industry is in the early stages of market growth, which if all holds true the industry will continue to gain in consumer acceptance of products and services.

Coming to terms with consumer behavior is the key to success in the marketplace. Timeshare developers are constantly looking at owner purchasing and consumption patterns to predict future trends. To familiarize oneself with purchasing and consumption patterns, the developer has to engage in a structured process of collecting, analyzing, and using demographic information, past purchase patterns, and consumption of onsite and offsite services to better understand and predict the behavior of existing and prospective owners for business decision making. Once this information is mastered, the timeshare developer is well on her way to promoting the product, with a very identifiable target market in mind. Armed with this information the timeshare developer can generate a satisfactory tour flow so that costs associated with sales and marketing efforts are more than sufficiently offset. The concept of tour flow is intricately woven into the sales and marketing design, with the sole purpose being to maximize organizational profits. The purpose of the marketing division is to profile prospects, stimulate their interest, and attract them to the resort site through a variety of promotional activities. Once the consumer is onsite, the sales division takes over and engages in a consultative selling process whereby any objections the prospect might have are overcome, and before the prospect leaves the resort the sale is made. The next step in the timeshare sales process is to present a consumer loan package that is appealing enough that the purchaser will leave the resort with a contract in hand.

This chapter highlights the processes, terms, and conditions that encompass the consumer loan process as practiced by the timeshare developer. Specifically, the chapter discusses consumer loan metrics, the basic principles surrounding onsite financing, consumer rescission rights, developer recourse rights, and federal consumer protection legislation concerning the consumer loan process. All these procedures are based on case law and federal legislation that provides a template that all developers need to follow with extreme due diligence.

An Overview of Timeshare Financing

The timeshare industry is here to stay and has become a major vacation alternative for those seeking sophisticated, personalized, and private condominium-style accommodations. This sophistication has attracted Wall Street's notice, as observed by Kathryn Plouff (2002):

> [T]he vacation ownership industry, in its early stages, was entrepreneurial and less corporate than Wall Street liked. Now the industry's maturation and growing interest from Wall Street are ushering in a new era with more sophisticated standards and procedures. (p. 20)

Because the timeshare industry is in the early stages of growth, there is tremendous potential for additional product proliferation and market penetration. The number of households that have expressed interest in owning a vacation-style type of accommodations is still on the increase (ARDA, 1999a; RCI, 2003; PriceWaterHouseCoopers, 2003). This fact, in combination with the massive number of baby boomers who are known to be seeking vacation experiences, indicates that the industry is projected to continue to grow at its current pace for the next decade or perhaps longer. Approximately 4 to 5 percent of eligible household buyers now own a timeshare, and annual surveys of owner satisfaction yield an 80 to 90 percent owner satisfaction rate (Ragatz and Associates, 2003).

Key Point 6.1

The majority (69.6%) of timeshare purchasers finance their purchase with the developer while onsite.

	Timeshare Resort Average Interval Price
United States	$14,500.00
Worldwide	$10,600.00
Average Timeshare Sales Price Trend Analysis	
Developer price/week (not points)	$14,500.00
Annualized rate of increase since 2000	4.30%
Annualized rate of increase since 1996	6.50%
Annualized rate of increase since 1978	4.90%

Table 6.1 Average Developer Sales Price per Interval

What pricing points do these baby boomers incur? Table 6.1 shows that the average purchase price for a timeshare interval is hardly a low-involvement decision-making process and as such requires consumer financing at the point-of-sale. According to a financial impact study released in 2003 by the American Resort Development Association, the average timeshare candidate is 55 years old, with an average household income of $110,000, and is signing an end-loan to purchase his or her timeshare at 14.3 percent for a period of six years.

All these facts taken in the aggregate indicate that the timeshare industry contributes to society by enhancing consumers' recreational and leisure lifestyles; stimulating additional resort development in national and international vistas; and contributing to the local economy in which the resort resides.

Chapter 2 discussed the necessity of acquiring funds from an outside lending agency for the purpose of acquiring land, developing the land, and developing additional resort phases. This is just one element of the financing process and is associated with the preconstruction to the development phase of the resort. Once that phase is complete, the developer quickly transitions into a revenue-generating mode. It is at this point of the resort's life cycle that the emphasis on

Price per interval	2003 interest percent rate
<$10,000	15%
$10,000–14,999	14.8%
$15,000–19,999	13.5%
$20,000+	12.5%
Percent of dollar value of timeshare sales financed in 2003	69.6%
Percent of dollar value of timeshare sales financed in 2002	69.7%
Overall range of interest rate charged on consumer purchase	9 to 18%
Overall interest rate charged on consumer purchase (Average)	14%

Source: American Resort Development Association, 2004

Table 6.2 Consumer Loan Profile, 2003

selling the resort units takes center stage as the primary revenue generation vehicle for the developer.

Table 6.2 shows that timeshare developers rely quite heavily on the convenience of offering consumer loan financing at the point-of-sale. The observation that 69.6 percent of all timeshare sales are financed via inhouse financing with a downpayment range of 10 to 30 percent with the overall downpayment average of 14.6 percent attests to the importance of offering inhouse financing to the consumer. This interest rate is obviously higher than the consumer would be offered if he took out a loan from a bank but oftentimes the matter of convenience in obtaining onsite financing is a powerful incentive that is linked to the consumer's immediate gratification. Aside from this consumer benefit there can be no doubt that convincing the consumer to finance onsite is a main part of the developer's revenue strategy. This is rather obvious given that the rate of financing internally is often twice the average percentage rate offered by an outside lending agency. The two primary revenue-generation sources are therefore the original sales price plus the interest charged on the purchase price. In this manner, the financing of a timeshare purchase is very similar to the purchase process of automobiles and to some degree homes.

The average consumer loan as financed by the timeshare developer is typically higher than what the consumer would be offered from a bank if he decided to exercise that option.

The Flow of Money

The timeshare industry is a very lucrative venture from the timeshare developer's standpoint. However, the resort financing process, in combination with the operating expenses associated with resort development and promotional activities, is not for the operator who does not have a sound grasp of the flow of money within the timeshare organization. This statement is supported by ARDA's 2004 financial performance report which found 11.6 percent of timeshare developers reported general and administrative costs as less than 5 percent of net sales, 37.2 percent reported general and administrative costs in the 5 to 10 percent range, 25.6 percent had general and administrative costs in the 10 to 15 percent range, and 25.6 percent reported general and administrative costs higher than 15 percent of net sales. Furthermore, developers reported on average that they paid out 13.6 percent of net sales in commissions to their sales force and that their sales and marketing costs hovered at 34 percent of net sales, which is a drop of 13.7 percent from the previous year. These statistics indicate that operating a timeshare business requires extensive financial knowledge from project inception to consumer loan financing. If this knowledge can be mastered, then the developer is on the right path to success. Perhaps this requirement of savviness in the arena of project and consumer financing is yet another reason that hotel brands became interested in timesharing.

Reflective Practice

Interview a marketing director of a timeshare company to determine the procedures that this organization has in place to control development costs. In this process, you are to get a general understanding of percent of costs relative to net sales. Once you collect this information, you are to discuss how this organization's figures compare to the national figures reported by ARDA in its *Financial Performance of the U.S. Timeshare Industry* (2004).

From a developer perspective, the timeshare concept has been strongly embraced by many of the hotel brands that have high recognition by the leisure and business traveler. Hotel lodging providers such as Marriott, Starwood, and De Vere have discovered that the timeshare product has made significant contributions, as evidenced by revenue gains and earnings before interest, taxes, depreciation, and amortization (EBITDA). Gose (2003, p. 4) noted that "timeshare EBITDA accounted for about 8% of Starwood's overall 2002 EBITDA of $1 billion, and timeshare revenues accounted for 9.3% of Starwood's $3.9 billion in revenues." Therefore, reported financial indicators from branded companies offer testament to the overall impact that these respective timeshare divisions have made to the overall financial portfolio of their parent companies. As a result of these financial gains, major hotel chains tout their timeshare operations to their shareholders because these divisions generate cash from sales and financing, as well as produce ancillary revenue in onsite resort restaurants, golf courses, and other retail shops (Gose, 2003).

To reach this level of sophistication, not only have timeshare product offerings advanced in quality and offerings, but the services offered by the developer have improved as well. One such service that has become a cornerstone of packaging the timeshare product for consumer consumption is that of consumer financing, also known as end-loan financing. This service is offered onsite directly after the sales representative has made his "pitch" to an interested consumer. If the consumer agrees to become an owner, the sales representative immediately introduces the prospect to an onsite contract officer who discusses the terms of the contract in accordance with various consumer protection and financing regulations.

The Sales Transaction

The first step in selling a timeshare interval is to get the prospect (typically a family) to the resort for a firsthand tour. To do so, the developer designs and deploys various marketing programs that stimulate the prospect to book a tour of the resort. This first step (as discussed in Chapters 4 and 10) is a fairly expensive proposition to the developer; therefore, proper targeting of prospects is instrumental for successful sales. Once marketing has done its job and the prospect has arrived at the resort, the focus shifts to the sales function. All tours commence at the resort's welcome center, at which time a timeshare sales representative walks the prospect through the entire sales process via a masterpiece of visual, auditory, and tactile sensations that are designed to create a lifetime of vacation memories that can be easily obtained.

The sale consists of purchasing a specified amount of time, known as an *interval*, at a specified resort. The typical length of a timeshare interval is one week per year; however, multiple-week products are available as well. The exact terms of the contract include all pertinent information as required by law. This can be a little daunting for the first-time purchaser, given the plethora of information that the law requires the purchasing contract to contain. These terms and conditions are quite exhaustive ranging from the name of the resort, taxation and assessment issues, and rescission rights to use of an escrow agent who holds timeshare owner monies for monitoring purposes and release of funds for legitimate reasons.

Key Point 6.3

By U.S. law, consumer purchase funds are placed in an escrow account for monitoring and disbursement purposes. This action follows the same procedures placed on all other real estate actions and falls under the umbrella of consumer protection law.

Committing purchase funds to an escrow account is a legally provided mechanism by which the consumer can protect his or her financial investment in the event of developer default. Table 6.3 provides details related to the release of escrow funds. Escrow companies provide an experienced

Occurs when title is free of all liens

The property has a clear deed; it is signed by all parties of interest

Occurs only when the full amount of purchase funds are in the account and verified as a full payment on the contract

Occurs when an existing mortgage is released

The property management entity or the homeowners association notates that there are no outstanding assessment or liens against the timeshare unit

Table 6.3 Release of Escrow Funds in the United States

professional service regulated by law to protect the interest of both the buyer and the seller. As such, an escrow is the process of closing a real estate sale in which a licensed third party prepares the documents and handles the closing between buyer and seller. For the protection of buyer and seller, all funds are required to be held in a special secure trust account until closing, at which time the escrow officer disburses funds according to identical escrow instructions signed by buyer and seller.

Other important parts of consumer protection that are a customary element of the contract are the nondisturbance provision and the nonperformance protection clause. A nondisturbance clause ensures that the consumer continue to use her unit in the event that a default claim is filed against the developer or management firm. A nonperformance protection clause allows the consumer to keep her ownership rights, even in the event that a third party is required to buy out the consumer's contract.

Key Point 6.4

A nondisturbance clause protects the consumer in situations where a default claim is filed against the developer.

There are other elements than just an escrow account, nondisturbance clauses, and nonperformance clauses that comprise a timeshare contract. The extent of these items can be quite daunting and typically require a read by an individual trained in such matters such as a real estate attorney. An example of the extensive nature of purchasing contract information is displayed in Table 6.4.

Chapter 721.6

(1) Each seller shall utilize and furnish each purchaser a fully completed and executed copy of a contract pertaining to the sale, which contract shall include the following information:

    (a) The actual date the contract is executed by each party.

    (b) The names and addresses of the developer and the timeshare plan.

    (c) The initial purchase price and any additional charges to which the purchaser may be subject in connection with the purchase of the timeshare interest, such as financing, or which will be collected from the purchaser on or before closing, such as the current year's annual assessment for common expenses.

    (d) Any annually recurring use charge and the next year's estimated annual assessment for common expenses and for ad valorem taxes or, if an estimate for next year's assessment is unavailable, the current year's actual annual assessment for common expenses and for ad valorem taxes.

    (e) The estimated date of completion of construction of each accommodation or facility promised to be completed which is not completed at the time the contract is executed and the estimated date of closing.

    (f) A brief description of the nature and duration of the timeshare interest being sold, including whether any interest in real property is being conveyed and the specific number of years constituting the term of the timeshare plan.

    (g) Immediately prior to the space reserved in the contract for the signature of the purchaser, in conspicuous type, substantially the following statements:

    You may cancel this contract without any penalty or obligation within 10 calendar days after the date you sign this contract.

    If you decide to cancel this contract, you must notify the seller in writing of your intent to cancel. Your notice of cancellation shall be effective upon the date sent and shall be sent to (Name of Seller) at (Address of Seller). Any attempt to obtain a waiver of your cancellation right is void and of no effect. While you may execute all closing documents in advance, the closing, as evidenced by delivery of the deed or other document, before expiration of your 10-day cancellation period, is prohibited.

    (h) If a timeshare estate is being conveyed, the following statement in conspicuous type:

    For the purpose of ad valorem assessment, taxation and special assessments, the managing entity will be considered the taxpayer as your agent pursuant to section 192.037, Florida Statutes.

    (i) A statement that, in the event the purchaser cancels the contract during a 10-day cancellation period, the developer will refund to the purchaser the total amount of all payments made by the purchaser under the contract, reduced by the proportion of any contract benefits the purchaser has actually received under the contract prior to the effective date of the cancellation. The statement shall further provide that the refund will be made within 20 days after receipt of notice of cancellation or within 5 days

(Continued)

after receipt of funds from the purchaser's cleared check, whichever is later. A seller and a purchaser shall agree in writing on a specific value for each contract benefit received by the purchaser for purposes of this paragraph. The term "contract benefit" shall not include purchaser public offering statements or other documentation or materials that must be furnished to a purchaser pursuant to statute or rule.

(j) If the timeshare interest is being sold pursuant to an agreement for deed, a statement that the signing of the agreement for deed does not entitle the purchaser to receive a deed until all payments under the agreement have been made.

(k) At the time of offering a unit for sale the developer must disclose any leans or encumbrances and ownership structure of the development. These disclosures include:

1. The names and addresses of all persons or entities having an ownership interest or other interest in the accommodations or facilities; and

2. The actual interest of the developer in the accommodations or facilities. As an alternative to including the statement in the purchase contract, a seller may include a reference in the purchase contract to the location in the purchaser public offering statement text of such information.

(l) If the purchaser will receive an interest in a multisite timeshare plan pursuant to part II, a statement shall be provided in conspicuous type in substantially the following form:

The developer is required to provide the managing entity of the multisite timeshare plan with a copy of the approved public offering statement text and exhibits filed with the division and any approved amendments thereto, and any other component site documents as described in section 721.07 or section 721.55, Florida Statutes, that are not required to be filed with the division, to be maintained by the managing entity for inspection as part of the books and records of the plan.

(m) The following statement in conspicuous type:

Any resale of this timeshare interest must be accompanied by certain disclosures in accordance with section 721.065, Florida Statutes.

(n) A description of any rights reserved by the developer to alter or modify the offering prior to closing.

Internet site reference: http://www.flsenate.gov/statutes/index.cfm?App_mode=Display_Statute&Search_String=&URL=Ch0721/Sec06.HTM

(2) An agreement for deed shall be recorded by the developer within 30 days after the day it is executed by the purchaser. The developer shall pay all recording costs associated therewith.

(3) The escrow agent shall provide the developer with a receipt for all purchaser funds or other property received by the escrow agent from a seller.

Table 6.4 Florida State Chapter 721.06 Contracts for Purchase of Timeshare Interests

Loan Assistance

The availability of consumer financing at the point-of-sale is more than just an added convenience for the consumer. Offering onsite loan service is designed to reduce buyer's remorse by alleviating the additional time to ponder the merits and demerits of the purchase. Developers offer the purchaser the option of taking out a loan at a percentage rate that is higher than similar loans obtained from external lending agencies and for a payment cycle that is of a shorter duration.

It is a common misconception that quick money can be made in the timeshare business by simply selling a single unit fifty-two different times. Certainly, significant profits can be obtained, but not without considerable financial savvy in estimating expenses, containing costs, and sustaining a revenue stream as calculated on a five- to seven-year window of return. Within this cycle, the developer's sales engine remains the primary source by producing an overall return in the 20 percent range (Gose, 2003). Specifically related to the sales process, a secondary source of revenue is acquired from the contracting process. The provision of consumer loans via a specialty lender is another rich source of revenue. It should be understood that timeshare developer success is measured in part by how the developer's portfolio of notes receivable (end-loans/consumer loans) performs. According to Herz (2003: p. 1), "the timeshare industry, like any other commercial endeavor in which the seller also provides financing to its consumer to facilitate the purchase of its product, is engaged in a credit extension finance business." This credit extension business is characterized by offering consumer loans at an approximate 10 percent downpayment that boasts a five- to ten-year repayment period with an interest rate hovering in the 11 to 18 percent range (Spaulding, 2004; ARDA, 2004a and b). This annual percentage rate is indeed well above the lending level that the consumer could obtain in the broader lending market, but the developer's higher percentage rate reflects the added convenience of completing the business transaction on the same day of purchase. It is at this point that the purchaser signs a promissory note specifying the interest rate, monthly installment fees, beginning and ending date of payment, overall payment due to the seller (in this case the developer), interest rate of the loan, and terms and conditions of late-fee payments. The truth of the matter is that financing a timeshare is a similar process as financing an automobile. Certainly the consumer can obtain a lower annual percentage rate from an external lender, but the immediate convenience of closing the deal and therefore receive any kind of offered price concession is associated with onsite financing. From the developer's perspective this is a good business strategy because financing consumer loans is a main part of the developer's financial strategy.

Key Point 6.5

Promissory notes are also used in the timeshare industry as a legally binding contract stating monthly fees, loan payment dates, interest percentage, and late-fee terms and conditions.

This point-of-sale financing is commonly known as notes receivable financing. Not only is the offering of consumer financing a matter of convenience, but it also impacts the developer's ability to seek out acquisition, development, and notes receivable funding for future projects. In this regard, it is of prime importance for the developer to minimize risks associated with consumer loan defaults by conducting a credit report on each loan transaction. If done so, the developer's credit rating improves accordingly owing to the application of sound financial management principles that also are reflected in the developer's ability to maintain a respectable cash flow.

Rescission Laws

Rescission rights are a legally mandated consumer protection in regards to the timeshare product. The net effect of rescission laws is twofold. First, a regulatory body gives assurance that timeshare purchasers have a right to cancel their contract within a specified number of days after signing, with a full refund. The purchaser does *not* have an indefinite period in which to "return" the interval to the developer. In fact, all states restrict their period of rescissions from three to fifteen days depending on the state in which the timeshare is sold. This period of rescission is advantageous to the consumer because he or she can, for whatever reason, rescind the agreement within the proper time frame. The second and opposite effect is that the developer must contend with the additional costs associated with marketing and selling this recycled interval. This is problematic for the developer because it negatively impacts the cash flow for the period *and* if rescission rates rise above industry norms the developer's lender may consider the developer a high-risk venture and therefore limit or not fund future developments.

The theory behind the concept of rescission is closely related to Leon Festinger's theory of cognitive dissonance. This theory asserts that behavior that contrasts with an established attitude demands change. This change usually takes the form of altering the individual's original attitude to conform to expected behavior. Moreover, when a person engages in behavior different from the norm, the individual will change his attitude about himself. The theory of cognitive dissonance further asserts that people are motivated to change and act consistent with their beliefs, values, and perceptions when there is psychological inconsistency or disagreement between two pieces of information. The conflict between these incongruent viewpoints produces dissonance. As a result, the individual doubts previously held rationales, beliefs, or values. These doubts generate uncomfortable feelings that often interfere with the ability to act in a rational manner. The resolution of dissonance occurs when one factor is seen to be more attractive than the other option. Prior to the resolution of the dissonance, the dilemma between the conflicting factors causes an impasse, which in turn leads to a high level of confusion and frustration. When dissonance is resolved, the person begins to act in agreement with the more commonly accepted viewpoints because beliefs, values, and perceptions agree with the displayed behavior (Haber, Leach, Schudy and Sideleau, 1982; Festinger, 1957).

Timeshare developers are keenly aware that timeshare purchasers can have immediate doubts about their purchase so they engage in activities designed to alleviate the purchaser's cognitive dissonance. One such strategy is to show streamed videos of recent and existing purchasers that are similar in demographic or geographic characteristics of the purchaser. The main intent in doing so is so that the purchaser will identify with individuals that are similar to themselves and therefore become more comfortable with their purchase decision.

Key Point 6.6

Consumers have the right to rescind their purchase by law. The time varies by state as to how long this period extends.

Developer's Recourse

In the timeshare industry, excluding the rescission period, if an owner stops making payments on her loan (e.g., note), the developer has the right to engage in collection procedures. The collection procedure can be conducted either inhouse or by an external collection agency. The decision on which option to choose depends on the availability of resources internal to the organization and is a matter of desired control over the process. The customary collection procedures include sending the owner a late notice, engaging in telephone contact procedures, and if need be, initiating collection procedures that include third-party collection procedures, skip tracing, and report of the bad debt to credit-reporting agencies. The collection process is the last recourse available to the developer and is exercised only when the owner's account is defaulted for nonpayment prior to the closing and title process.

Key Point 6.7

Developers also receive protection under law for payment of a binding consumer loan contract. If a consumer defaults on the loan, the developer has the legal right to follow standard collection procedures set forth by the federal government.

Engaging in collection procedures from a service perspective is the least favorable option available to the developer. This is because timeshare developers prefer to keep their owners active rather than consider them to be an immediate credit risk. To avoid this scenario, the developer might modify the mortgage payments in an effort to keep the customer in good standing. The net effect is to turn a potentially demeaning situation into a win-win situation for both parties involved. Unfortunately, this outcome cannot always be achieved, and at times the developer is forced to exercise its collection procedure privileges as assigned by federal law.

Consumer Protection Legislation

The task of offering onsite consumer financing is not without considerable external oversight from the appropriate regulatory bodies. The fact that the timeshare product is sold either as a deeded or a leasehold type of offering places this product squarely in the realm of real estate, and as such it is commonly viewed as a major purchase that entitles the purchaser to various levels of protection. It is at this point that consumer protection legislation plays an integral part in how the developer conducts the services provided to consumers. The following pieces of legislation that regulate timeshare purchases in the United States are not specific to the timeshare industry. Indeed, these laws are broadly encompassing laws that cover business-to-consumer transactions of a public nature. The laws addressed here are the Equal Credit Opportunity Act, Fair Credit Reporting Act, Fair Debt Collection Practices Act, Federal Consumer Credit Protection Act (Truth-in-Lending Law), and Real Estate Settlement Procedures Act (RESPA).

Key Point 6.8

Many of the consumer protection laws were not developed specifically for the timeshare industry; instead, these laws were designed for the broader context of real estate transactions. These laws are binding for the timeshare industry as well.

Equal Credit Opportunity Act

This consumer protection law was created to avoid discrimination in obtaining credit relative to sex, age, marital status, race, color, national origin, receipt of public assistance or one's rights under consumer protection laws. More important for the timeshare developer is the fact that advertisements cannot either orally or in writing discourage consumers protected by the above categories from applying for credit. From a practical perspective, this law presents a unique challenge to some timeshare developers based on the argument that certain nationalities are not inclined to purchase their product, and therefore it is not an efficient use of their marketing and sales resources. In spite of this argument, the equal credit opportunity law is designed to offer equal access to credit to anyone who might possibly seek this service. Table 6.5 presents a general guideline as to what a creditor cannot state in its communications to potential purchasers.

Fair Credit Reporting Act

This law covers the consumer's right to review and correct any erroneous credit information that a credit bureau might

---

A creditor is not allowed to . . .

Ask for the sex, race, color, religion or national origin of an applicant. They can, however, ask about permanent residency or immigration status.

Ask about plans for raising or having children. The creditor can, however, ask about the number of dependents and dependent-related financial obligations.

Discount income because of your sex or marital status. For example, a creditor cannot count a man's salary at 100 percent and a woman's at 75 percent.

Ask whether you receive alimony, child support or separate maintenance payments *UNLESS* you will rely on that income to pay back credit. But the lender must first explain that the income from these sources need not be revealed unless the applicant wishes to rely on it to establish creditworthiness.

Discount or refuse to consider income because it comes from part-time work, pension, annuity or retirement benefits.

Profile the consumer based on sec, race, color, religion, or national origin in an effort to refuse credit services.

Adpated from: http://www.bankrate.com/brm/green/loan/loan1a.asp September 18, 2004

Table 6.5 U.S. Fair Credit Reporting Guidelines—What a Creditor Cannot Do

hold relative to the consumer's personal file. According to the Fair Credit Reporting law, an individual has the right to obtain his personal credit information once proper identification is provided to the credit bureau. If the consumer detects any inaccuracies in the credit record, the credit bureau is obligated by law to research and rectify the entry (if it is in error) and then notify all companies that have requested the consumer's credit information over the preceding six months.

Fair Debt Collection Practices Act

The Fair Debt Collection Practices Act is a federal law that outlines what information debt collectors can gather on the consumer. It contains specific rules on how debt collectors can communicate with the individual at home and at work. These bill collector rules are designed to protect the consumer from abuse, harassment, false and misleading tricks, and illegal debt collector tactics. The language in this legislation is very specific, covering a range of abusive, deceptive, and unfair collection practices in an effort to protect the consumer from overzealous collection agencies.

This law permits a collection agency to contact a consumer in person, mail, or phone between the hours of 8 A.M. and not after 9 P.M. at home or at work, unless the employer restricts the latter hour. If the collection agency has difficulty getting in touch with the consumer, it has the right to contact previous employers, relatives, and other sources for the sole purpose of locating the debtholder. In doing so, the collection agency cannot indicate that the debtholder owes money, nor can it contact a source more than once. Furthermore, the collector cannot indicate that "nonpayment of any debt will result in the arrest or imprisonment of any person or the seizure, garnishment, attachment, or sale of any property or wages of any person unless such action is lawful and the debt collector or creditor intends to take such action." This summary is an excerpt of the U.S. federal regulations that apply to the Fair Debt Collection Practices Act. A full accounting of this law can be found at http://www.ftc.gov/os/statutes/fdcpa/fdcpact.htm#808.

Case Study 6.1

Bob and Sue Thomas purchased a timeshare two years ago but never found the time to use it because of their hectic work schedule. They contacted the developer to resell the timeshare, to which they received a sharp response that the developer did not buy back timeshare units and that the Thomas's must continue making their payments. The interaction deteriorated at that point, after which the couple decided to quit making payment on their loan. The developer leveraged its right to engage in collection procedures and began to call their employers, friends, relatives, and previous employers, implying that garnishment was a distinct possibility.

Reflective Practice

Did the developer follow the correct collection procedures? If not, why? And how should this situation have been handled?

Federal Consumer Credit Protection Act

The Federal Consumer Credit Protection Act of 1968, also known as the Truth-in-Lending Law, is designed to inform consumers of the total costs associated with taking out credit for the purchase in question. The practical purpose of highlighting the exact terms of the loan is to enable the consumer to compare cost structures from various lenders. Even though this law is typically associated with services offered by automobile dealers, home mortgage brokers, banks, and professional providers (such as attorneys and medical doctors), the timeshare industry also falls under the scrutiny of this law. The reason is that the developer is extending credit to the purchaser for purposes of personal or family acquisition of a real estate-based product.

This law specifies in a uniform manner the quoted costs associated with obtaining credit from the developer. These uniform, quoted costs must include the total direct and indirect finance charges the purchaser must pay in order to complete the purchase of his timeshare interval. These costs can include title fees, recording fees, document preparation, loan service charges, and credit report. One of the more critical pieces that must be included in this statement concerns the total amount of the finance charges, which is commonly known as the annual percentage rate (APR) of the loan. This percentage rate is not capped by the federal government but can be limited by state usury laws. The developer is not allowed to charge an APR that exceeds the annual percentage rate established by the state. All elements that comprise the loan must be clearly specified in a disclosure statement that is to be reviewed onsite with a purchaser by a contract verification officer. A thorough review of this disclosure agreement is a mandatory requirement per the Truth-in-Lending Law. A thorough review of these items is necessary for the timeshare purchase to be complete because engaging in a detailed review with concomitant feedback for all items will reduce purchaser rescission after the deal is sealed.

Real Estate Settlement Procedures Act

The original Real Estate Settlement Procedures Act (RESPA) was passed in 1974 with the designated purpose of enabling consumers to become better shoppers for settlement services. In this capacity, RESPA involves the purchaser receiving disclosure of certain pieces of information at various points during the purchasing process. The general information that is to be disclosed concerns costs associated with the settlement, lender servicing and escrow account practices, and a description of the business relationships between settlement service providers, if such a relationship exists.

When the lender submits a loan application, he is obligated to provide the purchaser with a Settlement Costs booklet (a federal government document) that describes the consumer's rights under federal law; a good faith estimate of the estimated closing costs; a mortgage servicing disclosure statement that discloses to the purchaser whether the lender will service the loan or whether an outside provider will be used. If this information is not provided, the lender must mail these documents to the purchaser within three days of signing the loan application (unless the loan is rejected).

At the time of closing, the developer must provide the purchaser with a disclosure statement concerning the exact costs associated with the settlement. The actual settlement costs include the initial escrow statement estimating taxes and other charges to be paid to the escrow account for the period of the mortgage loan.

Reflective Practice

1. Discuss the importance of the Fair Credit Reporting Act.
2. Discuss the importance of the Equal Credit Opportunity Act.
3. Discuss the importance of Fair Debt Collection Practices Act.
4. Discuss the Fair Consumer Credit Protection Act.
5. Discuss the Real Estate Settlement Protection Act.

Conclusion

The timeshare is continuing to contribute to local, state, and national economies. The timeshare developer concentrates on the revenue centers of timeshare unit sales and, to a lesser degree, on consumer loan financing. Both require extreme attention to consumer demographics in terms of purchasing patterns and usage patterns. Products and services have to be properly aligned with the needs, wants, and expectations of present consumers because prospects with similar needs, wants, and expectations will be enticed to be owners as long as what is offered appeals to their interests.

Once the marketing and sales portion of the timeshare developer's enterprise has successfully attracted a purchaser with a propensity to purchase and this propensity is turned into a desire to purchase the product, the developer offers the added enticement of onsite loan services. The majority of timeshare purchasers do indeed take advantage of this onsite loan financing service, which implies that the developer must actively reinforce the owner's decision with a timespan immediately following the purchase. Otherwise a rescission might occur with an established legal timeframe. This consideration is important for two reasons; first, the purchase of a high-ticket item such as a timeshare is certain to generate some cognitive dissonance immediately after purchase because the consumption (therefore the reinforcement) of the product is not always consecutive with the purchase; second, rescission laws allow the consumer to rescind his purchase without recourse within a specified time period following the original purchase. These rescission laws in combination with the principle of cognitive dissonance means that it is in the developer's best interest to prevent rescission from happening by deploying personal contact and information dissemination.

Finally, developers are required to comply with consumer protection legislation as it relates to the purchase of a real estate product for personal or family use.

CHAPTER 7

Managing Human Resources in Timeshare Operations

Learning Objectives

After studying this chapter you should be able to:

- explain the role of emotions in timeshare encounters.

- analyze the role of emotional intelligence in services.

- critically discuss empowerment.

- evaluate human resource management practice.

Introduction

Timeshare operations involve service interactions whereby the nature of the frontline staff performance has a major impact on customer evaluations of service quality (Langhorn, 2004). Timeshare operations are different from traditional services because they are linked to the emotional experiences associated with hospitality, and the relationship between guest and host as well as between domestic and commercial dimensions of hospitality (Lashley, 2000; Lashley and Morrison, 2003; Lashley, Morrison, and Randall, 2004). Traditional service quality management instruments rarely recognize the strong emotional dimensions of the service interaction in the context of hospitality (Parasuraman, Berry, and Zeithaml, 1991) and consequently underplay the importance of the emotional performance of frontline staff and line management for effective performance. Even those who do recognize that it takes "happy workers to create happy customers" (Barbee and Bott, 1991) fail to recognize the emotional complexities concerned, and so they rely on the reproduction of a "Have a Nice Day Culture" (Mann, 1998; 1999).

Given the importance of frontline employee performance to guest satisfaction, managers must understand the dynamics of service encounters, particularly as these might involve emotional labor (Hochschild, 2003), resulting in emotional stress and negative behaviors toward customers. In addition, managers need to be able to recognize the emotional needs of customers and identify the employee performance most appropriate to support customers (Anderson, Povis, and Chappel, 2002). Emotional intelligence (Goleman, 1998), reflects the ability of managers and frontline employees to recognize their own emotions and the emotional needs of others, and understand how to manage the emotional dimensions of human interactions.

These emotional demands on both service workers and their managers have implications for the way employees are managed, as well as for employment practices and techniques. Empowerment has the potential to engage employees not only in delighting customers through the quality of their personal performance, but also in developing more emotional harmony. Empowered employees are likely to feel more satisfied in their work and not experience the stresses arising from emotional disharmony (Mann, 1999). Empowerment has the potential to give frontline employees the freedom to meet (or exceed) customer service expectations, and to improve their job satisfaction and commitment to the firm and its objectives (Parson, 1995).

All this confirms the importance of some basic human resource management practices. In the first instance, it is essential that the "right" people are recruited from the start. Selection and recruitment practices should be carefully defined and planned. Erecting "high barriers to entry" will ensure that entry to jobs in timeshare occupations goes beyond "breath on the mirror" approaches, whereby anyone demonstrating signs of life is deemed employable (Lashley and Rowson, 2000). Careful and considered recruitment is concerned essentially with recruiting the "right person" with high levels of social skill and emotional intelligence (Langhorn, 2004). Where necessary, the skills are further developed by planned and targeted staff development, and the retention of staff of emotionally intelligent staff is given a high priority by managers who are themselves providing "emotional leadership" (Lashley, 2004).

Emotional Dimensions of Timeshare Service

Chapter 4 discusses consumer motives and behaviors in detail, but it is important to point to the emotional dimensions of the service encounter and the emotional aspects of service performance in timeshare operations. The emotions of hospitality and hospitable behavior, and the study of hospitality as human activities, with deep cultural and domestic, as well as commercial, roots suggest that hospitality is more than a service encounter (Lashley and Morrison, 2003).

Recent work exploring the nature of hospitality (Lashley and Morrison, 2000; Lynch, 2005; O'Mahony, 2003) and hospitableness (Telfer, 2000) provides insights into the service expectations of timeshare customers. On one level, timeshare operations often encompass what might be classed as commercial hospitality industry activities, "the provision food and/or drink, and/or accommodation in a service context" (HEFCE, 1998). Even though individual timeshare owners may "self-cater," the resort in which properties are located typically includes restaurants, bars, clubs, leisure facilities, shops, and other recreational venues that contribute to the vacation experience. The timeshare owner's service experience, while in the resort, is comprised of the sum total of these service encounters.

On another level, timeshare ownership has some interesting features that encompass both domestic and commercial dimensions of hospitality. Some timeshare owners are buying a permanent piece of a second home. Unlike a hotel stay, timeshare ownership brings with it a sense of belonging, permanence, and embeddedness. Even owners who exchange their weeks and locations are to some extent buying into an ownership relationship that hotel occupancy does not involve. These notions of domestic space in "foreign" settings have deep resonances with guest and host relations. In particular, some people regard domestic hospitality with an authenticity that is not to be found in commercial hospitality (Warde and Martens, 2000). In some ways, timeshare ownership involves a "stranger becoming a friend," a fundamental element of the relationship of guest and host, because the timeshare property enables an ongoing relationship between the guest (owner) and the host (operator).

Historically, various terms such as sojourner, alien, traveler, and foreigner have been used interchangeably for stranger (Bratcher, 2002). They represent individuals who were literally homeless, having been displaced, for whatever reason, from their usual activities, relationships, and sense of place. In a frequently hostile world, they relied on the host to offer a welcome to a stranger who was unfamiliar, unknown, and ambiguous as an act of faith and goodwill. The host provided a sanctuary or oasis that protected the stranger from estrangement, immorality, theft, and violence (Elwell, 1996). This allowed a person who is experiencing homelessness to have temporary access to shared social space in the context of a safe, friendly, and social relationship. The relationship between the stranger (guest) and the host is fundamental and one that can better inform commercial hospitality relationships, including those engaging timeshare owners. Examples from preindustrial societies around the world confirm that many societies have a moral imperative to be hospitable to strangers and "to turn a stranger into a friend." In commercial operations, as in timeshare resorts, it is frontline staff and unit management who will be in a position to perform acts of hospitableness and make the owner feel welcome and valued as a friend.

Telfer (2000) provides a philosophical insight into genuine acts of hospitableness. She states that hosts are concerned for a guest's well-being and comfort while under their care, but good hosts also need to be skilled in managing situations and in preventing disputes. A good host, however, is not necessarily hospitable because the host may have an ulterior motive for tending to the guest and exercising hosting skills. For example, the host may be attempting to manipulate the guest so as to gain favor, or for purposes of self-display and vanity. Genuine hospitality is driven by motives that stem from friendliness and concern for others. Hospitableness suggests a warmth and affection for other people, a desire to protect and nurture and perform acts of hospitableness. The motives of those involved in host relationships with guests are fundamental, even in commercial settings. Those selected to serve in frontline hospitality settings, including timeshare, need to understand, display, and genuinely feel emotions consistent with being hospitable.

Key Point 7.1

People selected to work in frontline positions and line management need to understand and perform their role in a way that is genuinely hospitable.

The importance of the emotions of hospitality is further reinforced by work on the emotions of "special meal occasions" (Lashley, Morrison, and Randall, 2004). Respondents asked to describe their most memorable meal identified the emotional dimensions that make meal occasions, and thereby hospitality, special. The occasion of the meal or holiday is often a celebration of bonding and togetherness with family and friends. The company of others and the atmosphere created by the setting, other people, and their treatment by hosts give emotional dimensions to meal occasions which are vital to creating memorable occasions. Interestingly, few of the respondents mentioned the food consumed as part of their descriptions. The dominant impression is that these emotional dimensions of hospitality make these meal occasions special, and it will be these emotional dimensions of their stay that will make timeshare owners' vacations special.

Respondents in this research used language that links their experiences to domestic hospitality. The need to feel welcome and friendliness from hosts, to be secure in a nonthreatening environment, and to experience comfort and warmth were all words used to describe guests' emotions. Commercial settings are not always a lesser form of hospitality; they engage guests with some different emotions, but there are some important overlaps. Fundamentally, guests evaluate hospitality experiences primarily in emotional terms. Providers of hospitality experiences in timeshare resorts need to be aware of these emotional dimensions of the customers' experiences and how to meet these emotional needs.

Case Study 7.1

Fiona described her most memorable meal:

I was included in the dinner party along with the birthday girl's family. On arrival at the restaurant we were greeted by two friendly staff and I was surprised at their pleasure at our arrival and their knowledge in remembering the names of my friend's family. They talked to her Dad as though they were old acquaintances and put me at ease. We were led into the restaurant, where most of the staff greeted us with the same enthusiastic reaction.

Overall I had a very good time, and I felt this was due to the warm welcome and good service I received from the staff, which I believe is the most important element in a good meal. The way

> the staff had a desire to please us showed they weren't only there to make a profit, and this was very satisfying and gives an advantage over other restaurants. The company also made it worthwhile as we all got along tremendously, which led to it being such a laugh. I don't believe it was the occasion that made it so; even if it hadn't been my friend's birthday, we would still have had a fabulous time, although the food and drink being delicious was also a strong element in making it an enjoyable experience.

Herzberg's study (1966) of motivation provides a useful metaphor for the physical aspects of the resort, the quality of the décor of the lodge or property, facilities, the meal and drink are all potential dissatisfiers. If standards do not meet expectations, customers will be dissatisfied, but exceeding their expectations in these aspects will not produce satisfaction (Balmer and Baum, 1993). Customer satisfaction will be generated by the quality of the emotions generated from their experiences; staff performance, the qualities of hospitableness, fellow diners, and the performance of line management are the key sources to generating customer satisfaction. Long-term customer loyalty and repeat visits to the resort are dependent on the emotions generated by these elements. Highly satisfied timeshare visitors are more likely to return to that resort or to recommend the property to family and friends.

Operators are aware of the importance of having the right kind of emotions on display in service encounters—hence their concern that staff display emotions appropriate to the service offer (Hochschild, 1983). Usually this is typified as smiling and the "Have a Nice Day Culture" (Mann, 1999). The problem is that the specific features of the hospitality service interactions relevant to timeshare operations are "more than a service encounter" (Lashley, Morrison, and Randall, 2004), and the emotional dimensions of performance need to be given a preeminence that they rarely receive in performance monitoring and quality management systems.

Furthermore, Hochschild's (1983) seminal work suggests that service workers are prone to provide emotional labor that can add to job stress, which results in burnout and staff retention problems. Emotional labor is the result of having to display an emotion that individuals do not feel or that result from the need to mask emotions that are felt but are not deemed to be legitimate for the service encounter. For example, an employee may be required to smile even though s/he may feel angry and upset, or to restrain anger when the employee is dealing with an awkward and complaining customer. Mann (1999) suggests that there are potentially three emotional states when dealing with customers. Each of the states is created as an interaction between the emotions felt, the emotions displayed, and the emotional performance required of the job role.

From a service perspective, *emotional harmony* is the desired state because it requires less emotional labor, it causes less stress and is more acceptable to customers, and the emotions expressed are those genuinely felt and required of the job holder. Langhorn's (2004) study of emotional performance and emotional intelligence in a UK popular restaurant chain found that the staff who were able to display "service emotions" which they genuinely felt were perceived by customers as giving better service and better value, and as generating a desire to return to the restaurant. Emotional dissonance and emotional deviance are less desirable. Emotional dissonance is the classic state of providing emotional labor, and apart from the negative effect on employees, Langhorn's study suggests that customers are less impressed with staff performance when the person appears to be acting and is trying to hide emotions felt. Emotional deviance will create a negative customer response, resulting in poor evaluations of the service experience, because the emotions being expressed are not appropriate for the service encounter. Timeshare operators need to consider these dimensions of the service interaction, and how to support their emotional laborers, because they are key to good customer relations and the generation of loyal customers.

Key Point 7.2

Emotional labor resulting from emotional disharmony is an important aspect of service work and one that needs to be managed so that frontline service workers provide the emotional performance that creates positive customer service experiences.

Work on emotional labor has stimulated interest in the emotional dimensions of organizational life (Fineman, 2000). The impact of emotional intelligence has been seen as a key influence on business success in commercial organizations, with particular relevance for services. *Emotional intelligence* has been described as key to organizational success, with particular relevance in organizations like timeshare and hospitality services, where employee (internal customer) relations impact directly on external customer experiences. Goleman (1998) puts emotional intelligence at the leading edge of business success. "The business case is compelling: companies that leverage this advantage [emotional intelligence] add measurably to their bottom line" (p. 13).

The notion of an Emotional Intelligence Quotient is being widely promoted by many consultants and is said to underpin the most effective business performance and successful lives (Cooper and Sawaf, 1997). Those who are emotionally intelligent are said to have abilities in five domains. They

1. recognize their own emotions and express them to others.

2. recognize and understand the emotions of others.

3. use emotions with reason and emotional information in thought.

4. regulate and manage their own and others' emotions.

5. control strong emotional states, anger, frustration, excitement, anxiety, and the like.

Timeshare operators might be able to improve business performance and customer satisfaction with management practices rooted in emotional intelligence practices. Langhorn's (2004) study mentioned earlier, also found that managers with higher emotional intelligence scores were positively related to improved profit performance, customer satisfaction, employee satisfaction, and team performance. Employee emotional intelligence scores were positively linked to customer perceptions of service quality and value, and willingness to return. Improvements can be made in operational performance through recruitment and training practices, as well as performance and service quality monitoring that use emotional intelligence as a key business concern.

Key Point 7.3

Emotional intelligence measures indicate the sensitivity of individuals to recognizing their own emotions and the emotions of other, and manage emotions in personal interactions.

The emotional dimensions of hospitality, including timeshare, make the relationship between host and guest, or timeshare owners and management company, more than an ordinary service encounter. Owners are likely to evaluate the totality of their experiences on the basis of the feelings generated in their various encounters with immediate resort frontline staff and managers, as well as the personnel from other organizations involved in the complete holiday experience. An awareness of these emotional dimensions leads to a concern for the emotional labor undertaken by frontline employees, and the conditions needed both to remove negative impacts and generate emotions that are genuinely hospitable. Recent interest in assessing, recruiting, and developing the emotional intelligence of service workers offers one interesting avenue for the improvement of service encounters. Employee empowerment also has the potential to create the conditions that will improve employee service performance by creating the conditions that are likely to result in emotional harmony.

Empowering Service Excellence

Employee empowerment is one of those management terms that sounds good because of the meaning that empowerment has in everyday language. The Collins English Dictionary (1993: 498) provides two meanings: "1. to give or delegate power or authority to; authorize. 2. to give ability to; enable or permit." Yet examples of empowerment in practice cover a whole host of different practices, some of which encompass these definitions and others that clearly do not.

In the Accor group of hotels, for example, empowerment has been used to describe the use of quality circles; suggestion schemes in McDonald's Restaurants; "Whatever it Takes" employee training programs in Marriott Hotels; employee involvement in devising departmental service standards in Hilton International Hotels; semiautonomous work groups and removal of levels of management in Harvester Restaurants; and the delegation of greater authority to hotel general managers (Lashley, 2001). In fact, these examples cover quite different arrangements in the way managers and employees interact. Some are participative and involve employees making decisions that might have been made by a manager or supervisor in more traditional organizations. In other cases, the relationships are more consultative—employees make suggestions, but managers make the ultimate decisions. In some cases, employees merely act on instructions given by managers. Empowerment as a management technique is therefore confusing and covers quite different experiences for employees and managers.

The work of Conger and Kanungo (1988) is helpful because they define empowerment as being both **relational** and **motivational**. Their model is useful because it allows consideration of initiatives that alter the relationships between managers and the managed, as well as those initiatives that structurally leave the relationship substantially unchanged but that do produce feelings of empowerment to be considered.

Table 7.1 suggests that empowerment takes a number of forms that identify different relationships between managers and those they are aiming to empower. Empowerment through participation covers a number of initiatives whereby employees make decisions that would previously have been made by a manager or supervisor. Empowerment through involvement includes initiatives that are mostly consultative; employees are asked for their ideas and suggestions, but managers make the final decision. Empowerment through commitment describes arrangements that attempt to engage employee feelings of being empowered in structures that are traditionally command and control oriented. Empowerment through delayering is concerned largely with the organizational

Managerial Meaning	Initiatives Used
Empowerment Through Participation	Autonomous Work Groups Whatever It Takes Training Job Enrichment Works Council Employee Directors
Empowerment Through Involvement	Quality Circles Team Briefings Suggestion Schemes
Empowerment Through Commitment	Employee Share Ownership Profit Sharing and Bonus Schemes Quality of Working Life Programmes - job rotation - job enlargement
Empowerment Through Delayering	Job Re-design Re-training Autonomous Work Groups Job Enrichment Profit Sharing and Bonus Schemes

Table 7.1 Managerial Meanings of Empowerment

hierarchy by removing levels and making the structure "flatter." In these circumstances, junior managers or frontline staff take on some of the decision-making roles of some of their more senior colleagues.

While these differences in managerial meanings of empowerment result in different working arrangements, and relationships between managers and staff, the key defining feature of empowerment is that people *feel* empowered. In Conger and Kanungo's terms, they engage with the motivational dimension of empowerment. If empowerment can be differentiated from other employment initiatives, it engages employees at an emotional level, and it is individual and personal. Empowerment is about discretion, autonomy, power, and control. Whatever the manager's intentions the effectiveness of empowerment as an employment strategy is determined by the perceptions, experiences, and feelings of the "empowered."

Fundamentally, these feelings will be rooted in a sense of personal worth and ability to affect outcomes, of having the "power" to make a difference.

Empowered employees are supposed to display greater control (Koberg et al, 1999), have a greater sense of personal power, together with the freedom to use that power (Potterfield, 1999), and possess a sense of personal efficacy and self-determination (Alpander, 1991). They have to feel that they have power and can make a difference and that they have choices and can exercise choice (Johnson, 1993). Empowerment provides employees with a sense of autonomy, authority, and control (Heslin, 1999) together with the abilities, resources, and discretion to make decisions. Empowerment, therefore, claims to produce an emotional state in employees from which derive the additional commitment and effort.

As service organizations increasingly require frontline service personnel to manage their emotions appropriate to the given situation, they use employment practices to create an emotional culture that is consistent with the offer being made to customers (Leidner, 1994). "Through recruitment, selection, socialisation and performance evaluation, organisations develop a social reality in which feelings become a commodity for achieving instrumental goals" (Putnam and Munby, 1993: 7). The use of employee empowerment might also be added to this list. Bearing in mind that empowerment takes a variety of forms, it is hoped that these initiatives which involve employees enable them to participate in decisions and generate high levels of commitment that will result in an increased sense of ownership of the service encounter and generate the required emotional display more easily. Through empowerment, employees are expected to genuinely display the warmth to customers required of the organization. In terms of the model outlined in Table 7.1, empowerment has the potential to produce emotional harmony. Empowered employees deliver greater customer satisfaction because they are able to respond quickly to customer service needs, but they are also happier in their work and present customers with service interactions that reflect their happiness.

Key Point 7.4

Employee empowerment is a potentially useful management technique because it can improve the work experiences of service employees and positively impact on customer service experiences.

Managing as Though People Mattered

This chapter has argued that the management of people in timeshare and hospitality operations has some important differentiating features. Hospitality experiences require employees to produce performances that meet customer needs on an emotional level, and the management of employees has to be consistent with practice that will contribute to the creation of appropriate emotional dimensions of the customer experience. Table 7.2 lists some of the issues of concern. Ensuring that jobs are designed in a way that encourages positive experiences, recruiting and selecting the right kind of people, and ensuring that skills are developed and that performance is monitored and rewarded in a systematic and consistent manner are all important.

In recent years, many firms in the service sector have redesigned jobs in a way that deskills the work. Job holders can complete job tasks with limited skills, and by requiring low levels of training. Recruitment is easier because potentially a large pool of labor is available. Pay rates are lower

Job design	Skills and discretion required
Job description	Describing the job to be done
Staff specification	Describing the ideal recruit
Labor market	Source of potential employees
Recruitment	Attracting suitable applicants
Selecting	Choosing the right person
Inducting	Settling the person
Training	Developing required skills
Appraisal	Reinforcing and extending performance
Reward and development	Motivating

Table 7.2 Human Resource Management for Service Excellence in Timeshare Operations

and training costs are lower. These trends have been called McDonaldization (Ritzer, 1993; 2000), but they essentially involve techniques first developed in manufacturing. Scientific management, as defined by Taylor (1947), includes redesigning jobs into small component parts; individuals specialize in working on one small part of the job. As Ritzer's term implies, McDonald's is an obvious example of the application of these techniques, but many other organizations are redesigning their offer to customers, and the jobs need to service them in ways that extend *"efficiency, calculability, predictability and control"* (Ritzer, 1993). Although the processes involved appear to be rational, there is an *irrational dimension* to supposedly rational decisions. High staff turnover and low levels of employee satisfaction experienced by many hospitality and timeshare organizations are, in part, caused by job designs that produce low-skilled, boring, and monotonous work experiences.

Designing and Defining the Job

Jobs should allow some degree of autonomy or individual interpretation so that employees are less likely to be bored. Several techniques developed in manufacturing can be applied to hospitality and timeshare organizations. *Job enrichment* is a technique with some overlaps with "participative forms of empowerment." Jobs are redesigned to build skills and judgments back into the work so that job holders have more autonomy to make decisions that are appropriate to the job. *Job enlargement* involves broadening the scope of jobs. So the skill levels and decision making are relatively simple, but the job is enlarged to include more tasks at the same level. The aim is to create more interest because the job involves a wide range of tasks. *Job rotation* involves moving people around different jobs. Again the jobs themselves remain largely simple and require limited judgments, but individuals are moved around jobs so as to reduce boredom and monotony.

Some organizations dealing in hospitality and timeshare use job rotation to good effect. By creating a *functionally flexible* workforce, organizations can move individuals between jobs as demands shift and change. Studies on hotel productivity (Jones, 2002) found that this approach to job design reduced the number of employees required to staff from 100 to 97, with the same level of customer sales and service.

Before activating the recruitment process, it is important to systematically define the job and duties involved, as well as the ideal candidate required. Recruitment and retention problems in hospitality and timeshare operations frequently occur because managers do not take the time to describe the job that is to be done and the duties involved. The *Job Description* defines the job; it also includes the job title, the position in the hierarchy—superior and subordinates (where appropriate), the main duties, occasional duties, and potential limits on authority. The job description is a rational outline of the job to be done and can be used in the recruitment process and in the development of individuals. The *Staff Specification* describes the "ideal candidate." Typically, this includes consideration of those factors that are *essential* and those that are *desirable*, across areas such as physical makeup, education and training, work experience, personality, and personal circumstances. The Staff Specification is helpful because it provides a blueprint of the sort of person who will be able to undertake the duties outlined in the job description. It can help prevent recruitment practices that select "the best of the bunch" rather than the person who meets the needs of the job to be done. A common problem experienced in hospitality and timeshare firms is that recruitment is hurried and not focused on a systematic understanding of the job to be done and the sort of person needed to do it.

Key Point 7.5

Systematic recruitment starts with careful consideration of the job to be done and the person required to do it.

Attracting Recruits

Before commencing the recruitment process, it is worth considering the labor market for the candidates for the post to be filled. Any one timeshare operation may be recruiting from a number of different labor markets. Cleaners and others undertaking "routine unskilled labor" are likely to be recruited from the local area. There is likely to be minimal travel involved. It is important to consider current pay and reward levels being paid by competitors. Employers are sometimes unaware of how the rates being paid measure up against those being offered by firms in not just competitor hospitality firms, but also in the retail, leisure and other sectors. While these employees are potentially plentiful, many other employers are offering jobs of a similar type. A UK study (Lashley, Thomas, & Rowson, 2002) found that hospitality firms were finding it difficult to retain staff because their rates were often 25 percent below the rates being paid in competitor firms.

Maintenance, receptionist, and gardening staff may be recruiting from a slightly different labor market because they are more skilled and fewer in number than for the "routine unskilled" labor discussed earlier. There may be more obvious competition for their skills, and they may travel from slightly further afield; alternatively, they may be recruited with an accommodation package, whereby they live onsite.

Managerial, sales, and marketing staff may be different in that they are fewer in number and may be recruited from a more regional, or even, national labor market. The seniority and rarity of the post, and the person required to fill it impact on the local, regional, or national source of potential recruits. Again, a clear understanding of competitive terms and conditions is required. A failure to match market rates may result in recruitment difficulties or problems retaining staff once recruited.

In all cases, recruitment and retention difficulties are increased in times of low unemployment. More competition for the fewer people looking for work and more alternatives for existing employees increase the competitive pressures. A firm may deliberately position itself as the "employer of first choice" by paying better wages, offering better employment terms, and suggesting career prospects (Lashley, Thomas, and Rowson, 2002). This enables the firm to have the pick of staff and to retain existing employees more easily.

Before exploring external sources of recruits, for some posts, internal sources may be appropriate. Moving individuals from casual to full-time employment, or promoting from within can be a quick way of filling vacancies and have a motivating effect on the workforce because it demonstrates the potential for career development. Asking existing staff if they know someone who might be interested in applying for the post is another potential "internal" source of recruits. This has the advantage of building team links and group dynamics as the recruits and existing staff are known to each other. While the benefits of internal recruitment are important, the major disadvantages are related to the match required for the post to be filled. The point is to recruit the person who best matches the job requirement, and there may be no one with this match in the organization. In other cases, recruiters are looking for new people who will bring in fresh ideas and skills from other employers.

Once the decision to recruit externally has been made, the source and method for advertising the post have to be taken. Typically, the more specialized the post to be filled, the more likely that post will be advertised using wide circulation media and "display advertisements." When recruiting management personnel or sales and marketing staff, job advertisements will likely be placed in regional, national, or trade journals. Advertisements for cleaners, bar, and restaurant staff may well be placed in the local paper using classified advertisements (Mullins, 2002).

Good job advertisements are designed to attract sufficient well-suited applications for the recruitment process to make a successful appointment. The recruitment team does not want to be swamped with lots of unsuitable candidates. The advertisement should therefore *attract* the attention of candidates, *interest* the person in the post, stimulate a *desire* to follow up, and inform the candidate of what *action* needs to be taken and by when.

Once applications have been received, the applicants need to be sifted for match against the Staff Specification so as to decide on the short list of candidates to be interviewed. If the advertising process has been successful, all applicants should be suitable on paper, although there may be differences in the extent to which they match desirable and essential qualities required from the staff specification. Recruiters use a number of techniques to assist in the shortlisting process, but the key requirement is to be objective and fair. Usually a system using a scoring process and involving more than one person making the selection overcomes some of the potential biases. Ethical recruitment processes avoid prejudgments and filtering people on superficial grounds, such as ethnicity, gender, or disability. Ultimately, the process has to be open to ethical scrutiny.

Key Point 7.6

Before commencing the selection process, the effective process considers the potential sources of recruits for the post as well as the terms and conditions to be offered so as to secure the services of a person to meet the needs of the job.

The Selection Process

At its most basic, the selection of candidates for employment involves some form of interviewing process. The interview is by far the most widely used selection technique. Interviewers feel comfortable with the process, though research suggests that this confidence is often misplaced. Interviewers tend to adopt a number of techniques that can result in overemphasizing the strengths of some candidates and the weaknesses of others. Some organizations try to overcome these problems by using more than one interviewer and more than one interview. In other cases, selection decisions are informed by aptitude and attitude tests, personality profiles, and/or role plays. The use of Emotional Intelligence Quotients is one example of a test being used by some firms in the sector. "Pret-a-manager," a UK-based sandwich chain, recruits new staff only after the individual has worked with the team for a shift and the team elects to recommend appointment. In TGI Fridays, new staff are subject to as many as four interviews and role-play situations.

Where interviews are used as part of the selection process, it is important to approach them in a planned and coordinated manner. *Prior to the interviews*, the interviewing team decides on the structure and timing of the interview, confirms that they are familiar with the applicants, and allocates sufficient time for the interviewing to take place. *During the interview*, candidates need to be given a chance to show their strengths, and questions should be asked in a way that encourages a discussion. The management of the interview should allow sufficient time for each candidate and should recognize that the interview is a two-way process whereby the candidate is also selecting the firm. *After the interview*, interviewers need to make the selection in a rational manner. Again, a scoring system can be useful because it enables the decision to be made on the basis of comparing the candidate against the requirements of the job, as defined in the job specification.

References supporting the candidate's application can be taken up before or after the interviewing process. References supplied prior to the interviews can help support the selection process; those taken after interviews can be used to confirm the impressions gained at the interview. In both cases, references are not always strictly accurate. Referees are sometimes loath to be overly critical of an applicant. In other cases, referees may be giving an unrealistically favorable picture of the applicant because of personal ties or because an existing employer wants to be rid of an unsuitable employee.

Key Point 7.7

Effective selection processes involve considered steps and stages that allow for the selection of individuals who match the needs of the job and that avoid prejudgment and discrimination.

Case Study 7.2

Recruitment of Sales Personnel at De Vere Resort Ownership

De Vere Resort Ownership sites select sales personnel who will act in a way that supports the company's business relationship with its owners. Whenever a vacancy occurs, the local sales manger for resort properties consults with Craig Mitchell, the senior executive for the resort ownership division. The first consideration is to explore the existing workforce to determine whether a member of the team might be promoted and trained for a sales role. In all three De Vere ownership sites there are sales team members who have previously worked on sales reception, or have been "owners" hosts.

If there is no suitable internal candidate, the local sales manager generates an advertisement for the vacant role, shortlists applicants, and arranges an interview schedule and asks Craig Mitchell to interview and select the person. Though involved in the decision, the local manager does not make the decision without the involvement of the senior manager. Staff turnover is quite low, and the senior manager is determined to retain control of the recruitment of sales personnel. He knows that the first contact with customers has to be carefully managed. An overly pressured sales pitch or a dishonest approach to the sale will be counterproductive and will both lose the sale and potentially damage the company's reputation. Equally, the manager wants to generate as many sales as possible because the generation of "leads" is costly and time consuming.

Although characteristics appear to differ in that some team members are more comfortable with different market segments among the contacts, sales personnel seem uniformly comfortable with other people. They all share an ability to make customers feel at ease.

Induction and Employment

Once the successful candidate has been selected, it is important to plan an induction program for the new recruit. Induction programs should formally introduce the recruit to the organization, work colleagues, and role. A well-planned induction program recognizes that the new recruit has anxieties and needs, and that the program is as concerned with meeting these needs as it is with making the recruit an effective employee as quickly as possible. The induction program may extend over several days and weeks, covering a range of issues that will help the recruit in understanding the organization and its employees' role within it. Lashley and Best (2001) found that many hospitality firms claimed to have an induction program, but it was often limited to its ability to meet legislative requirements. Some firms had a structured program that identified a range of skills and competences to be developed. In other cases, the programs were informal and restricted to showing new recruits the basic job tasks. In none of the surveyed firms did the induction program address the recruit's emotional needs.

Induction training is part of the induction process and is essentially concerned with ensuring that employees learn the skills required to be effective in the job. Formal training that has clear objectives and structures tends to help recruits become effective more quickly and achieve higher levels of long-term output (Eaglen, Lashley, and Thomas, 2000). Research on the benefits and costs of training and development (Eaglen, Lashley, and Thomas, 1999) shows that employee training produces an array of business benefits, including increased employee productivity. Although productivity is a complex concept in hospitality services, formally trained frontline service staff tend to serve more customers and have higher average transaction values than employees who learn in informal ways—that is, who learn without the benefit of a formal program. In addition to improved productivity, formally trained employees are also less likely to leave the firm or to take absences. They register higher levels of personal job satisfaction, produce better service quality, and have more satisfied customers. They are also more confident, more flexible, and more likely to accept change. This range of benefits covers both tangible and intangible benefits. A problem faced by many hospitality and timeshare firms is that performance management systems are frequently limited to financial performance. Often, they are incapable of capturing the benefits flowing from training and development, and as a consequence they tend to see training as a luxury. In reality, failure to train is costly and leads to lower productivity, higher staff turnover, lower customer satisfaction, and so on (Eaglen and Lashley, 2001).

Ongoing staff performance appraisal helps to produce a climate of continuous professional development. The development of individuals ensures that individuals are performing effectively, but control of individuals should not be the main motive for appraisal systems. Best practice suggests that appraisal is concerned primarily with development and gaining insights into the appraisee's experiences and ambitions. In some cases, a *360 degree* process involves the staff member appraising the manager as well as the manager appraising the employee. Appraisal systems vary in their scope and frequency; typically, they occur on an annual basis, though in some instances the appraisal takes place more regularly—every six months or so. Appraisal assists communication processes between staff and managers, and ensures that managers understand employee aspirations. This helps minimize employee frustrations and most importantly, ensures that managers understand sources of satisfaction and rewards that are most appealing to staff.

Rewards from work can be identified under two headings: extrinsic and intrinsic rewards. *Extrinsic rewards* originate outside of the individual. They are best understood as material rewards such as pay rates—bonus schemes, tips, commission, performance-related pay, share option schemes, and so on. Research shows that managers have a general tendency to think these incentives are more important to employees than they are to employees in reality (Lashley, 2000). That is not to say that people will not want to improve their income; however, people are not usually driven to maximize material rewards at all costs. Most people strike an *effort reward bargain*, whereby they will increase work effort to increase income to a point. In addition, financial incentives can distort the priorities pursued by individuals because individuals may prioritize those activities that maximize income at the expense of other outcomes. For example, timeshare sales personnel in some firms have been criticized for being overly concerned about making a sale with the use of high-pressure sales techniques. Commission-linked sales targets may result in sales but also in some poor public relations impacts and ultimately dissatisfied customers.

Intrinsic rewards are those rewards from work that do not materially benefit the individual but make the post holder better off. The nature of the work itself, the feel of control and effectiveness, and the skills needed for the job are all influences that help a person feel good about her work. According to Rodwell, Keinzie, and Shadur (1998), several surveys show that employee satisfaction levels are positively linked to personal autonomy and to possession of some degree of choice as to how tasks are completed. Effective communications are also a key ingredient of enabling employees to clearly understand what is expected of them and where the organization is going. The role of the immediate supervisor is also positively linked to employee satisfaction levels (Argenti, 1998). The supervisor's management style and use of praise to subordinates have a key impact on generating these intrinsic rewards from work. Concerns to redesign jobs in the ways outlined earlier are all examples of approaches to job design which are enhancing intrinsic rewards from work—empowerment, job enrichment, job enlargement and job rotation, and emotional leadership are all in different ways linked to helping employees feel better about work.

Key Point 7.8

Once employed, recruits need to be managed in a way that stresses their importance and value to the organization through ongoing programs of development and rewards that meet their full range of aspirations and needs.

Conclusion

Human resource management practices have a crucial contribution to make in hospitality and timeshare service operations because of the emotional dimensions present in customers' decision to use commercial hospitality services and to buy into a timeshare. Fundamentally, the links between the emotions of hospitality and the performance of frontline staff require careful consideration and management. These considerations need to go beyond the current practice of demanding an emotional element to employees' performance as exemplified by the "Have a Nice Day Culture." Important though this consideration is, these emotional demands can lead to emotional disharmony, emotional labor, and added job stress that feed into staff turnover and poor service levels.

Emotional laborers need to be supported by managers. Training and the development of coping strategies assist frontline staff to deal with these emotional demands. To do this, managers have to be able to recognize their own emotions and to work with the emotions of others. Emotional intelligence is required of both managers and staff to better operate in hospitality and timeshare operations.

Given the key significance of employee and management performance to customer satisfaction levels, and ultimately to the ability of organizations to build competitive advantage through quality customer experiences, the management of people has a central significance. The design of jobs in the first instance, and the recruitment of the most suitable employees, their development and rewards, are issues to be carefully planned and executed. People are more than a production cost to be minimized so as to extract extra profit. People are a key asset of the timeshare business and need to recognized as such through the use of techniques built into organizational performance reviews.

Managing Service Quality in Timeshare

After studying this chapter you should be able to:

- critically evaluate the distinctive features of time-share services.

- contrast and compare approaches to service quality management.

- discuss Total Quality Management approaches to timeshare service management.

- define the critical success factors for timeshare service quality delivery.

Introduction

Visits by timeshare owners, exchangers, or guests to resorts create the total service experience from which each evaluates the quality of both their purchase and each individual visit. Apart from the immediate services associated with the lodge or apartment, the bar, restaurant, leisure, and other services provided at the resort need to match, or even exceed, customer service expectations. It is for this reason that ARDA's Code covering *Standards of Practice in Professional Hospitality Management*, for example, "is intended to ensure high quality to owners and guests" (ARDA, 2002b: 240). Quality management in hospitality services presents both customers and managers with some problems because of some general features of service quality delivery and because of some unique features of the hospitality relationship.

The nature of services themselves reflects the difficulties of definition, standardization, and control. In timeshare operations, the combination of benefits, and the importance of employee and customer perceptions of service expectations, together with variations in evaluations of successful service encounters, all make for a complexity in managing service quality that is not found in other sectors. Mudie and Cottam (1999: 1) sum up the dilemma for service organizations in general; "For the customer there may be little evidence, in advance, of what to expect. The service provider has often to produce the service under the watchful gaze of customers. Finally both parties may fail to agree what constitutes quality service." Both academic commentators and practitioners have attempted to overcome these difficulties by developing a range of analytical tools through which to measure customer assessments of service quality and service encounter success.

Timeshare services vary in the amount of interaction between the customer and the service organization. However, service interactions that have been under the most intense investigation are those that rely on the interface between employees and customers. This is the key determinant of customer satisfaction, repeat business, competitive advantage, and commercial success. The employee's performance is the means through which the timeshare resort operators deliver service quality and customer satisfaction. Paradoxically, it is precisely these frontline staff who have been regarded by many hospitality service organizations as a key cost area and have used labor costs as a source of cost reduction and profit. Typically, the person fronting the customer has been the lowest paid and least trained member of the organization (Barbee and Bott, 1991). Traditionally, many of these firms have adopted a cost leadership strategy that has been at the heart of policies relating to low levels of training, sloppy recruitment, poor induction, and remarkably high levels of staff turnover. Interestingly ARDA's "hospitality management code" requires that "Management should have qualified staff that are trained to perform at a professional level, and should provide continuing education for all staff" (ARDA, 2002b: 240).

Against this background, some hospitality and timeshare organizations have recently been concerned about gaining greater competitive advantage by addressing issues of service quality, through initiatives such as Total Quality Management, the development of service cultures, and so on. An important ingredient of these strategies has been their empowerment of employees to meet customer needs as they arise. In addition, some commentators and researchers are suggesting that exploration of hospitality as fundamentally involving the relationship between *hosts* and *guests* considers hospitality as delivering a series of emotional experiences that mean they represent "more than a service encounter" (Lashley and Morrison, 2003). Service quality management in hospitality and timeshare operations needs to focus on these emotional dimensions of the encounter because it is through these that customer loyalty is built and maintained.

Understanding Services and Service Quality

Hospitality services share some features in common with services in general, and some of the debates about service quality management apply. The distinction between goods and services has been subject to a great deal of debate as different writers choose to argue that all goods contain some intangible elements (Levitt, 1972) or that services have distinct characteristics that cannot be captured by generic analysis (Lovelock, 1981). In practice, there is likely to be a clustering of both tangible and intangible benefits associated with most goods and services. These differences are best demonstrated by Figure 8.1, which shows an array of timeshare products and services, for example, that provide varying amounts of tangible and intangible benefits. Services in general have been defined: "The production of an essentially intangible benefit, either in its own right or as a significant element of a tangible product, which through some form of exchange satisfies an identified consumer need" (Palmer, 1994: 3).

Customers buy timeshare property weeks as a combination of tangible and intangible benefits. The apartment, lodge, or suite is tangible. The décor and equipment, the resort property, and accompanying facilities are clearly all tangible and can be the subject of a checklist of features and qualities. Being tangible, they can be defined and specified. Customers are able to identify and itemize what it is they are buying. Tangible benefits are subject to deterioration over time, and maintenance and replacement of equipment are important influences on customer perceptions of quality. Once grand, well-equipped and well-appointed property can become a little tired if not properly maintained.

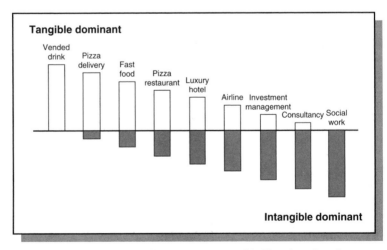

Figure 8.1 The Continuum of Tangible and Intangible Timeshare Benefits

Key Point 8.1

Customer experiences of timeshare services consist of a number of tangible (measurable) and intangible (difficult to measure) benefits.

Once the customer has become a resort owner, customer satisfaction is much more dependent on the influences of the core features of service. Intangibility, inseparability, variability, and perishability (Cowell, 1986; Mudie and Cottam, 1999) all present timeshare service organizations with management difficulties.

* The *intangible* aspects of services make it difficult for customers to verify the benefits to be gained from a service prior to the purchase. This can only be done as a result of receiving the service. In addition, it is difficult to assess the expectations of customers, service employees, and managers in what the intangible benefits should deliver. Consumers face uncertainty when choosing between competing services, say whether to eat on the resort's premises or whether to go outside the resort. The response of many service producers has been to increase physical evidence and to produce strong brands. In recent years, many hospitality organizations have begun to advocate competitive advantage through focus on the intangible elements of the service encounter. This is less easily copied by competitors. In particular, brand values that stress emotional benefits require employees to produce the emotional performance required. It is in this area that empowerment is said to be valuable, though the general approach to employment practice is key. Well-paid, well-motivated, and well-trained employees who work for the same organization over many years are more likely to deliver the professional service quality advocated by ARDA's hospitality code.

* The *heterogeneity* of services is another feature that distinguishes them from typical manufacturing production. Service delivery is frequently variable and difficult to standardize because of the personal nature of the contact

between the customer and the frontline employee. Thus, individual employees may well vary in their interpretation of customer needs. Elements of human chemistry may interfere with the performance, and some employees are more personally committed to successful service encounters than others. Customer expectations of satisfactory service vary and are difficult to predict. Hence, it cannot be said that service delivery is homogeneous. Even where the service is relatively simple, service encounter is never the same; each interaction is a unique encounter.

There is variety between different types of services and the degree of standardization and within the services provided. Some firms are able to standardize the tangible elements of the service encounter. Many fast-food deliverers, branded restaurants, and hotel operators supply standardized products to customers who demand the predictability and security of the branded service (Ritzer, 2002). The success of many timeshare operators associated with well-known hotel brands—Marriott, De Vere, and so on—is due to the standardized offer. Customers know what quality to expect from the facilities. Some firms have also attempted to standardize the intangible elements of the service encounter by scripting employees, training them to use certain phrases and words during service. McDonald's Restaurants and Disney World are well-known examples of organizations that seek to standardize the service encounter in this way.

Other service organizations are in positions where the encounters with customers are more individualized and difficult to predict. Successful encounters are dependent on the individual service deliverer being able to interpret the requirements of customers and adapt the service delivered to their wants. Other organizations may well require that frontline staff deliver a standardized product in the tangibles but then require a more individualized, or personalized, service in the intangibles. A themed and branded restaurant may offer a standardized menu for food and drink, but expect staff to personalize their relationship with the guest.

Key Point 8.2

Customer expectations of timeshare services vary according to the degree of standardization and customization they require.

- The production and consumption of the service should also be *inseparable*. Consumers of the hospitality service are themselves participants in the service delivery, say as customers in a restaurant, bar, or resort facility. They interact with the service deliverer, the environment, and other consumers. Customers are party to the service interaction and partially shape it. Their perceptions of the service encounter are developed through their perceptions of the service environment and of fellow customers.

  Similarly, the relationship between customers and service deliverers is not uniform. In some cases, the service interaction will be simple, requiring a limited range of short (and predictable?) transactions between customer and service deliverer: a fast-food or take-away operation is typical. In other situations, customers will expect ritualized performance, where employees need to appreciate the expectations of customers as in an haute cuisine restaurant. The ability to balance customer expectations of formality with service accessibility is an important consideration. In other situations customers are buying into the hospitality service operation as "theater"; employees are expected to provide the appropriate performance. American bar and dinner operations are examples, though to some extent employee "performance" is a feature of most service interactions (Deighton, 1994; Lashley 2000).

- Typically, hospitality services are subject to *perishability* because they are time specific. Bed spaces in hotels, timeshare weeks, or seats in restaurants represent capacity for a given period. Thus, it is not possible to store up sales and satisfy them at another time. Nor can any loss of service output be made up at a later date. The service is temporal and once lost is gone forever. Hence, the empty hotel bed, vacant timeshare property, or unsold restaurant meal represents revenue never to be regained. Hospitality service deliverers are not able to stockpile services, or make up lost service production through overtime working, or multisource services to allow for fluctuations in the demand and supply of services.

Perishability presents several key problems for hospitality and timeshare organizations. Service quality faults cannot easily be reworked and given back to the customer, as commonly happens with a manufactured product. Demand has to be satisfied as and when it is required, so there is difficulty in planning service delivery to meet demand. Typically, demand is not evenly spaced out over time. Not surprisingly, restaurants find that demand peaks at traditional meal times. Timeshare weeks are more popular when associated with school holidays, summer periods, or snowfall patterns in ski resorts. In other situations, demand may be influenced by factors difficult to predict, such as the weather or political events. This creates circumstances where there are limits to capital resources usage, and human resources are needed for short, intensive periods. Seasonal demand for a resort may create difficulties for revenue generation and for continuity of employment of staff.

Finally, hospitality services are supplied to customers who do not "own" the service as supplied; they cannot take it away or return it if unsatisfactory. Because of the intangibility and perishability features, customers are frequently buying the right to a service or an experience. This creates problems of loyalty and memory. Unlike the possessors of a tangible product, service consumers rarely have permanent reminders of the product's features or benefits. Repeat purchases will be based on a bundle of remembered experiences and expectations. Individual perceptions and differences become important issues.

Key Point 8.3

Successful service management recognizes the importance of the four key features of services—intangibility, heterogeneity, inseparability, and perishability—and the crucial contribution frontline staff make to service quality provision.

Early attempts to define service quality tended to distinguish between those aspects that were capable of objective measurement and those that were more subjective. Thus, the objective category might include the tangible aspects of the customer offer—say, the size and quality of a meal or accommodation against standards, and those aspects of the service that can be measured—the time taken to be served and the like. Gronroos (1984) identified *technical* and *functional* elements of service quality. Technical aspects were those elements of the service that were quantifiable—time taken to answer the telephone, waiting times in a bar, and so on. Here the customer is making judgments about the service on the basis of a set of personal standards that are capable of measurement. Functional elements were more concerned with customer judgments of service based on the interactions between the service deliverer and consumer—that is, on how the technical aspects of the service were delivered and might include the appearance and attitudes of staff, the physical environment in which the service was being delivered, together with the management of the processes involved in delivering the service. In all cases, customer expectations form the basis on which they evaluate the success or failure of the service encounter.

The problem for management is in understanding what these expectations are and then sharing them with employees on the frontline who will deliver the service in a way that satisfies customer expectations. "The general absence of easily understood criteria for assessing quality makes the articulation of customer's requirements and the communication of the quality level on offer much more difficult than is the case for goods" (Palmer, 1994: 175).

Consumer expectations of service quality become an important feature of service quality when set against experiences of the service. Customers vary in their expectations: customers with more experience of a service may well have higher expectations than those who have less experience of it. Organizations and their image may have a role in shaping customer expectations; advertising and other promotional activities influence consumer expectations. Customers have a base level of expectations of the service—the minimum they expect. They have a level of expectations about what the service should be like—about what they want. In addition, customers also predict what they expect the quality to be like (Zeithmal, Berry, and Parasuraman, 1993). The work of Herzberg (1966) on employee motivation has been used to explain aspects of customer expectations (Balmer and Baum, 1993). Thus, it is possible to consider states of service *dissatisfaction*, but an absence of dissatisfaction does not lead to customer motivation. There are likely to be a set of key (perhaps mostly intangible) elements that will produce *customer satisfaction* and motivation to return.

Parasuraman et al. (1991) propose that service organizations need to be much more systematic about capturing their customers' expectations of the service. They suggest that "[c]ustomer service expectations can be categorised into five overall dimensions: *reliability, tangibles, responsiveness, assurance* and *empathy*" (1991: 41). These dimensions are reproduced in Table 8.1. Reliability is concerned with service outcomes, whereas the other elements are concerned with process. Three of the elements point to *employee performance* as key to customer expectations: *responsiveness, assurance,* and

Dimension	Definition
Reliability	The ability to perform the promised service dependably and accurately
Tangibles	The appearance of physical facilities, equipment, personnel, and communication materials
Responsiveness	The willingness to help customers and provide prompt service
Assurance	The knowledge and courtesy of employees and their ability to convey trust and confidence
Empathy	The caring, individualized attention provided to customers

Source: Parasuraman, Berry, and Zeithaml (1991).

Table 8.1 The Five Dimensions of Service

empathy. These three elements are related to the service process and "the opportunity is present to surprise customers with uncommon swiftness, grace, courtesy, competence, commitment or understanding, and go beyond what is expected" (1991: 41). In the context of the Herzberg conceptual framework, reliability relates to the "hygiene factors" whereby customers have an expectation of what the service should be like. Real motivation to use the service repeatedly, however, will be built through attention to the process element and service employee performance in particular.

Parasuraman, Berry, and Zeithaml have developed a measure of service quality which asks customers twenty-two questions exploring the five dimensions of service. Hospitality service providers in timeshare resorts can use SERVQUAL to compare customers' expectations with their experiences and thereby show where service delivery has strengths and weaknesses. The performance of different competitors can be compared with the service organization's own performance. "The SERVQUAL model highlights the difficulties in ensuring high quality service for all customers in all situations" (Palmer, 1994: 181). In particular, it reveals "five service gaps" where there may be a mismatch between the expectation of the service level and the perception of the service delivered. These gaps focus on the points at which expectations of service requirements by management, the standards set, the standards achieved, or the service standards communicated to customers produce a situation where customer perceptions of the service delivered do not match with the expected service. Figure 8.2 presents an application to a fictitious restaurant.

Rust and Oliver (1994) suggest that the management of service quality requires the recognition that "[s]ervice quality is by nature a subjective concept, which means that understanding how the customer thinks about service quality is essential to effective management" (p. 2). Specifically, they suggest a need to disentangle three related but distinct concepts—customer satisfaction, service quality, and customer value. Customer satisfaction results from a service encounter and from comparing the experience with expectations. Customer satisfaction relates to process theories and to the states identified earlier in which "satisfaction is viewed as

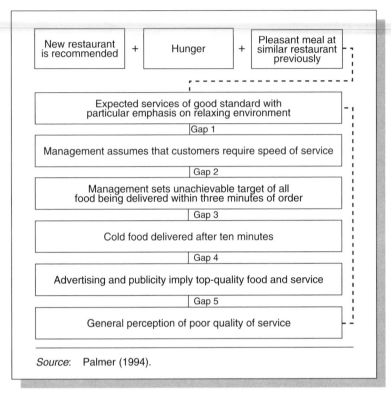

Figure 8.2 Source of Divergence Between Service Quality Expectation and Delivery

largely based on meeting or exceeding expectations" (Rust and Oliver, 1994: 4). In essence, customer satisfaction arises from experience. Service quality can be judged against a set of ideals, "Thus the SERVQUAL instrument illustrates the core of what service quality may mean, namely *a comparison to excellence* in service *by the customer*" (Rust and Oliver, 1994: 6). Service quality is said to be the customer's overall judgment about a firm's excellence or superiority (Bitner, 1990). Value includes quality and price, though it might also include other economic and psychological benefits. "Ultimately, it is perceived value which attracts a customer, or lures a customer away from the competition" (Rust and Oliver, 1994: 7). When arriving at a perception of the value of a service, customers are in effect considering the benefits received and the sacrifices made in the service encounter.

Key Point 8.4

Customer evaluations of service quality are shaped by their expectations of service quality. SERVQUAL provides a technique for measuring the gaps between customer expectations and customer experiences of service quality.

In summary, the nature of services in general—their intangibility, heterogeneity, inseparability, and perishability—create difficulties for resort managers, employees, and customers. The role of perception of needs, source of satisfaction, and the success of the service encounter and differences in expectations provide organizations with service management difficulties. Recent research suggests that resort organizations need to better understand customer expectations of service quality, the source of customer satisfaction and elements that shape customer evaluations of value. In particular, the performance of employees in service interactions plays a significant role in shaping customer evaluations of satisfaction, quality, and service value.

Employees and Customer Satisfaction

Frontline employees have a key role in all hospitality and resort services. The customer visits the resort to receive the service, whether restaurant, hotel, bar, or leisure facility. In many resorts, half the customer's total expenditure at the resort will be in these settings. Ensuring customer satisfaction when they visit the bar, restaurant, or hotel has a major impact on the customer's experience at the resort. Employees are key to shaping customer perceptions of service quality and satisfaction. From the customer's point of view, the interaction *with* employees is *the service.* Even allowing that customer perceptions of an organization's quality will be a product of the organization's image and its promoted offer to customers, the actual service experience is the point of contact where preconceptions and expectations result in either favorable or unfavorable evaluations of the service delivered.

Paradoxically, many hospitality and resort organizations fail to grasp the importance of the employee's role. Indeed, many managers have seen employees as "the single most controllable cost" (Pannel Kerr Forster Associates, 1992). Given that labor costs represent significant proportions of total costs, cost reduction strategies have tended to focus largely on labor costs. Many organizations pay low wages, invest little in training, and practice numerical flexibility through the use of large numbers of part-time staff or through the ready acceptance of high levels of labor turnover (Wood, 1992). The result has been that "frontline employees are not trained to understand customers and do not have the freedom and discretion in the ways that ensure effective service" (Bitner, Booms, and Tetreault, 1990: 71). Although the strategy is widespread in hospitality firms, cost leadership strategies are incompatible with quality-based strategies.

Barbee and Bott (1991) point out that the link between employee satisfaction and customer satisfaction has been understood for some time. They refer to the comment made by J.W. Marriott Sr., which gave high priority to employee satisfaction as a necessary ingredient to generating customer satisfaction. Firms that give high priority to exemplary service delivery tend to understand how employee behavior generates feelings of customer satisfaction even in adverse situations. Bitner et al.'s (1990) study of *critical incidents* in service delivery helps to build a picture of how employee behaviors can be crucial in determining customer satisfaction.

Bitner et al. describe a critical incident as one that "contributes or detracts from the general activity in a significant way" (1990: 73). In their study, they focused on those incidents that involved interactions between employees and customers, and that resulted in the customer being *very satisfied* or *dissatisfied*. Their findings suggested three broad groups of incidents: employee responses to service delivery system failures; employee reactions to customer needs and requests: and unprompted and unsolicited employee actions. Each group represented a cluster of incidents in which employee behavior could result in either customer satisfaction or customer dissatisfaction.

Employee responses to service delivery failure could be turned into incidents that employees use to advantage and generate customer satisfaction. An employee may react quickly to service failure by responding sensitively to customer experiences—say by compensating the customer or by upgrading a customer to a higher status service. More frequently, however, staff responses are likely to be a source of a dissatisfaction: the employee may fail to provide an apology or an adequate explanation or may argue with the customer. *Employee responses to customer needs and requests* come into play when requests are made to provide a service that is not normally incorporated in the offer. Again, employee reactions can be a source of both satisfaction and dissatisfaction. For example, the customer may have a "special" need or preference, or the customer may have made a mistake by ordering dishes not on the menu. Employees' responsiveness, flexibility, and confidence that they can match whatever the customer needs are important sources of a positive customer response. Similarly, employee intransigence, inflexibility, and perceived incompetence are all potential sources of customer dissatisfaction. The Bitner et al. study suggested that, generally, employee responses were a greater source of satisfaction than dissatisfaction when meeting unusual requests. *Unprompted and unsolicited employee actions* incorporated actions that were outside of the customer's expectations of the service encounter. This might involve employee behaviors that made the employee feel special, or an act of unexpected generosity that took the customer by surprise. Customer dissatisfaction may be the result of a failure to give the customer the level of attention expected, or inadequate information, or it might involve inappropriate behavior such as the use of bad language or drunkenness.

In all these situations, service interactions involve critical incidents whereby employee responses are fundamental to the customer's satisfaction or dissatisfaction with the service provided. To effectively participate in the service, employees need to be aware of customer expectations and perceptions, they must have a sense of engagement and concern for customer satisfaction, and they need to have a sense that they can make a difference to the service encounter. In another study, Bitner (1990) evaluated service encounters and the effects of physical surroundings and employee responses on customer perceptions of service quality and made a number of conclusions for the managers of service organizations. It is important to manage and control each service interaction. If the service does not match customer expectations, opportunities still exist to create customer satisfaction if the employee understands the processes through which customers lay blame for the incident. They are much more likely to accept a service breakdown if they are given a logical explanation for it and are compensated in some way. Indeed, these incidents can be turned into "memorable incidents" if the employee is quick to offer an explanation and compensation.

Key Point 8.5

Resort operators should focus on critical incidents as a way of ensuring that the employee performance promotes positive behavior in all contacts with customers. Even customer complaints can be turned to advantage with the right staff actions.

Apart from the role employees play in shaping customer experiences of service quality and generation of customer satisfaction through the service encounter, service employees play a key part in helping to "personalize" services for consumers. It is possible to see some tensions in customer needs from service organizations. As we have seen, a service purchase can create difficulties for customers because it is difficult to know what the service will be like until it has been received. Given the poor image many customers have of timeshare, this issue of expectations is particularly important. A consequence has been the growth of branded services, through which service providers send messages that help to establish customer expectations of the service encounter. Through a standardized offer, customers are assured of the quality and attributes of the service to be supplied. The branded, standardized service helps to meet customer security needs, but can leave customers feeling unimportant and anonymous. Increasingly, branded and standardized service firms have been looking to various forms of personalization to help overcome these negative customer feelings. Suprenant and Solomon (1987) identify personalized service as occurring when the "customer role is embellished in the encounter through specific recognition of the customer's uniqueness as an individual over and above his/her status as an anonymous service recipient" (1987: 87). Again, they point to appropriate employee performance to be matched with the forms of personalization being offered by the organization.

The issue of employee performance and customer satisfaction takes on added urgency when firms begin to consider the costs of lost business and the benefits of generating customer loyalty. Dissatisfied customers who no longer use the resort, or predominantly use off-resort facilities represent lost income. For example, it was found that on average timeshare customers of the DeVere group spent £450 per week in the hotel and resort facilities associated with their properties. This equates to approximately 50 percent of the total spent for their week's stay, over and above service and maintenance fees. This extra expenditure generated by timeshare visitors can result in high additional income to both hotel or resort properties as well as to local businesses outside the resort. Lost business due to customer dissatisfaction can result in substantial reductions in income. Furthermore, dissatisfied customers frequently share their dissatisfaction with others. Each customer will tell ten or fifteen others if they are unhappy with poor service. Conversely, personal recommendation from satisfied, loyal customers has much greater impact in generating sales than any other promotional form. Loyal timeshare customers will tell friends and relatives about their experiences and generate strong prospects. Loyal customers are also a good source of additional sales. In the hotel sector, Carper (1992) estimated it costs seven times more to generate a new customer than to get back an existing customer. Heskett, Sasser, and Hart (1990) maintain that "[c]ustomer loyalty and profitability go hand in hand" (p. 31). They explain this through the reduction in costs of servicing new customers and the effect that loyal customers have on recruiting new customers.

These dimensions have particular importance for time-share, where "cold calling" takes place against popular perceptions of timeshare as being riddled with unethical business practice. Loyal and satisfied customers can help overcome anxieties among family and friends as a source of potential customers for the timeshare offer. They themselves are also an important source of added sales; as satisfied customers, they are likely to want to repeat their happy experiences by buying additional weeks. Among the two largest European timeshare-owning countries—Great Britain and Germany—almost 50 percent of owners own more than one week. Hence, existing customers are a crucial source of sales in these countries.

The financial implications of customer satisfaction, and the key role employees play in the service encounter, have prompted concerns about equipping employees to maximize their effectiveness. Harris (1991) emphasizes the need to "invest in your staff" (p. 236). Figure 8.3 provides a graphic representation for the links made between customer satisfaction and turnover, and employee satisfaction and turnover. In the upper part of the diagram, a virtuous cycle results in continuous improvements in all the elements. The lower portion of the diagram, on the other hand, presents a vicious cycle in which declining customer satisfaction results in reduced customer retention, which results in employees having to work harder to recruit new customers, which reduces employee satisfaction and increases employee turnover, which in turn impacts on customer satisfaction.

A result of all this analysis of the commercial imperative associated with service quality and service employee performance, particularly by service marketeers, has been the establishment of a metaphor that describes employees as internal customers. As such, employees are involved in a value chain that interlinks the stages of the production of the service within the organization backwards with suppliers and forwards with customers. Internally, employees are both customers of other employees at an earlier stage in the production process and suppliers to other employees at later stages.

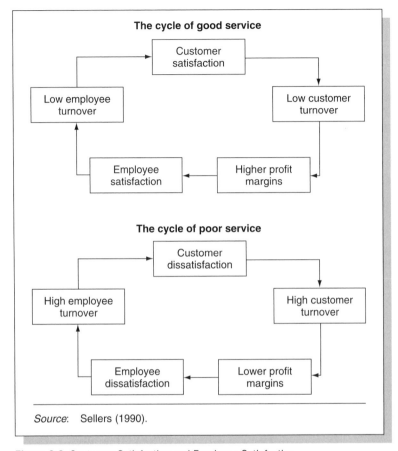

Figure 8.3 Customer Satisfaction and Employee Satisfaction

In addition, service employees have been subject to "the tools of the marketeer" (Harris, 1991: 239). This notion of the employee as *internal customer* on one level suggests that frontline employees are integral to customer satisfaction and employee morale and in creating "happy customers." On another level, the inconsistencies and potential conflicts between the needs of external and internal customers do limit the usefulness of this metaphor. Rafiq and Ahmed (1993) point to the difficulties that arise if internal customers in a restaurant do not want to work "unsocial" hours. As with many of these pronouncements, the phrase "internal customers" has a symbolic attraction but does not stand close scrutiny and is of limited use as an analytical tool.

Managers of resort organizations face two key dilemmas.

1. In most services, labor costs represent an important element of total operating costs. In the past, many organizations have used the manipulation of labor costs as a source of cost reduction. Frontline service employees have been poorly paid and poorly trained with low motivation, causing high job dissatisfaction and high labor turnover (Bitner et al., 1990). This situation has resulted in customer perceptions that "the observable symptom is decreasing quality in . . . the service encounter" (p. 71). Both academics and practitioners have attempted to develop a better understanding of customer perceptions of service quality and the critical incidents in the service encounter that lead to perceptions of satisfaction. It has therefore become obvious that those firms wishing to gain competitive advantage through service quality have to address the means by which they engage employees in the service encounter. To be effective, employees need to be appropriately trained, to be given adequate information, and to develop a strong commitment to delivering successful service encounters.

2. The second dilemma relates to the need to control employee performance in a situation where service interactions are complex, interpersonal, and not easily subject to scrutiny. Given the importance of each service interaction in shaping customer perceptions of service quality and satisfaction, there is a need to reexamine the way employees are managed and how their performance is controlled. In some cases, customer expectations are for a standardized and highly predictable service encounter. Here service delivery can be best planned using mass production techniques to deliver standardized experience. In other cases, service encounters may not be so easily predicted, and opportunities to standardize interactions are limited. Here the very lack of predictability creates difficulties of control because managers have no way of either knowing what customers want or of being party to every transaction.

It is here that empowerment appears to offer the ability to square the circle. Empowerment, with its win-win rhetoric, appears to be the device that will give employees the motivation to be involved and committed to customer satisfaction. Employee empowerment promises to be a technique managers can use to produce employee commitment, ownership, and sense of personal efficacy through which customer satisfaction can be delivered. It also seems to shift the locus of control from the supervisor/manager to the individual employee. Each person internalizes the service standards and works to these. Empowerment appears to offer the possibility of making frontline employees more responsive to customer needs while at the same time providing a means through which management costs can be reduced.

Key Point 8.6

> *Frontline employee performance has an immediate impact on customer service experiences. Employee empowerment has been suggested as one way of managing employees in a way that ensures improved service quality.*

In the chapter entitled "Mobilizing People," Heskett et al. (1990) suggest that service organizations need to "become employers of first choice ... develop and retain such people through ... ministering ... promote good managers towards rather than away from the customer ... dieting the organisation, especially at middle levels, ... [and] empowering frontline managers while maintaining adequate control" (p. 194). Much of these concerns and considerations were built into an apparently "unified" body of ideas through the advocacy of Total Quality Management as the business strategy for the management of service organizations in a more competitive era.

Total Quality Management and Timeshare

General concern for quality improvement, initially in Japan and then in most Western economies in the 1980s and 1990s, resulted in the launch of an array of quality improvement techniques that moved beyond checking for and measuring faults. The emphasis shifted, even in manufacturing, to the prevention of quality breakdowns rather than the detection of faults that had occurred. Given the nature of services, the fault detection avenue was not a feasible option. Services cannot be sent back to be reworked. Services have to be designed and delivered in a way where faults are designed out of the system, or the point at which faults are likely to occur are identified.

In some cases, service organizations wanted to adopt quality assurance systems that were based on "designing quality into the process" or "getting it right first time" through the production of standard procedures manuals that were verified through ISO 9000. "ISO9000 is a quality monitoring process. You decide what you want to do, write it all down and monitor whether you are doing it or not" (McDermid, 1992: 14). In fact, this approach might be okay for timeshare unit design or for servicing the lodge, but it is not useful when dealing with service interactions. Consequently, few service organizations adopted this approach, and those who did tended to have marketing reasons for doing so because it gave them access to customers. Service industries require quality systems that are holistic enough to allow for the characteristics of services and the varied perceptions of customers. Total Quality Management appeared to offer service organizations the system needed.

Almost every edition of the journal *Service Quality Management* contains at least one article advocating the use of Total Quality Management (TQM) as a way of improving service quality. In many of these articles, the link between TQM and employee empowerment is also made. Chopin (1994) has been a regular contributor on the subject and states that "[i]t is not helpful to define Total Quality Management. Such a definition would either be too simplistic, leading to the cynical charge that it is all puff and no substance, while a detailed definition would be too prescriptive (p. 44). TQM, it appears, "is for dreamers" (p. 44). Later, Chopin goes on to describe sixteen principles of TQM in services (see Table 8.2).

Chopin's sixteen principles cover several broad features of TQM that are found in most descriptions of the initiative. The

1. Highest priority is given to quality throughout the organization.

2. Quality is defined in terms of customer satisfaction.

3. Customers are defined as those who have both internal and external relationships with the organization, including employees, shareholders, and the wider community.

4. Customer satisfaction and the building of long-term relationships are at the nub of the organization.

5. The organization's aims will be clearly stated and accessible to all.

6. The principles, beliefs, values, and quality are communicated throughout the organization.

7. Total Quality Management creates an ethos that pervades all aspects of the organization's activities.

8. The core values of honesty, integrity, trust, and openness are essential ingredients of TQM.

9. The Total Quality organization is intended to be mutually beneficial to all concerned and operates in a climate of mutual respect for all stakeholders.

10. The health and safety of all organization members and customers are given priority.

11. Total Quality offers individuals the chance to participate and feel ownership for the success of the enterprise.

12. Commitment is generated in individuals and teams through leadership from senior management.

13. TQM results in an organizationwide commitment to continuous improvement.

14. Performance measurement, assessment, and auditing of the organization's activities is a common feature of TQM.

15. TQM aims to use resources more effectively, and members are encouraged to consider better ways of using resources.

16. TQM requires appropriate investment to ensure that planned activity can occur.

Source: Chopin (1994).

Table 8.2 Principles of Total Quality Management

initiative locates a commitment to quality services as a core organizational concern. The commitment of senior management is crucial, and the approach has to permeate every aspect of the organization. The approach has been particularly attractive to service organizations because it aims to create a cultural environment in which employees, operating independently, are guided by a commitment to delighting customers because they have internalized the organization's objectives and values. These internalized values, beliefs, and objectives ensure that employees aspire to customer satisfaction and quality improvement, without extrinsic controls or inducements. The Total Quality Management philosophy has much in common with systems theory, particularly when linked to the metaphor of internal customers. Each subsystem is regarded as the customer of a supplier to other subsystems. "The objective of TQM is to optimise these relationships at every subsystem boundary" (Johns, 1993: 13).

Employee empowerment enables employees to respond to unusual customer requests, or to use their experience and creativity to delight the customer. These aspirations for TQM and empowerment are relevant to the three employee customer interactions that Bitner et al. (1990) identified as critical to creating, or damaging, customer satisfaction. In dealing with service failures, responding to requests for unusual service, and providing extraordinary interactions, employees can impact customer satisfaction and perceptions of service quality either positively or negatively. TQM provides an organizational setting in which empowered employees, through a heightened sense of their own personal efficacy, will respond in the desired way.

The naming of initiatives that prioritize customer service quality vary; Total Quality Management, Customer Service organization, and Total Quality organization are all variations of an approach that has similar intentions, conceptual origins, and ideological roots. All basically suggest that service organizations and resort operators can benefit from an organizationwide commitment to quality, development of a customer quality-dominated culture, employee empowerment, and so on. Many of these approaches recognize that delivering consistent service quality and ensuring customer satisfaction can produce competitive advantage. Each identifies employee performance as playing a crucial role in pointing to potential faults and thereby continuously improving performance, and in interacting with customers in ways that will deliver customer satisfaction.

Ideologically, these approaches lead to a somewhat distorted and temporally located management analysis of organizational behavior and their relationship with employees in particular. The list reproduced in Table 8.2 embodies a unitary perception underpinning many of its prescriptions. The supposed evenhandedness of stakeholder interests is a case in point. When push comes to shove, shareholders are the key interest group, and although it might be effective to promote the idea that "employees are our most important asset" when times are good, a trade downturn and a few resulting redundancies show just how important, because they expose the cost driven priorities of business decisions.

Key Point 8.7

Timeshare resort operators could benefit from adopting Total Quality Management approaches within their organizations. In this way the total customer experience would become the core consideration of everyone in the organization.

TQM and employee empowerment can provide both managers and employees of service industries with benefits that can improve service quality and customer satisfaction, while giving employees more control over how they organize and complete their tasks. These techniques can produce win-win situations, but they can also be used as rhetoric that ultimately provides a situation where the "route to TQM is integral to workforce consent to a new set—often far more intensified—work relations" (Tuckman, 1995: 56).

More than a Service Encounter?

The preceding discussion has highlighted much of the traditional service quality management models in the study of all services, including those offered by timeshare and hospitality operators. Over recent years, however, there has been growing interest in studying commercial hospitality interactions from another perspective. The study of hospitality as a human interaction involving hosts and guests possesses highly significant dimensions that are not captured in the traditional service quality management instruments and literature. The emotional dimensions present in hospitality encounters, and how they might best be delivered, have important implications for both hospitality service quality management and the development of a loyal customer base.

In Search of Hospitality: Theoretical Perspectives and Debates (Lashley and Morrison, 2000) opened up the study of hospitality from a range of social science perspectives. Certainly, the study of host and guest relationships reveals some common features across cultures and throughout time. All major religions make some comments on the duties and obligations of hosts to protect guests while they are under the host's protection. With some small variations between societies, most cultures require that the host offer sanctuary to strangers as guests, share food and give sustenance, welcome the stranger, and establish bonds of trust. Many cultures simply affirm that hospitality involves turning "strangers into friends" (Lashley, 2000).

Telfer (2000) states that genuine hospitality has to be driven by a desire to be hospitable. Hospitable behavior is motivated by a desire for the company of others, the pleasure of entertaining, the desire to please others, concern or compassion to meet others' needs, and allegiance to the duty to be hospitable. These motives create bonds and long-term relationships between host and guest. Telfer argues that ulterior motives such as the desire to manipulate others or motives associated with vanity will not generate these bonds and feelings. Genuine hospitality is motivated by a concern for the guest's pleasure for its own sake. To some extent, the fact that genuine experiences of hospitality are rarely experienced in the hospitality industry has caused some to refer to these commercial activities as the "inhospitality industry" (Ritzer, 2004).

Understanding hospitality from the perspective of these fundamental motives and relationships provides an opportunity for critical analysis of hospitality and resort operations, and suggests how customer experiences can be improved so as to establish long-term loyalty. "Turning the customer into a friend" (Lashley and Morrison, 2004) through acts of genuine hospitality will ensure the loyalty of customers, who will act as champions for the resort organization among family and friends.

The study of hospitality from wider perspectives also opens up the study of hospitality in three dimensions. First, the *social domain* suggests that different societies place different degrees of importance on these obligations to be hospitable and that these obligations may change within any one society over time. Second, the *private domain* suggests that acts of hospitality and obligations to be hospitable can be studied in the private domestic domain. Some argue that these domestic experiences are "authentic," whereas the *commercial domain*, the third dimension, offers experiences that are "inauthentic" (Warde and Martins, 2000). These domestic experiences of hospitality appear to provide measures of hospitality in commercial settings. Lashley, Morrison, and Randall (2004) found that respondents evaluating special meal occasions in commercial settings said that "they made me feel at home," "they made me feel really welcome," and "the staff seemed genuinely interested in meeting our needs."

Timeshare operators need to understand these expressions of hospitality for two reasons. First, the motives to buy timeshare in some cases are concerned with establishing a "home from home." The private domain which the timeshare purchase represents provides a location in which familiarity with the space and familiarity with the resort community are built. Some of the quotations included in Chapter 4 confirm these important dimensions of the purchase and pattern of usage. Second, the visit to the resort, regardless of purchase motives, involves interactions with hospitality operations in bars, restaurants, and the like. If customer satisfaction is to be maximized and customer loyalty developed, it is necessary for operators to consider service interactions that involve genuine hospitality. Each service encounter involves the visitor (guest) or stranger in a relationship with the employee/manager (host).

Hospitality service operators have long understood the significance of the employee's emotional performance as a contributor to customer evaluations of service encounters. Displaying the "Have a Nice Day" (HAND) persona (Mann, 2000) is a required feature of staff training and performance appraisal in many resorts, bars, and restaurants. However, this feature is often poorly managed, and as a result, employees have to display one set of emotions while feeling quite another. The resulting "emotional labor" (Hochschild, 1983) causes tension and job stress, and adds to job turnover. The emotional dimension of hospitality interactions needs to be more clearly understood and managed. Employee training and performance appraisal need to reflect customer satisfaction as dependent on delivery of genuine hospitable behavior rather than the somewhat formulaic HAND culture that dominates much hospitality management practice. Langhorn (2004) suggests that emotional intelligence is key to successful hospitality operations. Managers and staff register significant individual differences in emotional intelligence, and those who register higher emotional intelligence demonstrate higher levels of customer satisfaction along with an increased willingness to return to the restaurant.

Key Point 8.8

The relationship between guests and hosts is a core feature of hospitality experiences. The emotional dimension of the hospitality service experience provides opportunities to develop loyal customers through ties of friendship, as hospitality traditionally converts strangers into friends.

Conclusions

Resort visitors, whether timeshare owners or just transferees from another resort, experience the tangible, physical, and measurable benefits of the resort, such as cleanliness, décor, and equipment specification, or size of portions and quality of food in the resort's restaurants. As such, these dimensions can be easily defined and evaluated. Other dimensions of the resort visitor's experiences are not as easily defined, measured, or predicted. These intangible aspects of the service encounter are dependent on the human chemistry between customers and those who interact with them.

Bearing in mind the intangible nature of the service encounter and the uniqueness of each service incident, customers increasingly look to brands as a means of ensuring predictable experiences. Timeshare operators linked to major hotel brands are a powerful aspect of the industry. But even though customers are attracted to the security of the standardized hospitality experience, they also want to be served as individuals. Consequently, a number of approaches to managing service quality point to the unique features of services, and in particular to the paramount importance of employee performance in delivering consistent service quality to customers.

Total Quality Management techniques, together with employee empowerment, provide resort operators with an approach that can deliver genuine benefits for the organization. A Total Quality culture creates a context in which service faults are "designed out" of the organization, as much as they can be in a service context. Employee performance, however, is flexible, adaptive, and engaged in the mission to ensure customer satisfaction. The emotions associated with encounter play a vital part in building customer perceptions of being welcome and valued as a friend. Well-motivated staff, encouraged to engage in genuinely hospitable behavior, provide the mechanism for achieving these emotional attachments.

Home Owners Associations and Stakeholder Management

After studying this chapter you should be able to:

- critically discuss timeshare stakeholders and needs.

- evaluate approaches to reflecting stakeholder interests in business performance evaluation.

- critically analyze long-range techniques for maintaining stakeholder loyalty.

- identify and evaluate provisions for ensuring that home owners associations protect owner interests.

Introduction

On one level, the relationship between timeshare home owners and resort operating companies is similar to that of any other organization and its customers. Customers are seen as king but in reality are individually often quite weak in relation to the large organization. Hence, the phrase widely used in English-speaking countries, "let the buyer beware," has come into play. According to the law of contract, an agreement to buy something from the organization stands, providing the individual has entered into the sale freely. Customers are not free to ask for their money back or to change their minds because they no longer want to make the purchase. Clearly, some of the malpractice suits launched against sales teams in the past were won because buyers made judgments based on sellers' lies and cheating business practices. Industry codes and statutory provision allow purchasers to have a cooling-off period, or give them the right to *rescission*, which allows the customer to withdraw from a signed contract within an agreed-upon time period.

On another level, the long-term relationship that the owner enters into requires that property quality and service delivery be consistently delivered over a long period of time. The owner is therefore in a position where she may enter into ownership with a resort operator who in the longer term may allow property to deteriorate or service standards to fall. As with the above example, in effect a potential conflict arises between the organization stakeholders and customers. Some timeshare organizations put shareholder interests before those of customers by not maintaining the property, thereby returning a healthy profit for the shareholders/owners. As a result, the property the customers purchased is no longer at the same level it was as when they bought it.

On yet another level, service interactions involve potential conflicts between the three key parties in the interaction—customer, service deliverer, (employee), and management/owners. Although customer satisfaction is the declared object of the organization, conflict between the different needs of the three parties can result in customer dissatisfaction, producing employee frustration and employer difficulties. Customer satisfaction may be achieved at the expense of extra staff effort or increased costs to owners. Thus, during hospitality service interactions at the resort, owners will evaluate the service delivered and rate it as improved or declining compared to earlier visits or to other resorts.

Differences in perceptions, needs, and evaluations of performance between different organizational stakeholders result in tensions and frustration. Over the last few decades organizations have increasingly undertaken stakeholder analysis as recognition that various organization members see things differently (Mullins, 2002). This has moved many to consider the mechanism for evaluating organizational success from the perspectives of the different stakeholders. Balanced scorecard techniques in particular help organizations to consider a range of measures that include customer and employee experiences and perceptions as well as those of shareholders. In some cases, organizations have put in place more participative management practices as a way of recognizing that customers and employees are best suited to manage themselves. This chapter focuses on the use of these democratic and participative techniques to run the resort and property maintenance programs. Home owners associations take on the responsibility for managing property maintenance in recognition that resort management will not be directly involved and that owners will collectively manage upkeep of the resort.

Stakeholders in Timeshare Organizations

Traditionally, organizations are viewed in terms of their economic role in delivering benefits to society. Friedman (1970), for example, sees organizations in Western societies as the democratic manifestation of customers' "votes" through their collective purchases. According to this view, organizations need to be free to meet the needs of their customers, and there are no conflicts of interest between owners, employees, and customers. Fox (1974) describes this as an essential unitary view of organizations. There is a unity of interests, and each part of the organization is in harmony owing to the common purpose of all. If problems occur, they are due to a breakdown in the natural order of the organization—the result of some "illness." Timeshare developers and operators who hold this view are uncritical of potential difficulties inherent in the timeshare business model. In the more unscrupulous cases, timeshare organizations operated with but a single objective—to maximize profit and to show little concern for the needs of customers or staff.

This unitary view of organizations has been criticized because it fails to reflect the tensions in organizational life (Lashley, 2001). Timeshare operators have begun to adopt a stakeholder analysis of their organization's recognition of a plurality of interests within them. Fox describes the view of organizations from the plurality perspective, as organizations that are not single entities. Organizations have relations with groups within the organization itself and with external agencies such as customers' communities and government bodies, all of whom have different interests in the organization and different perceptions of the organization's success (Mullins, 2002).

Stakeholder analysis, therefore, stems from an understanding that organizations represent a plurality of interests and that the management of organizations needs to adopt strategies and tactics that give voice and power to these different groups. By bringing together the different sets of interests and managing in a way that reflects the range of interests, conflict can be avoided. Mullins describes stakeholders as "those individuals or groups who have an interest in and/or are affected by the goals, operations and activities of the organisation or behaviour of its members" (2002: 145).

Employee perceptions of organization success focus on employment—pay rates, training, opportunities for development and promotion, fair treatment, social justice, and consistent management. Many hospitality and timeshare organizations experience high levels of staff turnover and low levels of retention in part because of the limited recognition of these needs in the employment practices of hospitality and tourism organizations. In organizations with low trade union membership, employees frequently take individual rather than collective actions to resolve grievances (Lashley and Lee-Ross, 2003). Hence, high numbers leave, take days away from work, or deliberately sabotage product or service quality. Employer actions that recognize these employee perceptions will involve various forms of consultation, participation in some service decision making, and empowerment.

Customers/owners have a range of needs that require contact with staff and the organization, which may lead to conflict. Timeshare customers in particular have long- and short-term needs with regard to the organization and other stakeholders. In the long term, they have a property interest that is located at a particular resort. They have interest in the value of the property, and in any resort operator's decision that may impact property values. Poor property maintenance and failure to upgrade the fixture and fittings within the property, or lack of action in developing the wider resort which either adds to or detracts from the investment are all issues that may cause customer conflict. Similarly, the service interactions which the customer experiences in the hospitality facilities are examples of potential conflict between customers and staff and customers and management. For example, staff may not be properly trained, or there is insufficient staff on duty to maintain customer service levels. Management decisions about investment and staffing levels have cost and finance implications and thereby implications for profits and shareholder value.

In **communities** where the resorts are located, the timeshare should benefit the community economically and any environmental impact must be kept to a minimum. Whereas some members of the community will become employees, others may become suppliers of goods and services, or use the resort and its services as a leisure facility. In each case, the resort management and the owners' actions may bring them into conflict with the community. The resort is often in a location that has an impact on the quality of life of community members who have no material gain or benefit from the resort. For these people, the resort may be regarded as generating only negative impacts—more visitors, more traffic, more congestion, less access to beaches and beauty spots. Walton's (2000) work on the history of the British seaside shows that different community members may be in conflict over the value of tourism and holiday makers. Concerns about the impact of visitors on the environment can be quite legitimate. Areas of outstanding natural beauty or of special environmental interest are often subject to pressures from demands to visit them, which in turn potentially damage the site itself.

Shareholders or business owners are concerned about covering costs, making profits and ensuring asset value growth. Short-term decisions, however, may create longer term problems. Delays in refurbishing property or attracting large numbers to use the resort may produce higher profits in one financial period but may help reduce property values in another period. Pay rates and training provisions impact upon operating costs and create potential conflicts with employees and customers because of the adverse effect on the service quality. Conflicts with other stakeholders in the community may arise because whereas stakeholders want to grow the resort and attract more customers, some community members desire a peaceful area. In larger organizations conflicts frequently develop among different shareholder interest groups. Small shareholders may invest in organizations because they have a personal interest in the organization as customers, employees, or local community members. They have a loyalty to the specific organization, whereas some of the larger institutional investors have concerns that are more investment and returns driven and have limited loyalty to any one business.

Managers operate the business in the interests of the owners or shareholders; however, some commentators regard managers as having interests distinct from those of shareholders. As organization members, they have much in common with other paid employees, and there is evidence that managers may operate in a way that satisfices shareholders rather than maximizing their return on capital. Managers as stakeholders may have interests that are in conflict with those of shareholders when issues of management costs are considered, or where downsizing may involve reductions in the management hierarchy, or career development opportunities.

Government at local, national, and international levels is concerned with the legal performance of the timeshare resort organizations. These legal requirements are often designed to provide minimum protection against unscrupulous and dishonest practitioners. Often these legal provisions are devised to protect customers from certain problems—pressure selling techniques, dishonest claims at the point-of-sale, health and safety matters, and so on, in a way that requires organizations to be "lawful." The legal provisions provide an opportunity to shape the way organizations are allowed to trade, and are subject to inspection and review by governmental agencies, which can represent a form of interference by some operators.

Trade bodies representing timeshare operators and developers attempt to establish some common standards to which members will comply. In part, they are an attempt to create minimum standards of trading that improve the perceived standing of the sector, and in part they attempt to protect lawful and ethical operators from those who are less honest. As Chapter 10 argues, these are often minimum restrictions that reflect current legislative requirements, and they aim to preempt more restrictive legislation in the future. They are, in effect, steps taken by business competitors to agree on some minimum trading standards. Most trade bodies have a hierarchy of sanctions that may be taken against those who do not comply.

Key Point 9.1

Timeshare organizations comprise a range of different stakeholders, each with different perspectives on the organization and its success.

Recognition of the variety of groups with both similar and different interests requires organizational structures and controls to reflect the varied perceptions of organizational conduct and success. One response is to install a democratic or participative structure. Employees can be organized in ways that involve self-management in autonomous work groups. In addition, "worker directors" might be appointed to the board in order to make sure employee concerns and perspectives are taken into consideration. The culture of the management of the organization may be more empowering, with more delegation of decision making wherever possible. More customer surveys, unannounced customer visits, and

Stakeholders	Measures
Employees	Employee attitude surveys
	Staff retention and turnover
	Employee training activity
	Promotions from within the workforce
Customers	Customer complaints or positive comments
	Mystery guest scores
	Customer satisfaction surveys
	Customer suggestion schemes
Owners	Sales levels
	Profitability
	Cost management measures
	Share and investment value
	Public relations profile
Community	Complaints or positive comments made
	Jobs created
	Economic impacts
	Pollution and other negative impacts

Table 9.1 Potential Balanced Scorecard Measures

formal monitoring of complaints can help inform the organization of customer perspectives and views. In the timeshare sector, the setting up of home owners associations with responsibilities for maintaining and repairing resort property gives customers some control over what can be a highly contentious aspect of their relationship with the resort operator. The practical use of each of these techniques is listed in Table 9.1, and home owners associations are discussed more fully later in this chapter.

Tensions in Timeshare Service Interactions

Service interactions in the resort's bars, restaurants, and other leisure facilities all shape owner and visitor evaluations of the resort. These service interactions are based on the potential tensions that some have described as a three-cornered fight between employees, resort operator, and customers (Bateson, 1985). Figure 9.1 shows the potential tensions in the service interaction. The relationship between resort operator and

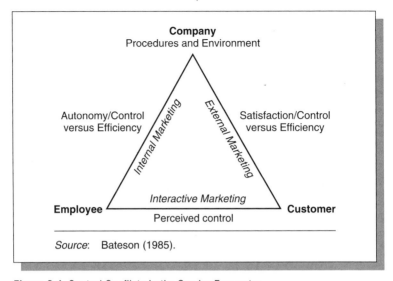

Figure 9.1 Control Conflicts In the Service Encounter

customers or visitors is often affected by tension caused by the operator's need to control costs and extend efficiency, predictability, and control. In branded contexts, customers' expectations are developed through marketing, public relations, and advertising activities. If customers' expectations are not met, dissatisfaction will occur. On another level the operator is managing a commercial activity where decisions about staffing levels, portion sizes, and prices may be in conflict with the visitor/customer. Income for the resort operator is cost to the customer or visitor. The price of goods sold is one obvious example of a potential conflict of interest. Staffing levels is another area where increased service to customers may result in increased staffing costs for the resort operator. The operator wants to satisfy customers but not at the expense of profits. Services supplied will enable this commercial dimension of the relationship.

The conflicts between customers and employees relate to the nature of the service encounter, the emotional performance, and the varied expectations that each might hold about appropriate levels of service. Customers want to be treated as individuals, not just as customers or tipping opportunities. The level of tip and the reasons for giving a tip also can cause confusion and conflict. Customer complaints can cause emotional stress among the employees, particularly if the customer complains in an aggressive manner. The whole emotional dimension of service performance can generally cause emotional labor for employees. The requirement to "smile through the tears" or to constantly provide a "have a nice day performance" leads to "emotional labor" as noted earlier (Hochschild, 1983). Responses to unusual customer requests are also potential opportunities for conflict, with customer and employee expectations at odds with each other.

Finally, the relationship between employees and the company can create conflict. Fundamentally, employee income is a cost to the employer. Training and support in the service encounter may also bring tension because training helps employees become more confident and effective, while it involves a cost to employers. The whole design of the job undertaken, the skill level required, the amount of autonomy given to the employee, and the amount of control exercised by the employer are causes of conflict. Under the influence of McDonaldization (Ritzer, 1993), the tendency has been to deskill jobs, work through standard procedures manuals, and generally reduce the autonomy and employee discretion required in jobs. The conflict it produces manifests itself in absenteeism, sabotage, low staff retention, and poor quality service.

Techniques for reflecting the range of stakeholder interests involve using a **balanced scorecard** through which to evaluate organization success. Traditionally, organizations evaluate performance using measures of interest to shareholder groups. Thus, the evaluation of performance in terms of profit growth, market share, investment and asset value, and return on capital are typically recorded in company reports and are used by investment advisers to analyze organizational success or failure. While these measures continue to have relevance to shareholders and owners of the business, other non-financial measures (discussed below) should be used to reflect the interests of other stakeholders.

For employees, measures of employee satisfaction, as well as staff retention and turnover, together with training and the volume of internal promotions are useful indicators of employee stakeholder assessment of organization performance. Using electronic databases comprised of this type of information, one can also measure changes in productivity levels through analysis of sales volumes, average transaction values, and so on. Customer stakeholder measures might include levels of complaints received, results from mystery guest visits, customer satisfaction surveys, and customer focus groups. Table 9.1 lists measures that timeshare resort operators can use to evaluate performance reflecting a wider array of stakeholder interests. These measures suggest that organizational success is likely to be a by-product of successful evaluation by the range of stakeholders involved. Traditional financial perspectives also suggest that profit and asset growth result from satisfied employees and loyal satisfied customers.

The management of organizations in a more stakeholder-sensitive manner implies that actions are taken in response to identified issues. If customers are consistently making the same set of complaints, there is a need to overcome the difficulty. If employee turnover is high, action needs to be taken to counter this problem. Resorts are often located in communities where not everyone is convinced of the benefits of additional tourists; in this situation, the local community relationship needs to be so managed that negative impacts will be limited.

Key Point 9.2

Resort operators need to manage the resort using insights gained from different stakeholder groups and to employ the balanced scorecard techniques so as to reflect the community of interests.

Stakeholder Management Techniques

The recognition that different stakeholders have different interests has resulted in the development of a number of techniques for managing timeshare organizations. Typically, organizations adopt those techniques that represent what managers consider adequate for the most pressing needs. It is highly unusual to see all techniques representing the full array of stakeholder interests. In contrast, writers such as

Senge (2003) believe that "learning organizations" are able to learn from all stakeholders and should be committed to reflecting views of employees and customers most immediately. Table 9.2 presents techniques that may be employed to manage a timeshare organization in a way that reflects these different interests.

Lashley and Lee-Ross (2003) identify a framework for understanding the "initiatives which are focused at improving employee involvement" (2003: 139). Employee views can be engaged through a range of techniques that span directive, consultative, and participative techniques, as well as approaches that involve all employees, or representatives of the workforce or financial forms; at a number of levels in the organization from frontline to board room; and including topics from task organization to pay and conditions and strategic decisions.

Stakeholder group	Initiative
Employees	Autonomous/Semi autonomous work teams Quality circles Team briefings Employee empowerment Employee Directors Consultation committees
Customers or visitors	Focus groups Owners committee
Owners	Home Owners Associations Focus groups Owners committee
Community	Community liaison committee
Managers	Autonomous work groups Delayering empowerment Consultation committees
Trade bodies	External audit Trade body participation

Table 9.2 Structural Responses to Different Stakeholder Interests

Employees

Employee stakeholder involvement encompasses initiatives that span participative, consultative, and directive forms, as well as initiatives that directly involve all employees or only representatives of the workforce as a whole. Typically, initiatives aimed at encouraging improved commitment to service quality and customer satisfaction focus on task-level decision making or consultation, while those that are more concerned with engagement in strategic decisions tend to be more representative. Those practices that have a democratic intent tend to be advocated by the workforce, while those that are aimed at improving operational effectiveness tend to be advocated by management (Lashley, 2001).

Customers

Resort visitors, whether they be owners, tenants, or short-stay visitors to the resort, have concerns about service experiences and operational policies that impact on the quality of the service experience. Apart from the devices discussed earlier that enable a benchmark approach to managing organizational performance, some techniques that can be used in organizational management are potentially more consultative.

Bringing together small groups of customers who are given aspects of company activities to discuss can be highly revealing about the meaning attached to particular actions, message, or impressions created by organizations. There are usually ten to twelve focus groups, and these groups are usually conducted by a consultant or someone with expertise in the field. Qualitative data often reveals more detail than questionnaires, though questions of how representative the sample is must be borne in mind. Topics for discussion are given by the group coordinator, and discussions are taped for analysis later.

Setting up *owners committees* to represent the interests and perception of customer are increasingly being used in the service sector. Essentially consultative in nature, they involve representatives of customer groups meeting on a regular basis to discuss company procedures, policies, and service quality.

Good relationships and customer loyalty are more likely to develop with insights for customers in this way. Typically, limits are put on the range of topics to be discussed so that there are limits on their impact on commercial outcomes. They have the benefit of improving the quality of communication between customers and managers.

Key Point 9.3

Resort operators can manage the business in ways that involve structures reflecting different stakeholder interests through participative, consultative, or fully democratic procedures.

Home Owners Associations

As a specific initiative for the timeshare sectors, some operators set up home owners associations so as to manage maintenance and refurbishment of properties. Owners automatically join the association and elect officers to run the club. The organization sets up the association and funds it through owners' maintenance fees. The association operates independently of the company, though within a framework established by the company. The benefit of these associations is that owners are in charge of the maintenance of the resort and the overall value of their asset. Since the company has relinquished control, the procedure is democratic in which the owner stakeholder group has control of their interest. By relinquishing control, the company increases potential customer satisfaction and reduces the potential for conflict with its customers. In many cases, the resort developer or operator is elected to manage the resort by the home owners association.

The daily or weekly functions of housekeeping, maintenance, registration, recreational, and other owner services must be managed in order to maintain the level of expected services and product quality. To ensure that a property is built, sold, and managed, many states have enacted laws that specify property management responsibilities. For instance, once the developer has obtained a specified level of sales, the management rights are typically transferred to a home owners association. At this preestablished level of sales, usually 80 to 90 percent of all available intervals, the timeshare owners are empowered to form a home owners association with a board of directors at the helm. This point is the time at which the developer relinquishes control to the home owners association. It should also be known that some statutes specify options for resort management entities. For instance, the managing entity can be the developer, a separate manager or management firm, or an owners association. Regardless of which course of management is selected, this entity assumes certain duties and responsibilities associated with the provision of resort services and general upkeep.

Key Point 9.4

Home owners associations allow owners of the properties to control the maintenance and upkeep of the resort. Typically, the day-to-day running of operations is then delegated to an elected board of directors and a subcontracted company.

To ensure protection to the association members (the time-share owners), various legislative provisions ensure that the association is truly independent and run by the members. Typically, this requires that articles of incorporation meet legislated standards, that the duties of specific officers are identified, and that procedures concerning conduct of meetings, voting, and creation of a board of directors with various officer positions are specified.

In these circumstances, timeshare resorts are run by a board of directors that serves as the representative of the larger home owners association. The board of directors, via legal empowerment from the home owners association, makes resort policies and is given complete legal authority over resort operations. In serving in this capacity, the board of directors is charged with duty of care, duty of loyalty, and duty of obedience (White and Gerstner, 1991).

The *duty of care* assumes that each board member is skilled and capable to serve in the role as designated by the home owners association. The implicit assumption underlying this concept is that each board member conducts him or herself in a prudent manner so that the timeshare owners' best interests are protected. This is a very large task given that a board of about six members is responsible and liable for the general oversight of the entire resort.

The *duty of loyalty* refers to the board member's commitment to the timeshare owners and in maintaining the upkeep of the resort. In agreeing to serve, the board member consents to devoting his or her undivided attention to making operational decisions that are in the best interests of the association. In short, this means that a board member cannot put his or her personal interests above the good of the whole *and* must act in the best interest of the organization.

The concept of *duty of obedience* refers to allegiance to the mission and principles associated with the timeshare plan. Granted mission statements are typically broad in scope with some element of flexibility assumed so long as those given the responsibility of applying the values embedded in the mission act with reasonable judgment concerning how the organization should best meet its mission. In doing so, the board member is not allowed to act in a way that is inconsistent with the primary goals of the timeshare plan. The basic rationale for this rule is based on the principle of promoting "goodwill and trust" for not only the timeshare owners but the industry as a whole. This is a very critical observation given the marred image that the timeshare industry has worked so diligently to overcome since its inception.

Board members are elected via an election process of unit owners in accordance with processes specified in the home owners association bylaws. This change of control from the developer to the board of directors (agent of the home owners association) occurs at a stated percentage of units sold. Once this level is obtained, the developer appoints the first board of directors (Gentry, Mandoki, and Rush, 1999).

The board of directors (hereafter referred to as the board) is elected by the timeshare owners to serve as the resort's governing body. The board is responsible for guiding the resort's administration; setting property policies; establishing property budgets (both operational and capital); managing its finances; managing owner assessments; establishing and monitoring vendor relations; and overseeing resort operations. The term of office is for a limited period of time, typically two years, with half of the board being elected in year 1 and the other half in year 2. If this process is followed, continuity in policy making is ensured. Furthermore, the board should consist of an odd number of members so a majority vote can be obtained.

The board plays a very important and legal role in the conduct of the timeshare resort's business by performing the following:

1. *Establishment of policies by which the resort operates.* Policies range from the hours of pool operation, retail hours of operation, collection of annual maintenance fees, owner misconduct to guidelines surrounding a rental program.

2. *Review of the resort's financial position* to ensure that the expenses are within the proposed budget.

3. *Communication with the ownership base* concerning topic issues and matters of importance such as elections and end-of-year reporting of reserves.

4. *Determination of the amount of annual maintenance fees* (regular property upkeep) and special assessment fees (nonschedule, one-time assessment for repair) where appropriate.

5. *Oversight of the property management function.* This assumes that a property management entity has been hired for management of daily resort operations and budget preparation.

6. *Hiring of the general manager or the property management firm.* This is a very important board function because board members are typically not present for the oversight of day-to-day operations, which means that management of personnel, provision of resort services, budget development, and income control procedures must be assigned to a property management entity, either operated by the home

owners association or vended to an outside contractor. Therefore, it is in the board's best interest to hire a qualified general manager (if management is done inhouse) or an experienced property management firm for daily operation conduct.

In essence, the global responsibilities of management and maintenance of all resort accommodations and facilities reside with the board of directors as empowered by the resort's timeshare owners. This is a rather exhaustive list that requires skills that the board members do not always possess, but are critically important to the conduct of the resort. These duties include collection of all assessments for common expenses, estimation of revenues and expenses, and development of an annual operations budget. The entire budget that is developed by the managing entity for the current fiscal year is to be shared with the timeshare unit owners for information purposes. Furthermore, most states require that each home owners association provide the state a copy of the finalized budget within a set number of days (e.g., 30) after the beginning of each fiscal year together with a statement of the number of periods of seven-day annual use availability that exist within the timeshare plan, including those periods filed for sale by the developer but not yet committed to the timeshare plan, for which annual fees are required to be paid to the state (Florida State Statute—Chapter 721).

Key Point 9.5

In many cases local statutes regulate the rights, conduct, and duties of home owners associations and their directors so as to ensure owners are protected from deceitful business practice.

The concept of home ownership associations was born of the need for an identifiable entity responsible for the oversight of common real estate facilities. State regulatory bodies recognized this need early on, so the concept of the Common Interest

Realty Association (CIRA) was enacted to resolve this problem which appeared as an outgrowth of the American Institute of Certified Public Accountants (2002). A natural extension of a CIRA is the application of association control to timeshare ownership because of a similar need for structure and consumer protection. As a direct result of this need for structure, state regulatory bodies have established statutes by which home ownership associations are to be formed, responsibilities and duties outlined, and related operational procedures defined. The reader should note that under a fee-simple transaction, ownership does not transfer to the owners until a specified level of sales of all available intervals. Under this scenario, the developer is required to provide the owners with a managing entity, which can be (a) the developer, (b) a separate manager or management firm, or (c) an owners' association.

The creation of a home ownership association occurs upon the first closing of the sale of a timeshare interest. Furthermore, when timeshare estates are sold, any contract between the owners association and a manager or management firm is automatically renewable every three years, beginning with the third year after the owners association is first created, unless the purchasers vote to discharge the manager or management firm. This vote is conducted by the home ownership association's board, which means that the board is very influential in operational conduct of the timeshare resort. The manager or management firm shall be deemed discharged if a specified percentage of voters agrees on the firm's removal. In the state of Florida, for example, removal of the management entity occurs when at least 66 percent of the purchasers voting with at least 50 percent of all votes allocated to purchasers vote to discharge. Once the manager or management firm is discharged, the board shall remain responsible for operating and maintaining the timeshare plan.

The Florida Chapter 721—Timeshare Plan provides a prescriptive range of duties and responsibilities that a management entity must fulfill in order to be representative of the resort's home owners association (see Table 9.3). This list is not exhaustive of all the duties and responsibilities contained in this statute; rather, it should be taken as an overview of critical functions that are very specific to timeshare plans.

Owner record keeping – maintenance fee payments, special assessment payments

Exchange company relations

Maintain confidentiality of owner and financial records

Facilitate home owners meetings

Reallocate reserves for deferred maintenance and capital expenditures when required

Monitor ad valorem tax escrow payments and release of escrow payments

Protect and update the names and addresses of all purchasers and owners of timeshare units

Monitor accommodation and facility usage – unit usage, reservations, and cancellations

Deny usage to owners or exchangers that are delinquent in assessment payments

Monitor resort rental program

Arrange for annual audit of financial statements

Schedule occupancy of timeshare units

Maintain all books and records concerning the timeshare plan and ready them for inspection

Be held accountable as a fiduciary to the purchasers of the timeshare plan

Invest the operating and reserve funds of the timeshare plan

Give greater weight to safety of capital versus production of income

Facilitate material alterations or additions to accommodations of resort facilities

Monitor the timeshare plan's trust fund

Table 9.3 Timeshare Regulation Entity Duties & Responsibilities

The primary focus of responsibility assigned to a designated management entity (e.g. home owners association) is in a fiduciary (e.g., responsible for what belongs to another) capacity. A quick glance shows that the management entity is directly responsible for various accounting and financial duties, as well as services that directly relate to tracking unit/villa usage. Noticeably absent from this list are duties that relate to the daily conduct of resort services. These duties can be quite intensive and require vigilant attention, which is exactly why property management services are vended out to the developer or some other property management firm (Florida State Chapter 720—Homeowner's Associations).

These management duties and responsibilities do not capture the unique challenges that exist in running the day-to-day resort operation. This is a full-time function that requires the presence of a full-time management staff. The duties and responsibilities described below reflect the complexity of the timeshare resort environment.

Management of a timeshare resort is a relatively flat structure representing the functional departments of registration (check-in), housekeeping, maintenance, and security with oversight by a general manager. Of course, other levels of management may be present at a timeshare resort, but that is dependent on the number of recreational services, retail outlets, units, and owners as mandated by the home owner association budget. It is this last point that actually determines the management and staff structure that is ultimately available at any timeshare resort. This influence is a matter of owner economics because management and staff salaries and benefits are directly supported by annual timeshare owner fees.

The general manager as an agent of the home owners association is in a precarious position in a context where owners typically see themselves as the employer of the general manager. The general manager has to be acutely aware of this sensitive relationship and cannot be deterred from speaking out on issues or events that concern the operation of the resort. In the role of resort "caretaker," management must openly carry out the directives of the home owners association, while ensuring that optimal service levels are attained regardless of the situation at hand, which may seem contradictory when the budget dollars are largely controlled by the home owner association board. Management must also behave in a manner that is above criticism. There can be no compromise on regulatory issues, on vendor contracts, *and* on association policies. In short, honesty is the best policy for members of management and of the resort's staff. The general manager is charged with oversight of the day-to-day operation of the resort, with special skills relating to (a) personnel management, (b) property, (c) equipment, furniture, fixtures, and inventory, (d) time, (e) servitude, and (f) financial resources (McMahan, 1989).

A common assumption made by the general public is that timeshare developers build their resorts and then move onto another resort project, giving little consideration to the previously constructed project. In many instances this is not the case because the developer has a stake in maintaining the property for reasons of (a) image and (b) revenue contribution. Image is extremely important to the timeshare developer because considerable pride is devoted to construction of the resort. Therefore, it is in the developer's best interest to maintain the physical structure and the corresponding standards that surround the furnishing, fixtures, and equipment of the entire resort. In short, potential negative word-of-mouth from the resort owners resulting from years of usage with substandard upkeep by another property management entity can be incorrectly associated with that of the original developer. Therefore, *image* is a legitimate reason why leading timeshare developers position themselves as the "preferred" property management firm for the resort's home owners association. This concept is no different than it is for the hotel industry where guests become loyal to a brand. Therefore, timeshare developers seek to leverage their brand name via association with the maintenance of their product line.

An added benefit of being the developer as well as the property management entity is that the developer can offer standardized operating procedures at their resort, which from the consumer's perspective is a very strong benefit. The second reason for wanting to enter into a property management agreement is that offering these services acts as an additional income source for the developer. The income generated by the property management division is less than the revenues generated from the original sale of the timeshare intervals; nonetheless, this division of the developer's portfolio leads to significant revenues for the company as a whole.

Key Point 9.6

Many timeshare resort developers continue to maintain resort properties, under license from the home owners association, because they have an interest in ensuring that the property continues to contribute to their image and brand characteristics.

From the home owner association's perspective there is a compelling need to hire a property management firm that is credible, respectable, honest, and knowledgeable, and has sufficient resources available to support the proposed delegated functions. In checking out these items, the home owners association should prioritize and then interview multiple vendors prior to making its selection. However, given the timeshare developers' experience in property management, accounting services, exchange services, financial investment strategies, condominium association management, owner services, and regulatory issues concerning timeshare resort management, it is difficult to imagine that an outside vendor will be able to satisfy these skill areas.

Conclusion

Timeshare organizations consist of stakeholder interests that need to be taken into account when deciding on priorities and policies for the organization's conduct. Each stakeholder—employees, visitors/customers, home owners, local communities, legislative bodies, and trade associations—as well as enterprise shareholders have differing needs and means of evaluating organizational success. Effective management needs to adopt a number of techniques to reflect all shareholders. In addition, service sector models of the customer interface with the organization suggest that tensions are inherent in the interaction. Customers, employees, and the company are in constant state of dynamic tension with each other. A three-way tie between the needs of these three has to be recognized and managed.

As a matter of service sector management practice, balanced scorecard techniques provide valuable information that can help manage the realities of organizational performance from the perspectives of the various stakeholders. Unlike traditional forms of organizational performance appraisal, which focuses on the organization's success as an investment, the balanced scorecard allows consideration of issues relating to employee satisfaction and employee retention as well as customer complaints. Registered levels of customer and employee satisfaction can, for example, round out the picture and present some valuable indicators of long-term success.

Taking a more structural approach to managing the organization in a way that is sensitive to stakeholder needs involves the use of more participative, consultative, and democratic techniques. A number of techniques can be used to reflect the perspectives of various stakeholders in the decision-making processes. In particular, the unique relationship between the timeshare owner and the resort has resulted in widespread use of home owners associations which manage the day-to-day workings of the resort. Home owners elect a board of directors that allocates the contract to manage maintenance and other resort services. Owners can decide on fee levels, maintenance and refurbishment patterns, and all other relevant policies. In practice, the resort development company often wins the contract to run the resort, but it is with the explicit support of the owners.

CHAPTER 10

Business Ethics and Ethical Practice

Learning Objectives

After studying this chapter you should be able to:

- critically discuss the need for a formal approach to business ethics and ethical practice.

- analyze variations in morality and ethics.

- critically analyze ethical values and behavior in the timeshare business.

- identify and evaluate ethical approaches to selling.

Introduction

From the early beginnings of the timeshare industry, industry associations have sought to develop codes of practice covering business ethics in the industry (ARDA, 2002a). In the United States the National Timeshare Council began to formalize a code of ethics in 1979. This code was further strengthened in the early 1980s. After the merger of several regional bodies in 1998, Organization of Timeshare Europe (OTE) developed codes to cover firms operating particularly in the European Union area, but also resort developers and operators in the European geographical area (TRI Consulting, 2001). These codes have been developed for two reasons. First, there are strong commercial drives for branded, reputable firms to counter the negative image of some practices of early resort developers. Negative publicity for major corporations is costly because it has a negative impact on the business as a whole. Also, the cost of legislation incurred by customers wishing to break contractual arrangements because of deceitful selling practices adds considerably to total costs. In addition, it is just bad business to enter into a relationship with reluctant customers. High levels of customer dissatisfaction can be avoided if customers enter timeshare arrangements willingly, having made an accurate, informed decision.

Second, for most developers self-regulation is preferable to government legislation. Self-regulation allows the industry to adopt codes of conduct that are devised by the industry and are sensitive to commercial needs. Legislated codes of conduct imposed by politicians are likely to be more punitive and more restrictive (Hendry, 2004).

The tension between commercial freedoms and the need to protect customers from "sharp practice" is at the heart of much of the debate and concern about business ethics and ethical practice across industry as whole (Hendry, 2004). Some argue that the "social responsibility of business is to increase profits" (Friedman, 1970: 122). For those holding this classical-liberal economic approach, firms and customers interact in free markets, which means that no individual has power over the markets and that the resulting transactions reflect society's wishes. For many who hold this view of markets and the role of business organizations within them, state intervention in the form of regulation of business practice results in unfair interference and inefficiency (Sorrell and Hardy, 1996). Those calling for tighter control of timeshare are often critical of the actual business practices of firms driven predominantly to increase profits and shareholder value. Increasingly, business organizations are suggesting that a stakeholder model of the firm and ethical relationships with customers, employees, and suppliers constitute a more sustainable approach to business management (Trevino and Nelson, 1999; Moon and Bonny, 2001). Ethical business practice is an essential element in building strong competitive advantage because it reinforces loyalties that are difficult to copy. Membership of trade bodies such as ARDA and OTE and their binding codes are voluntary; resort developers and operators are not compelled to join, and as a result, governments in many countries have enacted legislation that provides minimum safeguards to timeshare customers.

Key Point 10.1

The major trade bodies representing the timeshare industry have developed codes of conduct that penalize unethical and illegal business practice.

Some Key Issues in Business Ethics

To provide an overview of some of the ethical issues in business organizations and management, Fisher and Lovell (2003) provide a valuable grid devised from two continua. The first dimension relates the distinction between ethics and morality. In many cases, writers use the terms interchangeably, but an understanding of timeshare issues can be enhanced by seeing these terms as meaning different things. Current timeshare codes, such as those issued by ARDA and OTE, are concerned with ensuring that operators do no harm to clients and are examples of morality. Ethics, on the other hand, is more concerned with ensuring good behavior. "Ethics is a term that can be thought of as developmental, whereas morality is judgemental" (Fisher and Lovell, 2003: 30). Morality usually involves lists of rules, of codes of what not to do, and of restrictions on actions that might harm others. Ethics are virtues or desirable values that help people to do good actions. Variations along this continuum will be discussed later in this chapter, but the key point of this chapter is that timeshare organizations can gain competitive advantage by being concerned with ethics.

The second dimension in the grid devised by Fisher and Lovell relates to dimensions covering "right and wrong" and legal and illegal actions. Right and wrong refer to moral or ethical actions, while legal and illegal actions relate to actions in relation to the relevant legal codes. They identify four positions on this continuum.

Actions that are good and legal but not a legal obligation.
Given the ideology of many corporations which defines their key duty as increasing shareholder value, many timeshare developers may see good actions as unnecessary. Others might consider that they also have duties to other stakeholders, such as adding a park or nature reserve that can be enjoyed by the community in which they are based, or adding better than expected staff facilities.

Actions that are bad and illegal.
In some instances, high-profile cases have included examples of where purchasers have been given wrong information, inflated figures relating to letting revenues and resale values, and so on. These actions are wrong ethically because it is wrong to lie, and they are illegal under both civil and criminal law.

Actions that are legal but bad.
This category is the one most likely to involve business and management decisions in timeshare because they relate to the obligations of shareholders alone or to a wider set of stakeholder interests—customers, employees, suppliers, communities. In some cases, being "economical with the truth" — which falls short of telling lies but nevertheless does mislead the customer or cover up useful information. It might also include a decision to pay employees low wages or to cut back

on contributions to refurbishment budgets so as to generate added profits for shareholders in the short term.

Actions that are good but illegal.
This category includes actions that may be morally good but illegal. For example, during Apartheid in South Africa, several U.S. and British firms took the view that it was their global duty to adhere to an equal opportunities policy, and broke the South African law promoting black and colored workers and providing equal employment rights. Clearly, actions in this category led to some difficult considerations because organizations are not free to disobey laws or legal obligations just because they don't like them. In most countries they are free to lobby and campaign for legislation to be changed, and so decisions to disobey the law are unusual.

The point here is that, although timeshare firms are legally bound to be lawful, they can adopt one of a number of positions in relation to their business practice. As members of one of the trade bodies, they also accept obligations to abide by the association's codes, but do they exceed these legal obligations and codes in their business practice, or do they abide by the letter of the codes but otherwise adopt practices that break the spirit of them? To some extent, these questions can be better understood through the use of Fisher and Lovell's second dimension relating to continuum relating to ethics and morality. Figure 10.1 is adapted from their grid (2003: 34).

Key Point 10.2

Management actions can be ethically evaluated against two continua that identify the extent to which actions are either "good" or "bad," or legal or illegal. Marketing malpractice by some sections of the industry have typically been both illegal and bad.

The various positions identified by Fisher and Lovell are helpful because they show a number of different options for timeshare operators. These options display varying degrees of commitment to doing good or avoiding doing harm.

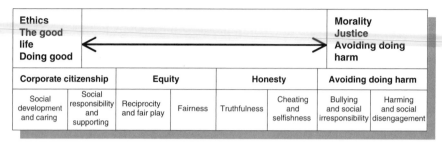

Figure 10.1 Mapping Ethics and Morality In Business Practice

Social Development and Caring

Organizations committed to taking action that improves the social, economic, cultural, or environmental conditions of a community or society are showing commitment to social development. Resorts located in an otherwise deprived country or region who then contribute to educational development or to the arts and recreational facilities for the community are examples of actions that are concerned with social development. Clearly, such acts have potential public relations benefits because the organization is seen to be contributing something more than what is needed to exploit a business opportunity. In some circumstances, considerable local opposition can be lodged to resort development and to flows of tourism to an area, so acts are not necessarily totally altruistic. The benefit to the community of having access to this added resource should not be underestimated, however, particularly as it may well benefit community members who are unlikely to gain from increased employment opportunities or the increased economic activity generated by the resort.

Social Responsibility and Supporting

Exercising social responsibility involves actions of the firm in a way that minimizes social impacts or damage to the environment. Often the actions of resort development firms can have devastating effects on communities and on the environments in which they are located. Behaving in a socially responsible manner involves taking actions that are sensitive to these impacts. For example, with regard to plans to cut local supplies and source from cheaper alternatives outside of the community, the social responsible action might be to phase in the change or to assist local suppliers in finding alternative markets. Similarly, if a resort needed to make large numbers of redundancies, the socially responsible action would involve support for redundant employees to find alternative jobs. Another act of social responsibility might involve careful consideration of the resort's impact on the environment and actions to minimize negative impacts. Again, the motives are not necessarily completely altruistic because some public relations benefits flow from these actions. However, the benefits are real enough and do provide some gain for those affected.

Reciprocity and Fair Play

Although some people view humanity as selfish and self-centered, others would argue that human history contains more evidence of altruism and actions in the interest of the collective good. Trade associations such the American Resort Development Association and the Organization Timeshare Europe involve individuals acting within common guidelines so as to promote the good of the industry. Obviously, members may, in principal, be competitors, but they cooperate for the long-term benefit of the community of providers. Some organizations do not join, and others join and then resign, perhaps for selfish and self-interested reasons. Other examples of reciprocity might involve resort developers working closely with other tourist attractions in a destination to promote a common destination profile. Key to the success of the approach is the punishment of cheats who act in self-interested ways and perhaps their expulsion from the organization, or fine. For example, ARDA's code includes the option to terminate membership for four months to two years, the length of time being determined by the seriousness of the failure to comply with the code.

Fairness

The distribution of resources among individuals, groups, and different stakeholders involves issues of fairness. "Resources can be money, respect or any possession a community can allocate between its members" (Fisher and Lovell, 2003: 48). Given finite resources in the forms of money and other rare resources, some fair system of distribution needs to be considered. Timeshare resort operators have to balance the resources allocated to meeting various stakeholder interests. Employment practices, for example, consider not just general levels of pay and employment conditions, but also how these are allocated among various employee groups. Typically, many hospitality employers provide the poorest pay and conditions to those employees who are in frontline positions because they are frequently recruited from sections of the labor market where labor is plentiful and cheap. Fairness would attempt to allocate rewards in different ways, so that those who benefit from the business most would attract a higher share in the results of the enterprise.

Lying

Lying is wrong in principle and undermines the basic common requirement of a business relationship, that is, honest dealing. What if everyone lied? How would the individual feel if she were being lied to? Certainly, lying under oath or in defined legal contexts carries with it a severe set of punishments, including fines and prison sentences. The issues are not as clearcut as they first seem: being economical with the truth, putting a favorable spin on things, and bluffing in business negotiations are widely practiced in business situations. However, long-term relationships with both employees and customers require openness and trust, so that lying even in these milder forms will undermine the relationship. At its most extreme, lying involves an intent to deceive others, and current codes of conduct for the timeshare sector proscribe deliberate intents to deceive. ARDA's (2002b) code contains a requirement to be both honest and to avoid deceit. The code states: "information, descriptions or disclosures required by this Code, whether oral, written, or graphic must be accurate and clear" (ARDA, 2002b: 231). The code also states that "Statements made in conjunction with development activities must not convey false, untrue, deceptive or misleading information through the use of statements, testimonials, photographs, graphics or other means. In addition, the Code requires you to disclose all material information, even if it will adversely affect the consumer's decision making" (ARDA, 2002b: 231).

Cheating

One must keep to the rules. Again, legal consequences may be imposed for not abiding by the terms of a contract, which can make the contract invalid. An injured party, whether it is the resort operator or the customer, can claim that the contract has been broken and that redress can be gained through the courts. Bending the rules, on the other hand, may be a way of expediting matters or of avoiding a greater injustice. As Oscar Wilde said, "Rules are for the guidance of wise men and the abeyance of fools." The important consideration in these milder forms of rule bending involves who is to benefit. If the rule bending is for personal or organizational gain at the expense of another, then the action is likely to be judged wrong. The key thrust of industry codes is to address the image created by cheating and deceitful practice in the past. "Clearly the strict application of the Code will address any myths and stereotypes that have been left by the unscrupulous actions taken by less than respectable developers from previous generations" (ARDA, 2002b: 229).

Bullying

Bullying involves relationships between those in different power positions in a relationship. It usually involves a misuse of power by the more powerful to abuse, humiliate, or cajole the less powerful person. There is no finite definition that fits all situations because assertiveness is not necessarily aggressiveness, and definitions between individuals may vary. In these circumstances, Fisher and Lovell (2003: 60) suggest, "One answer to the problem of bullying is to allow the victim to define. This empowers the weak against the strong by accepting that if someone says they are being bullied then they are." Obvious examples in work settings can involve a supervisor or manager harassing an employee with language, tone, and unfair treatment. Despite legislation outlawing many forms of prejudice, this sort of treatment frequently has a prejudicial dimension. Apart from this employment dimension, timeshare developers and operators have been accused of bullying in the sales negotiation. For this reason, both legislation and association codes allow for rescission rights — that is, the consumer's right to escape from the contract within a specified period. Typically, the minimum period allows the consumer to withdraw within ten days of signing the contract and to have all deposits refunded without charge.

Harming

Harming involves actions against individuals, institutions, organizations, living creatures, and the environment. Timeshare organizations can harm employees, customers, and communities, as well as the flora and fauna in which resorts are located. Discriminatory employment practices harm individual employees, mis-selling resulting in deceitful claims about the financial returns, or resale values may harm customers, and insensitive planning and design activities may damage communities and the local environment. The use of poor-quality building materials and the flouting of building regulation may cause physical harm if buildings collapse. ARDA's code, in the section dealing with *Standards of Practice in Professional Resort and Hospitality Management*, does make a general comment about the conduct of resort management and the need to avoid harming guests.

> Management must comply with all applicable laws and regulations, the legal documents of the association client. The safety and happiness of owners and guests are management's foremost concerns, and every effort must be made to resolve problems fairly and quickly. Clients should define the level of guest services they expect management to provide, and properly budget for it. Then, management is responsible for meeting those standards. (ARDA, 2003b: 241)

One way of understanding ethical business practice is through a continuum, which suggests that business behavior can be ethical and do good, or it can have negative effects and cause harm. Current codes issued by various timeshare associations such as ARDA and OTE are moral codes, which proscribe behavior that might do harm. By preventing harm, it is hoped that the member organizations can avoid some of the negative effects of past practice. The discussion has also suggested that individual companies might look toward a more proactive and deliberately ethical perspective. Ethical behavior might then be defined as including the following virtues of timeshare business behavior: social development; social responsibility; reciprocity; fairness; truthfulness; fair play; supporting; and caring.

Key Point 10.3

Timeshare codes of practice tend to be codes against wrongdoing and to be moral codes. Ethical business practice is concerned with doing good as well as avoiding doing harm.

Texas Instruments provides one of a number of ethical checklists that timeshare organizations, associations, and individuals might use to evaluate their actions (Table 10.1). Essentially, the list includes some general ethical principles that involve a consideration of doing to others as you would have them do to you and that concerns public disclosure of

1. Is the action legal?
2. Does it comply with our values?
3. If you do it, will you feel bad?
4. How will it look in the newspaper?
5. If you know it is wrong, don't do it!
6. If you are not sure, ask.
7. Keep asking until you get an answer.

Source: Fisher and Lovell (2003: 103).

Table 10.1 The Texas Instruments Ethics Quick Test

actions. The list is a valuable guide to individuals because some personnel may ignore both the industry's and the organization's codes of practice. This is a constant problem when individuals may be driven to maximize their income by pushing sales.

This brief discussion suggests that the issues are complex and that each of these virtues represents potentially a variety of positions. Some might attempt just to adhere to the codes and avoid the negative effects of punishment by the association. Others might even see these codes as a barrier to free market business practice and attempt to get around them. Still others might consider ethical business practice as a cornerstone of building a business reputation that will secure it a competitive advantage which other organizations will find hard to replicate.

Managing Ethical Business Practice

The preceding discussion has touched on some issues relating to the use of the codes of practice incorporated into the rules and regulations of major timeshare associations such as ARDA and OTE. In principle these codes aim to protect consumers from unscrupulous business practice. They represent attempts by the industry to self-regulate and to ward off government legislation. In addition, the reputable firms, with brand images to protect, are limiting the opportunities of less scrupulous firms to gain *unfair* competitive advantage. Business practices that increase short-term profits to the detriment of long-term industry reputation are discouraged, and minimum trading standards act as a common platform from which all must operate. While these concerns have specific relevance to the timeshare sector, a wider set of influences are causing many firms to explore more ethical ways of doing business.

Moon and Bonny (2001) suggest that changes within the world economy are causing many major business organizations to adopt more ethical practices. Specifically, they suggest that technological innovation, globalization, the importance of intangible assets, competition for talent, and the growing use of economic networks are leading to changes toward more ethical practice. In these circumstances, Moon and Bonny advocate an approach to business management which depends on forging business relationships with key stakeholder groups: "In the new economy the ability to forge relationships with diverse stakeholders, including employees, customers, suppliers, pressure groups and opinion setters is crucial. How they perceive a business and what they say about it has a direct impact on its reputation, success and, ultimately, its share price." (2001: 17).

Moon and Bonny advocate a model which they call Value Dynamics as a means of representing a business comprising an assortment of tangible and intangible assets. Most organizations, in line with traditional business reporting techniques, tend to include only physical assets and financial resources in their balance sheets. The Value Dynamics model suggests that intangible assets are important aspects of total company value and that these should be used to calculate worth. Figure 10.2 reproduces their model. Traditional indicators of company assets are listed on the left-hand side of the diagram, whereas intangible assets measuring the value of the organization's business relationships are listed below.

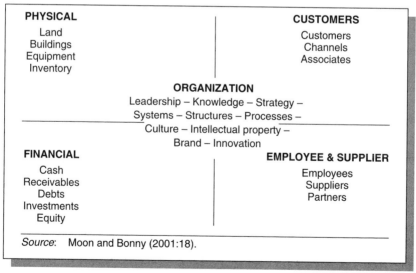

PHYSICAL
Land
Buildings
Equipment
Inventory

CUSTOMERS
Customers
Channels
Associates

ORGANIZATION
Leadership – Knowledge – Strategy –
Systems – Structures – Processes –
Culture – Intellectual property –
Brand – Innovation

FINANCIAL
Cash
Receivables
Debts
Investments
Equity

EMPLOYEE & SUPPLIER
Employees
Suppliers
Partners

Source: Moon and Bonny (2001:18).

Figure 10.2 Value Dynamics: Asset Relationships

The Value Dynamics model can be used to build a business case for stakeholder evaluation of timeshare organizations. It shows how stakeholders link with tangible and intangible assets, and it indicates that successful timeshare organizations are likely to most effectively manage the relationships between assets. Shareholders and other equity stakeholders invest money expecting a level of return on their investment in the form of dividends and asset growth. The value of the shareholder investment will in part be enhanced by levels of customer satisfaction that result in improved reputation, willingness to repeat, and recommendations to other potential customers. Shareholder value will also improve if the relationship with employees results in increased satisfaction and reduced staff turnover. This latter cost can be quite considerable, though it is rarely accounted for in hospitality and timeshare organizations. Improved retention of staff also improves the human capital that individuals accrue through increased knowledge of their jobs and customers. Improved links with suppliers can further add to business value as processes are more robust, and the reputation of the organization is enhanced as a fair business partner, and prompt payer for goods supplied. Though not included in Figure 10.2, the value of good community relationships also adds to the value of the business, through an improved public relations profile.

This move toward stakeholder accountability does not mean that sound economic principles are being abandoned. As Moon and Bonny (2001: 20) state, "Making money is being repositioned, not relegated." They report that over 40 percent of business leaders in one recent report believe that a company cannot succeed unless accountability goes wider than shareholders. Wider accountability involves a wider range of ethical dimensions that managers must manage because there are greater risks of ethical conflicts that can damage an organization. This is particularly relevant for timeshare resort operators because they know their cost, reputation is a significant intangible asset, and potential reputation damage is a key risk that the organization faces. Reputation is best understood as the goodwill of all stakeholders. The process of understanding stakeholder perspectives and views is fundamental, being able to manage reputation in a way that minimizes the risk of damage (Moon and Bonny, 2001).

Key Point 10.4

A stakeholder model for judging ethical business performance is required so that all the organization's constituent communities can be considered.

Key Ingredients for Successful Ethical Management

As a protection against ethical misconduct and wrongdoing, many companies are establishing ethics programs. Typically, these programs consist of policies, processes, and education and training courses that explain the company's ethics. Often these programs focus on workplace behavior and operating procedures that tend toward the avoidance of potentially damaging practice through compliance to codes. As we have seen, many timeshare codes consist of this approach to managing ethical behavior. A series of policies and processes identify desirable and undesirable actions. Increasingly, firms are looking to a more value-led approach through which to guide business behavior. The idea is that individuals use their internalized set of values to shape actions and behavior. Getting it right the first time is more likely to produce ethical behavior and thereby avoid potential problems. Whichever approach is taken, successful management of an organization's ethical behavior requires monitoring, and there are some important elements to successful implementation and management of these behaviors.

A recent U.S. study of nearly 3,000 firms (Moon and Bonny, 2001) suggested some common requirements of ethics and compliance management. Fundamentally, employees need to believe that the organization is serious about ethics and values, and that management actions and deeds match the policy. The process needs to appear to be fair to employees, ethical behavior should be rewarded, and there is open discussion about ethics and values. The more successful programs were value driven, resulting in lower incidence of observed unethical behavior, increased employee commitment, and greater confidence for employees to deliver bad news to management. The U.S. survey also suggested that if an ethics program was perceived to be exclusively concerned with protecting senior executives, it was considered worse than having no program at all.

A similar study of UK firms identified a number of potential problems in ethical policy management. The study found that in some cases codes of conduct were not handed to all employees and risked creating the idea that ethics was not a concern for some employees. Worse still, it reinforced the idea of an "us and them" culture. Because employees were rarely consulted about the code of ethics, there was little sense of shared ownership. Few had codes that were made publicly available, and thereby they missed opportunities to gain public relations benefits and confirm organizational commitment. Not all companies conducted ethics training for employees, and only six out of ten provided training to all employees. As might be expected, those who had received training were more aware of ethical issues. The content of training programs was generally restricted to the communication of standards and rules, and not to how these shape actual individual behavior. The study also showed that in the United Kingdom whistle-blowing policies are frequently ineffective. The ability of employees to report wrongdoing by managers and fellow employees is fundamental and requires that individuals feel confident that they can report these actions anonymously.

Evidence from these surveys provides some suggestions for constructing an effective model based on the best practice from industry examples (see Table 10.2). These suggest seven key ingredients: values, codes, feedback, responsibility, training, performance review, and external assessment. These represent a framework for managing ethical policies in a consistent way that is likely to reduce wrongdoing and help timeshare firms meet legal requirements, adhere to the industry association's codes, and protect the organization's reputation. The seven key ingredients follow three broad themes, namely, the need to identify the values and mission of the organization; to communicate these to internal and external stakeholders; and to build and maintain a decision-making culture.

1. **Values and mission statement** Create the mission and values that define what the organization stands for and how this impacts on the way it deals with stakeholders. Best practice suggests that a senior manager should be responsible for ethical practice within the organization. Management behavior must be consistent and in line with these values and mission.

2. **Codes of conduct** Codes of conduct are devised around a common framework to guide behavior. These codes should emphasize general principles so that employees can use them as a guide to their actions. Best practice suggests that these codes of conduct are developed by both management and employees. This aids buy-in from all organization members and increases the likelihood of producing a workable code.

3. **Feedback gathering and analysis** It is essential that the organization monitor and evaluate the conduct of organization members. This should include feedback from internal and external stakeholders. Instruments might include questionnaires, focus groups, and interviews. The process needs to consider identified problems and actions to correct them.

4. **Functional responsibility** Best practice indicates that ethical approaches work most effectively when responsibilities and accountabilities for ethical practice are clearly identified, unambiguous, and distributed throughout the organization. There should be leadership from the top and accessibility to senior offices for managers and employees. It is essential that all organization members have a sense of ownership to the ethical policy.

5. **Education and training** It is essential that all employees, regardless of level, job category, or tenure be included in the education and training program. The program should include examples of situations where wrongdoing occurs, its causes and consequences. Training should include realistic examples relevant to each group's work environment, thereby recognizing that the ethical issues faced at different points in the organization are different.

6. **Performance reviews and standards** Managing performance should use an array of measures of ethical performance as well as financial measures. Accountabilities and conduct should be measured against key performance indicators that include balance scorecard techniques. Responsible behavior should be rewarded, and wrongdoing should be identified and disciplined.

7. **External review** Best practice models suggest that externally conducted verification of the organization's ethical practices help to establish independence and public confidence in the process. External audits can generate useful information about best practice elsewhere and contribute to a culture of learning and continuous development.

Table 10.2 Best Practice Framework

Best practice suggests that the most effective way to promote ethical business practice is to embed it into the whole organizational culture and decision-making process. Ethical business practice extends beyond the avoidance of wrongdoing and the protection of the organization's reputation. There are clear messages that incorporate an ongoing dialogue with employees at all levels. Management decisions are permanently concerned to ensure that business practice continues to have an ethical dimension. Education and training extends beyond induction programs and potential disciplinary matters, but becomes a key process for helping all organization members understand how the organization's ethical commitments impact on them and the way they do their jobs. Implicitly, ethical organization demands a more empowered and participatory style of management and a learning organizational culture.

Key Point 10.5

Surveys show that ethical business practice is most effective when it is clearly articulated and managed. Specifically, seven key ingredients are required: values, codes, feedback responsibility, training, feedback, and external assessment.

Ethical Issues and Timeshare Management

Timeshare resort developers and operators are regulated at a basic level by government, and intergovernment legislation relating to timeshare business practice, and in more detail by industry association attempts to impose codes of conduct which promote more ethical behavior. In practice, both the legislative framework and the codes of conduct are attempts to prevent and discourage timeshare operators form doing harm to their clients.

The Legal Framework

Legislation relating to timeshare falls into broad categories. There is legislation generally relating to trade and sales agreements, finance antidiscrimination, for example, and there is legislation aimed specifically at the timeshare sector.

Each legislature frames its laws in its own way, but there are some general provisions that set a context for this discussion about ethics and moral codes, legal and illegal behavior.

The law of contract expects the "buyer to beware" and to be cautious when entering a contract to make a purchase. However, much consumer protection legislation is based on protecting "the mass multitude that includes the ignorant, the unthinking and the credulous" (ARDA, 2002a: 215). In particular, the laws protect the consumer in relation to use of the resort in the long term, stipulating that marketing and sales must accurately describe the facilities and services available. Consumer protection legislation makes it illegal to make statements that are lies, or to lead consumers to draw false conclusions, including exaggerating the quality of the resort units; making inaccurate statements about exchange opportunities and values; or misrepresenting the availability of recreational facilities, for example (ARDA, 2002b: 216).

Most consumer protection legislation also includes protection against unfair or deceitful practices in relation to the acquisition of contacts who are potential purchasers. Certain practices associated with promotional events are also the subject of much consumer protection legislation. In most cases, false competitions where all visitors to a resort are "winners" when there is no real competition; or falsely claiming that a person has been selected for a promotion; or failing to disclose information that might materially influence the purchase decision; or falsely claiming that there is a time frame within which the purchase has to be made are all examples of unfair and unlawful sales and purchase practice.

Similarly, legislation is in place in most legislative areas relating to the financial details of the purchase, for example, in overestimating future property values, exchange values, or rental incomes. Distorted information that might mislead the purchaser into overestimating the value of the purchase is also outlawed. In addition, legislation is in place that protects the consumer with regard to credit arrangements, say by underestimating the interest rates or misrepresenting the true full cost of the loan.

In addition to these general protections against unscrupulous actions in the purchase transaction, legislation also exists in most cases to protect individuals from discriminatory practice as would-be clients or as employees. It is illegal to discriminate on the grounds of race or ethnicity or gender. In many cases, legislation is in place which makes it illegal to discriminate on the grounds of disability. Increasingly, legislation is being introduced to promote equality of access to public places. This requires that resorts address the needs of a range of disabilities among resort owners.

Finally, current legislation gives customers rescission rights—the right to withdraw from a signed contract. Some individual states in the United States and the European Union have legislated the inclusion of a set amount of time in the contract for "cooling off." That is, customers have a set time during which they can cancel the contract and get their deposit refunded with no extra charge. Although individual member countries have increased this time period, the base provision applying to all EU member countries is ten days. In the United States, the base legislation requires that rescission rights be clearly stated in the contract, so that the time period for reconsideration, potential charges, and limitations on refund are accurately communicated in easily understood terms.

Association Codes

Most legal provisions are included in the relevant ARDA and OTE codes. Not only does the industry want to promote legal practice, but also through these codes they want to give more precise information and guidance on practices that support legal practice and avoid illegal conduct. ARDA's code, for example, includes ethics, standards, and ethical requirements that cover solicitation requirements (how contacts are obtained) and sales requirements (conduct of the selling encounter). The code also describes who is covered by the code and how the code will be administered, as well as the enforcement procedures and potential penalties for noncompliance with the code. Attachments to the code define standards of practice in Professional Resort and Hospitality Management, Off-Premises Contact, Applicability to non-ARDA-firms, Vacation Package Interpreting, and Timeshare Resale Interpretation Guidelines.

These examples of forms or processes give practical insights into general legal requirements for giving factual information, avoiding deception, or allowing management practices that put the consumer at a disadvantage.

Interestingly, association codes rarely consider other stakeholder interests. Apart from general requirements to abide by local planning, building regulations, and health and safety requirements, the codes do not discuss best practice models that include local community and special interest groups (say, environmentalists). Nor do the codes discuss employees and the requirement to provide ethical employment practice. By implication, timeshare developers and operators are required to abide by appropriate labor laws, but there is little comment about employees as stakeholders who need to be involved in the consultation process. In fact, these codes do not reflect a stakeholder model of ethical behavior as outlined in research on best ethical practice.

The development of these codes is generally "strongly market driven" (ARDA, 2002b: 229) and focused on regulating the relationship with "an increasingly sophisticated consumer" (ARDA, 2002a: 228). ARDA clearly states that the codes were developed as a way of distancing members from "questionable practices of its earliest days." For members it represented a "chance to move into a new and improved phase of sales and marketing" (2002b: 228). An interview with a senior executive at the De Vere Resort Group confirmed the importance of these issues for branded timeshare operators:

> The European timeshare directive has helped us, because it discourages hard selling. I know of one organization where over 90% of their sales withdraw during the EU cooling off period. That is such a waste of resources. Allowing people space to make their decision to purchase without pressure is much more effective. Customers feel comfortable and we spend less time and money generating sales.

These codes tend to be moral codes, using Fisher and Lovell's (2003) framework. They are concerned principally with avoiding doing harm by promoting honesty and avoiding deceitful, cheating, bullying, and harmful behaviors that put consumers at a disadvantage. As suggested earlier, both the associations and the individual members have considerable opportunities to go further than these codes. By adopting a more wide-ranging definition of ethical practice, they could take actions to improve the general good, through virtues that promote corporate citizenship and equity. Concerns for social development and caring, social responsibility and supporting, for reciprocity and fair play, and for fairness would help develop a more proactive approach to ethical behavior. Such an approach would represent a positive challenge to the unethical practices of the past. In effect, the sector would be saying, "We have not just stopped being bad, we are now actively promoting being good."

Key Point 10.6

The timeshare industry's codes tend to be concerned with limiting wrongdoing, which has caused problems in the past. There are opportunities to encourage more explicitly ethical business practice in the future.

The production and policing of these codes present some genuine dilemmas for self-regulation and the management of ethical practice across a large and diverse industry in a market economy. The ideology of the free market suggests that firms should be free to conduct trade as they see fit and that the marketplace is the ultimate judge. Consumers will avoid firms that trade in an unfair manner. In these circumstances, government regulation and legislation is unwelcome as it is seen to be an undue interference in the free conduct of trade. Consumers have been harmed by unscrupulous practice in the past, and as a result public perceptions of timeshare business operations are scarred and represent a barrier to trade in some customers. The development of industry codes is clearly a response to these perceptions and an attempt to positively change perceptions of the sector. The big dilemma for both associations and the firms is to determine how far they can go. If the codes become too restrictive, individual members may withdraw and may trade outside of the association. Without some legislative requirement for resort developers and operators to belong to the association, freedom to trade independently is likely to be an attractive option for some organizations. Others may take the view that more ethical business practices give them a distinct trading advantage compared to competitors. Still, others may argue that a tightly regulated environment will drive out the less efficient, unscrupulous developers and leave the market open to them. Certainly, some interesting tensions and questions remain regarding the future extent and scope of the sectors codes of practice.

Conclusions

Concerns over ethical business practice are not unique to timeshare practitioners, although the industry does have a track record that shapes particular problems and issues. Unscrupulous timeshare operators in the past have adopted practices that were both "illegal and wrong." Using the dimensions of actions that are either legal or illegal, good or bad, we can identify three broad ethical positions for timeshare firms. The first is that firms pursue business practices that are *legal but wrong*; that is, they adopt policies and approaches to customers that are within the letter of the law, but that are not totally open, truthful, fair, and selfless: notably, adopting spin and half truths with customers; being low-pay, high-turnover employers; treating local communities with disdain; or adopting selling practices that "use a lie when the truth would do," as one interviewee suggested. Some timeshare developers and operators also adopt approaches that are *legal but neutral*—that is, actions that are within the law and follow association codes but do not actively promote ethical business practice. The phrase *legal but neutral* is not identified in the Fisher and Lovell framework, but probably describes the position of many resort developers and operators. Such operators are principally concerned with avoiding wrongdoing and do not have actively defined ethical policy.

Individual timeshare firms can develop considerable competitive advantage by adopting ethical practices that are *legal and good*—that is, practices that go beyond the mere avoidance of wrongdoing and the protection of the organization's reputation. Indeed, association codes might benefit from ethical business practice that promotes doing good because this will counter the negative effects of questionable past practices. In these cases, ethical codes would need to define ethical practice from the perspective of all the key stakeholders, not just customers and shareholders. The code would need to consider ethical behavior as employer, as customer of suppliers, as a community and environmental asset, and as an organization of interest to a number of special interest groups.

Both moral codes designed to prevent wrongdoing and ethical codes designed to promote human happiness and goodness need to be adequately managed. The approach must permeate the whole organization, starting at the top and supported by adequate systems of accountability, control, and reward. Training staff and monitoring practice are essential. Certainly, a key requirement is consistency and avoidance of double standards and mixed messages. Research suggests that organizations that pay lip service to ethical policies, using fine-sounding words that are not put into practice, fare worse than organizations that have no policy at all.

The Future of Timesharing: A Matter of Strategy

After studying this chapter you should be able to:

- comprehend the processes involved in deploying a market position strategy.

- understand how deploying strategic demographic and lifestyle models will expand outreach and growth of the timeshare industry.

- understand how the application of economic models can be used to estimate the growth of the timeshare industry.

Introduction

The double-digit growth recorded by both the American Resort Development Association (ARDA) and Organization Timeshare Europe (OTE) has been fostered by altering demographic and usage pattern trends, economic stability within the worldwide marketplace, increased interest in the lending market to finance timeshare projects, continued establishment of regulatory bodies to impose and monitor adherence to existing timeshare laws, and the general dispersion of timeshare resorts, quality of product, and increased service levels from the resort and developer levels. The astute timeshare developer will take a proactive stance in the marketplace by planning for competitive, environmental, and consumer demand factors and by deploying short-range strategies that will position the developer's products firmly in the marketplace for a period of five to ten years.

According to Lovelock and Wright (1999), timeshare operators adopt a focused strategic stance in the short term because it is often very difficult to plan farther into the future, given the many unknown and uncontrollable variables that can surface. In doing so, the timeshare developer can continually monitor trends and react accordingly by adjusting their business strategies to account for shifts in demographic, economic, lending, and development trends as discussed earlier in this book.

Reflecting on the industry's demographic, economic, lending, and competitive development trends is just one piece of a concerted effort to effectively position the developer's products and services within a very competitive marketplace. The success or failure of a timeshare operator is intricately intertwined with the quality of the developer's market plan.

A timeshare developer could operate without a focused marketing plan, with the multiple outcomes being (1) the developer will have no established position in the marketplace because of little awareness, (2) the developer is forced to assume a market where no other developer wants to operate owing to low consumer demand, (3) the developer's product and services are misunderstood so that the resort(s) are not perceived to have a distinctive competence or legitimacy, or (4) the developer is confronted with intensive competition with other established developers (Lovelock, 1996).

The establishment and maintenance of a distinctive spot in the marketplace, otherwise known as a position in the marketplace, can indeed overcome these problems. Heskett (1997) asserts that organizations engage in positioning in an effort to distinguish their products and services from the competition. This is done by addressing six core questions: (1) how do consumers perceive the developer's products and services; (2) how do consumers view competitors' products and services; (3) to what differing market segments do the developer's products and services appeal; (4) what are the consumers' perceptions and usage characteristics of the products and services; (5) what changes does the developer need to make to enhance the current position within the marketplace; and (6) what is the long-term financial yield to the organization for each target market served? In accordance with strategic management and marketing literature, these questions require an analysis of internal and external factors, as noted in the following strategic positioning model discussion.

Conducting a SWOT Analysis and BCG Analysis

The SWOT (Strengths, Weaknesses, Opportunities, and Threats) framework is an analytical tool that allows developers to quickly concentrate on internal and external business variables that have potential impact on market considerations. As such, the SWOT analysis is useful when addressing a multifactor strategic business situation (http://www.netmba.com/strategy/swot/). Figure 11.1 shows how a SWOT analysis fits into a strategic situation analysis.

Key Point 11.1

Strengths, Weaknesses, Opportunities, and Threats analysis—the analysis of factors that potentially impact organizational success in the marketplace that is used in formulating strategic business plans.

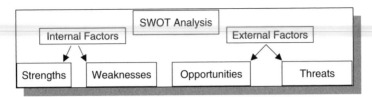

Figure 11.1 Modeling the SWOT Analysis

By developing a comparative grid, the developer can weigh the internal aspects of the company as strengths or weaknesses and the external situational factors as opportunities or threats. The general idea is that strengths lead to a competitive advantage in the marketplace and weaknesses may hinder this competitive position. Therefore, by reflecting on the individual SWOT components and their corresponding weights, the developer can design a strategy to leverage strengths, correct weaknesses, capitalize on market opportunities, and avoid potentially harmful threats.

Internal Analysis

The internal analysis is a comprehensive evaluation of the internal environment's potential strengths and weaknesses. Factors internal to the organization, as found in http://www.netmba.com/strategy/swot, include:

- Company culture
- Company image
- Organizational structure
- Key staff
- Access to natural resources
- Position on the experience curve
- Operational efficiency
- Operational capacity
- Brand awareness

- Market share

- Financial resources

- Exclusive contracts

- Patents and trade secrets

Case Study 11.1

David Jankers, vice president of marketing for the TRI Resort Group, had always wanted to find out why his major competitor was so successful with the European market. No matter what his organization did, it simply could not dislodge the tremendous hold that his competitor had on that market segment. After conducting an in-depth analysis of his competitor, David soon came to the realization that its culture was incredibly strong: it had executives with advanced college degrees, all of whom were seasoned veterans in sales, marketing, and finance. In addition, it appeared that his competitor's parent company was not at a loss for working capital, and it had a tremendous public relations campaign that was second to none. So now he knew the real story. . . .

External Analysis

In the world of timeshare development, the primary charge is to seek out and dominate markets via product development or service packaging that generate the highest yield per market. However, what might have been a golden opportunity can just as quickly turn into a major threat to the organization. When market position is threatened, the developer may decide to introduce new product or services into its offerings to remain competitive in the marketplace. Factors that comprise the external (and can be either a threat or an opportunity) operating environment, as found in http://www.netmba.com/strategy/swot, include:

- Customers

- Competitors

- Market trends

- Suppliers

- Partners

- Social changes

- New technology

- Economic environment

- Political and regulatory environment

The SWOT procedure for determining competitive positioning helps the timeshare developer define its strategies within the context of competitive environments and intervening factors. The SWOT decision-making tool encompasses a review of the organization's internal strengths and weaknesses, as well as the opportunities and threats found in the external marketplace. The SWOT tool can also be integrated with the Boston Consulting Group (BCG) matrix to give a composite picture of the immediate competitive landscape in which the timeshare developer already operates or plans to operate its resorts.

Key Point 11.2

The Boston Consulting Group matrix is a business analytical tool that assists developers in determining and positioning their products and services in existing or new markets.

By combining the SWOT process with BCG positioning matrix, the developer can analyze the validity of a strategy that has been proposed and recommend changes where relevant. The BCG Growth-Share Matrix (see Figure 11.2) is a planning model developed by Bruce Henderson of the Boston Consulting Group in the early 1970s. Therefore, the BCG positioning process takes into account strengths and weaknesses, as well as opportunities and threats, to highlight various strategic positions that the timeshare

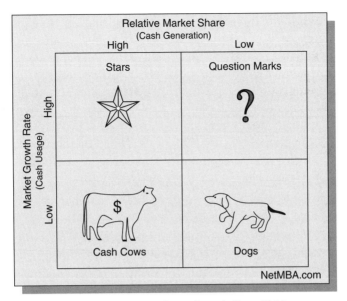

Figure 11.2 Boston Consulting Group Growth-Share Matrix

developer could deploy based on this combined information. In short, the BCG positioning matrix assists marketeers in identifying high- and low-potential business units or products. The BCG output is a two-by-two matrix that has, on the vertical axis, market growth rate, which provides a measure of market attractiveness and, on the horizontal axis, market share relative to the largest competitor, which serves as a measure of company strength in the market. The matrix therefore compares the developer's business unit positions within these two important determinants of profitability (Kotler, 2003).

The BCG matrix categories are as follows:

Cash Cow

The cash cow market is noted for its low-growth and high-market-share potential because it is capable of producing large amounts of cash while projected future growth is limited. If the SWOT and the BCG matrix indicate a cash cow market, a harvest strategy is usually recommended in which the developer reaps the highest level of profits possible while not investing back into the market. The industry as a whole is still heavily investing in new marketing technologies and products designed to maintain market share and defend a dominant position that does not lend itself to not reinvesting in the market because market positioning and penetration is a primary concern. Hence, it would not be unusual for a timeshare developer's BCG to reflect a cash cow market, with the focus being on domination instead of reaping maximum profits only to withdraw from the marketplace.

Stars

A market is considered a star when it is typified as high growth and high market share for the developer's product offerings. For this type of position, the developer's products bring in large amounts of cash that yield a dominant position in the competing market.

Question Marks

A market is described as a question mark when it is characterized as having high growth and low market share. When a developer operates in this kind of environment, its products are operating in a risky environment because its product offerings are profitable while securing a small share of the total market. The challenge for the developer that does not have a dominant position is that the present market leaders will continue to allocate their seemingly inexhaustible resources to make it difficult for the independent (or new entrant) to gain market share.

Dogs

The market described as a dog is characterized by low growth and low market share and therefore is limited in revenue-generation potential. A typical strategy associated with this type of market would be to sell the underperforming resorts in order to release money to support resorts that were functioning in rising markets (e.g., question marks).

Conduct an analysis of your local timeshare industry and discuss if there are any resorts (in the development phase) that could be classified as a star, a question mark, a dog, or a cash cow.

General Strategic Approaches

A timeshare resort developer has certain common tools at his or her disposal, as noted in the strategic management and marketing literature (Kotler, 1999). These organizational strategies are classified under four broad headings: growth, stability, retrenchment, and aggregate.

Growth

If the developer chooses to follow a growth strategy, the organization determines that internal resources and external possibilities are sufficient to maximize revenues and market share. In this strategic positioning mode, it is common to find evidence of refined sales, marketing, financial, accounting, legal, owner services, and property management services. This strategy also assumes that other developers in the same market are not entrenched and that sufficient consumer demand exists for timeshare products and services.

Stability

This positioning strategy assumes that the timeshare market is mature as noted by low growth or little growth by existing or new entrants into the market. Under this scenario, the developer would have already achieved a satisfactory financial performance level in the market and would have maintained this status for multiple years. Because there are very few, if any, new markets to be pursued, the developer focuses on its existing consumer base and refines the costs of its business and investment practices so as to increase return on investment levels. To achieve improved return on investment schedules, the developer relies on upper management to control expenditures and on sales and marketing to rejuvenate additional purchases by existing owners and on programs that enhance the organization's image.

Retrenchment

If a timeshare resort developer engages in a retrenchment strategy, the organization is reacting to economic vacillation that is negatively impacting the consumer's decision to purchase timeshare products. The developer expects this to be a temporary situation and anticipates that the market will rise again once the crisis has passed. Retrenchment is not the same as divestment strategy, in that it is the direct result of a temporary hardship whereas divestment represents a permanently failed market.

Aggregate

If a timeshare developer decides to pursue different strategies within separate product divisions of the organization (e.g., timeshare, fractional, private residence clubs), the developer is said to be practicing an aggregated strategy—that is, the pursuit of different strategies in separate strategic business units. The aggregate approach indicates that developers that operate different product types might not employ a singular approach for all their strategic business units. For instance, if the developer operates resorts in separate geographical regions or operates different product types such as timeshare, fractional, or high-end private residence clubs, the ownership base will mandate that different strategies be deployed. Still, this does not imply that the different product divisions of the organization will not operate from a unified organizational mission and value orientation.

Key Point 11.3

Each of the general product positioning strategies of growth, stability, retrenchment, and aggregate is associated with unique and specific positioning strategies.

From General to Specific Strategies—an Example of Growth

From the developer's perspective, these four strategies are very broad and require some specificity. Given the timeshare industry's sustained growth, it would initially appear that further delineation of specific growth strategies is in order. The common growth strategies of market development, product development, product differentiation, market penetration, and niche marketing are explored next.

Market Development

The timeshare industry as a whole has been in a market development mode since the 1960s both in the United States and abroad. The expansion of products into new geographical regions, national and international, and refinements in demographic and lifestyle markets indicate that the industry continues to expand into differing markets. One specific example of such an expansion is the introduction of private residence clubs in various tourist destination markets in recent years.

Product Development

Product development entails protecting or increasing market share by engaging in product improvements or enhancements. When an operator develops different types of resorts that cater to differing markets and lifestyles, he or she is actively reconfiguring existing architectural plans and services to meet the needs of an untapped market. Offering the "dude ranch" type of timeshare resorts in the western region of the United States, with trail guides, stalls, and tack services, is an example of a new product line that caters to a specific consumer clientele.

Product Differentiation

The deciding factor when using a product differentiation strategy resides in management of the consumers' perceptions of product and service quality as being distinctly different from the competition. Often this does not mean that the product is altered or improved to make the offering different. Instead, the strategy practiced is to build satisfaction and consumer loyalty to the brand.

Market Penetration

The primary objective under the market penetration strategy is to increase the sales of timeshare units by encouraging wider usage of existing products by owners, renters, or exchangers. In this scenario, the timeshare developer often devotes significant human and technological resources to tracking and communicating with their ownership, exchanger, and renter base, with special offers to purchase additional resort time or services.

Niche Marketing

A niche market is a gap in a market that is not being provided for by existing businesses in the industry. Therefore, a niche strategy focuses on areas where no other developer offers services. Thus, a timeshare developer will decide to concentrate on this narrowly defined and highly profitable market. An example would be the timeshare developer who offers a combined international air and weekend stay from London to Orlando for an exclusively upscale European clientele.

Key Point 11.4

The general positioning strategy of growth is associated with the specific strategies of market development, product development, product differentiation, market penetration, and niche marketing.

Practical Elements of a Competitive Advantage

Throughout the present work, the various national and international statistics have shown that the timeshare industry has continually grown in the metrics of ownership, number of resorts, number of new developers entering the market, proliferation of product types, and locations throughout the world.

As such, competition has intensified in a global fashion and is driving developers to adopt proven theories concerning market development and penetration. Therefore, the primary thrust of any timeshare organization is to work smarter at identifying certain target markets versus using a mass marketing approach to attract potential purchasers who have an inclination to buy their timeshare product. Accordingly, this chapter presents market segmentation models that assist developers in refining their marketing efforts by segmenting the broader market by segments that it can serve best. Roughly speaking, this means that the timeshare developer must engage in a market segmentation process that identifies those target markets with sufficient interest and yield.

The following paragraphs outline how three widely accepted segmentation strategies can be applied to the timeshare product. These segmentation strategies are known as Claritas, The Looking Glass Cohorts, and VALS. Within the timeshare context, market segments are defined as a collection of purchasers who share demographic characteristics, lifestyles, and consumption patterns. The foundation of any market segmentation theory is to accurately understand how the intended target segments view the developer's product offerings and *then* to properly position these products to appeal to these segments.

The Strategic Application of Demographic Projection Models

Promoting the timeshare product to consumers of seemingly different age ranges, ethnicities, and nationalities can be a daunting task. As with many products and services on the market, a shotgun approach to marketing will rarely yield significant gains in revenue or market share due to the lack of a concentrated plan. Therefore, it is in the developer's best interest to stay abreast of current and projected demographic and lifestyle trends as identified by industry experts.

Various consulting firms exist, so it is fairly easy to outsource the collection of this type of demographic and lifestyle information to proven experts. However, publications by credible agencies use leading methods such as the VALS instrument as produced by Claritas (http://www.claritas.com). One publication that merits review by any timeshare developer is *American Demographics*. Counterparts of this type of publication may be found in European, Asian, and other international markets as well.

Key Point 11.5

Timeshare developers can enhance their positioning efforts by employing demographic and lifestyle segmentation programs.

Current Industry Practices

The industry is beginning to embrace the concept of demographic and lifestyles when pinpointing its existing and potential customers. This is a radical departure from past practices and appears to be a less than focused approach to attracting potential purchasers. This explains why the timeshare industry has historically been labeled as aggressive in its sales and marketing approaches. For instance, Ragatz & Associates has diverged from existing thought by employing a demographic and lifestyle approach to categorizing timeshare owners through the Looking Glass Cohorts. This system is yet another market segmentation system such as PRIZM as described at the end of this chapter. The difference between Cohorts and other systems is that other segmentation systems are based on U.S. Census data that classify consumers into geographical areas of similar interest and are supposedly reflective of households in that geographical region. Conversely, Cohorts is based on the specific demographic and lifestyle characteristics of each individual household, in line with the demographic profile outlined in Chapter 3. The basic difference then is that *Cohorts* provides representation of individuals' likes and dislikes concerning marketing messages, products and services versus an 'assumed' for a group of people that reside in a specific geographical area.

Therefore the underlying difference between the Cohorts model versus other segmentation approaches is that the timeshare developer has a practical tool at his or her disposal. For instance, the timeshare developer can deploy marketing programs and sales strategies that are based on the expressed attitudes, interests, and opinions of existing Cohort types. The basic premise is that expressed satisfaction by existing owners (and of course specific Cohort types) can only lead to satisfaction of potential consumers that also fit the existing Cohort purchasers. A general description of the Looking Glass Cohort types are shown in Figure 11.3.

For a tangible application of the Looking Glass Cohorts (see the Appendix to Chapter 4), the 2003 resort timesharing

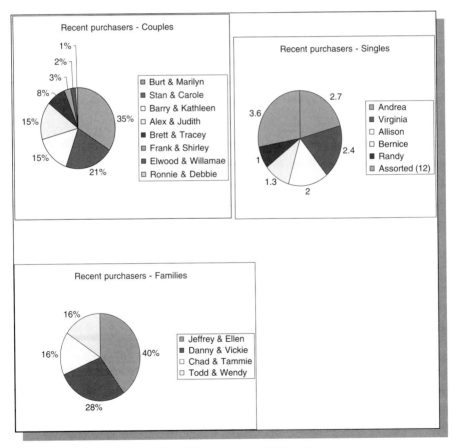

Figure 11.3 Cohorts Making Recent Purchases in U.S. Timeshare

report by Ragatz & Associates presents an excellent view into the future because past performance is often an excellent indicator of future performance. This study is not indicative of all timeshare properties in the United States because it represents only those reporting owners who use RCI's exchange company services. Under the couples category, the mature couples (Burt & Marilyn), upscale middle-aged couples (Stan & Carole), affluent professional couples (Barry & Kathleen), and affluent empty nesters (Alex & Judith) accounted for 48.4 percent of the timeshare purchasers. In the family classification category, the affluent couples with kids (Jeffrey & Ellen), teen-dominated families (Danny & Vickie), young families (Chad & Tammie), and back to school families (Todd & Wendy) commanded 30.8 percent of the recent timeshare purchasers. In the single category there were seventeen cohort groupings, with the top five accounting for 9.1 percent out of the overall 13 percent of single-timeshare purchasers. From a macro view this means that approximately 87 percent of the most recent purchasers were families, with only 13 percent being single households. For illustrative purposes, only the top two Cohort consumer groupings under the couples, families, and singles categories are described further.

The mature couples (Burt & Marlyn) cohort type placed a high level of importance on the timeshare company's credibility, were close to retirement with no children at home, were active investors, and were active travelers. The Stan & Carole type were an upscale middle-aged couple (49 years of age) that maximized their value by purchasing single weeks, biennials, or points, were drawn by the credibility of the timeshare developer, were not financially hampered by children, were dual-income households (median income of $73,500), and enjoyed outdoor activities. The Jeffrey & Ellen type were middle-aged (42 years of age) affluent couples (median income of $144,800) with children who purchased single- to multiple-week products in tourist destinations that favored snow skiing or tropical areas, lived in urban areas, were cultural connoisseurs, and were active in recreational activities. Danny & Vickie were teen-dominated families that were approximately 42 years of age with an average household income of $56,200. This cohort type was the most well-represented timeshare purchasing group, exhibiting a preference for three-bedroom villas, single weeks, and mountain and tropical locations. The Andrea cohort type earned a median income of $48,900, had a median age of 39 years, was a single-career-focused mom, purchased a two-bedroom villa, and had a preference for beach and entertainment locations. The upscale mature woman (Virginia) cohort type tended to acquire its timeshare via an inheritance, gift, or a divorce, preferred historical or cultural sites, was about 60 years of age (median) with a median income of $69,600, and enjoyed traveling during their retirement years.

Reflective Practice

Visit the Looking Glass Cohort web site and review its services. Are there other ways in which this company can position its product's timeshare developers?

The Looking Glass Cohort system can be used to project future purchasers, as is shown in a 2001 report by Ragatz & Associates using this same cohort tool. The differences between 2001 and 2003 show that mature couples (Burt & Marlyn) accounted for 12.5 percent in 2001 versus 19.2 percent in 2003; affluent empty nesters (Alex & Judith) for 16.2 percent versus 8.6 percent; affluent couples with kids (Jeffrey & Ellen) for 10.6 percent versus 12.4 percent; and upscale middle-aged couples (Stan & Carole) for 9.5 percent versus 11.9 percent. This comparison indicates that three of the consumer groups have become more representative, which indicates that this trend is likely to continue. The Cohorts system therefore has much to offer as a way of estimating and identifying potential consumers of timeshare products.

Future Developer Investment Projections

Financing a timeshare resort is a complex process that often requires an extensive amount of capital investment. That is why securitization and hypothecation investments are such important financial strategies for the timeshare developer.

Hypothecated receivables are the consumers' installment contracts that are pledged as collateral for debt. In 2003, hypothecation loans totaled $902 million at an average interest rate of 6.1 percent. In comparison, the average interest rate was 6.4 percent for funds borrowed against hypothecated loans. Lenders seeking to reduce the risk of the loan tend to limit the amount advanced to the developer for their hypothecated receivables. In 2003, the advance rate for a hypothecated loan was 86.1 percent versus 82.8 percent in 2002. Table 11.1 presents a two-year trend relative to advance rates on hypothecated loans. An assumption to be made relative to this table is that hypothecation is indeed a common practice in the timeshare industry, with the advance rates reflecting the level of risk associated with hypothecated loans. Based on this two-year comparison, the advance rate on hypothecated loan is expected to remain in the 85 to 90 percent range. This, of course, has the potential of being impacted by the economic conditions mentioned previously. If these come to fruition, consumers will become more restrictive with such recreational purchases, which in turn will result in lenders becoming more cautious in their advance rates.

Another financing option available to the timeshare developer is securitization. When a developer sells a collection of its receivables as investments on the open market (Baumann, 2003), the result is an immediate cash flow to the developer. The downside of seeking a securitized loan is that it requires an

Weighted Advance Rate on Hypothecated Loans			
Loan % rate	# of companies in 2003	# of companies in 2002	Difference
<80%	13	16	−3
80 to 84.9%	0	0	0
85 to 89.9%	32	28	4
90%	52	50	2
90%+	3	6	−3

Table 11.1 Advance Rate on Hypothecated Loans

intensive receivable pool in the neighborhood of $100 to $200 million. At this level of investment, this type of financing is typically not for small- or medium-size developers. This type of investment also carries considerable risks that are commonly associated with playing in the capital investment market. In a report on the financial status of the industry, the American Resort Development Association (2004b) reported that eight developers conducted twenty transactions for a total investment of $1.2 billion. In comparison to 2002, eight developers conducted twenty-one transactions for a total investment of $1 billion. The more telling result is that the advance rate for a securitization transaction in 2003 was 86.5 percent versus 91.1 percent in 2002. This two-year comparison indicates that securitized loans are sought out in moderation and that the risk of this type of investment, in combination with not understanding the timeshare industry, has resulted in a slightly reduced advance rate. Furthermore, the interest rate paid by the timeshare developer in 2003 decreased to 3.6 percent from 5.6 percent in 2002. If this trend continues, lending agencies will continue to offer securitized loans to the industry at increasingly favorable advance rates and interest rates that benefit both parties. This could be a very positive occurrence for small developers if they generate enough consumer receivables to enter into a securitized loan.

Resort Life-cycle Theory—Applied to Timeshare

As the timeshare product has matured, it has progressed through development stages that Butler (1980) has described as the resort life cycle. As shown in other chapters, the resort life cycle is similar in theory to the product life cycle in the retailing industry. Both theories posit that an organization gradually progresses through five distinct phases during the life of the business, with the exception being the rebound or rejuvenation phase. The distinct phases of the resort's life cycle are introduction, growth, maturity, decline, and rebound. In the introduction phase, the developer leverages intensive promotional campaigns to raise the level of public awareness. This is exactly why in the early years of timeshare development there was a plethora of off-site booths and mini-vacation offerings designed to intercept and attract a wide variety of consumers. During the growth phase (the 1970s to present), the industry was typified by the rapid development of resort tiers in an effort to cater to differing consumer groups, positioning of products and services aimed at differing recreation and leisure needs, and the expansion of timesharing into worldwide locations. Also in this phase, the timeshare industry witnessed the entrance of major hotel developers (Marriott, Hilton, Disney, Hyatt, Starwood, and Wyndham). Basically, the growth phase of the resort life cycle is characterized by gradual product differentiation, service differentiation, and sustained investment in sales and marketing programs in order to increase consumer trial and adoption of timeshare offerings.

Franchising Agreements

The best indicator of future growth is often reflected in the product and service changes that have occurred. A recent trend in timeshare development that is projected to expand current timeshare resort offerings is that of franchising. Franchising is not new to the hospitality industry and has been mastered by companies like McDonald's, Starbucks, Hilton, and Marriott in the restaurant and lodging sectors. However, the first published evidence of franchising in the timeshare industry occurred in 2004 as released in an article in the publication, *Lodging Hospitality*. The anonymous author of this work noted that Wyndham was rolling out its products to interested parties via a franchise agreement. As with other franchise arrangements, Wyndham's franchise agreement offers franchisees development support in terms of sales, marketing, feasibility, construction services, mortgage banking, and other services. Shortly after Wyndham's franchising announcement, Shell Vacations announced that it, too, was expanding its network of resorts via franchise agreements (Sherles and Lennon, 2004). If this trend follows the pattern established by the hotel industry, timeshare resort development is poised for rapid expansion in regional, national, and international markets. In doing so, the timeshare industry will enter into the main part of the growth cycle as posed by Butler.

Conclusion

It is difficult to project what any industry will do and what it will look like in the future. However, a developer can take certain steps that can better position its products and services. This chapter has offered such suggestions by reflecting on past industry practices and by considering national and worldwide economic trends, changing demographic trends, and lifestyle patterns. In doing so, the developer will be better prepared to adjust its development and operational practices to better service the marketplace.

A strength, weakness, opportunity, and threat analysis—a SWOT analysis—is helpful in exploring possibilities for new efforts or solutions to problems, making decisions about the best option available for products and services, identifying opportunities for success in the context of threats to success, and reviewing strengths and weaknesses to reveal market possibilities. In addition, the accumulation of this information enables the developer to adjust and refine plans midcourse so as to react quickly to competitive conditions. In short, SWOT is a business tool that offers timeshare executives a mechanism of communicating product and service programs in an effort to adjust, refine, or enter into new markets via a structured analytical review process rather than react to market conditions after the fact.

PRIZM

The popular PRIZM (Potential Rating Index for Zip Markets) system categorizes consumers by a standardized set of characteristics, known as clusters, within each ZIP Code in the United States. PRIZM information comes from census data and data from millions of purchase records and customer surveys. Once compiled, the composite zip code and psychographic analysis creates a fascinating look at the communities that comprise the United States.

In the PRIZM lifestyle segmentation system, every U.S. neighborhood is defined according to 62 distinct types or "clusters." These 62 PRIZM clusters reflect the variety of activities, interests, and

(Continued)

opinions that impact neighborhoods. In turn, each U.S. neighborhood is assigned to one of these PRIZM Clusters according to demographic projections taken from the current census year. These clusters are derived by a statistical classification procedure known as factor analysis whereby the collected census data are grouped into demographic and lifestyle variables that explain the differences between customer profiles. The 62 PRIZM Clusters are subdivided into 15 social groups as segmented by degree of urbanization (from the rural countryside to urban high-rises) and by degree of affluence or socioeconomic status (e.g., income, education, home value and occupation). In doing subdividing the geographic markets in this manner the marketer can group geographic groupings by lower, middle and upscale markets. The 62 geodemographic clusters are gathered in the following fifteen social groups as subdivided by psychographic variations (clusters).

PRIZM Geodemographic Density of 15 Social Groups as Stratified by 62 Clusters

S1 - Elite Suburbs
- 01 Blue Blood Estates
- 02 Winner's Circle
- 03 Executive Suites
- 04 Pools and Patios
- 05 Kids and Cul-de-Sacs

S2 - The Affluentials
- 18 Young Influentials
- 19 New Empty Nests
- 20 Boomers and Babies
- 21 Suburban Sprawl
- 22 Blue Chip Blues

S3 - Inner Suburbs
- 23 Upstarts and Seniors
- 24 New Beginnings
- 25 Mobility Blues
- 26 Gray Collars

U1 - Urban Uptown
- 06 Urban Gold Coast
- 07 Money and Brains
- 08 Young Literati
- 09 American Dreams
- 10 Bohemian Mix

U2 - Urban Midscale
- 27 Urban Achievers
- 28 Big City Blend
- 29 Old Yankee Rows
- 30 Mid-City Mix
- 31 Latino America

U3 - Urban Cores
- 45 Single City Blues
- 46 Hispanic Mix
- 47 Inner Cities

C1 - 2nd City Society
- 11 Second City Elite
- 12 Upward Bound
- 13 Gray Power

C2 - 2nd City Centers
- 32 Middleburg Managers
- 33 Boomtown Singles
- 34 Starter Families
- 35 Sunset City Blues
- 36 Towns and Gowns

C3 - 2nd City Blues
- 48 Smalltown Downtown
- 49 Hometown Retired
- 50 Family Scramble
- 51 Southside City

T1 - Landed Gentry
- 14 Country Squires
- 15 God's Country
- 16 Big Fish, Small Pond
- 17 Greenbelt Families

T2 - Exurban Blues
- 37 New Homesteaders
- 38 Middle America
- 39 Red, White and Blues

T3 - Working Towns
- 52 Golden Ponds
- 53 Rural Industrial
- 54 Norma Rea-Ville
- 55 Mines and Mills

R1- Country Families
- 41 Big Sky Families
- 43 New Eco-topia
- 43 River City, USA
- 44 Shotguns and Pickups

R2 - Heartlanders
- 56 Agri-Business
- 57 Grain Belt

R3 - Rustic Living
- 58 Blue Highways
- 59 Rustic Elders
- 60 Back Country Folks
- 61 Scrub Pines Flats
- 62 Hard Scrabble

For further clarification, two of the fifteen geodemographic lifestyles are:

Cluster 02: Winners Circle – Is classified as *executive suburban families* which are families with "new money" that live in expensive major metropolitan suburbs, are well-educated executives and professionals who are married with teenagers at home. Individuals in this classification are in their peak earning years, are big spenders and enjoy travel. They are independently wealthy, approximately 45–54 and 55–64 years of age, are predominantly white Caucasians or Asian.

(Continued)

Cluster 18: Young Influentials – Individuals in this cluster are known as upwardly mobile singles and couples. This group is high-tech educated individuals that hold managerial and professional jobs and live in urban high-rises. These individuals prefer sophisticated urban lifestyles that are supported by dual incomes. They are aged 25–34 and 35–44, are classified as upper-middle class, and are predominantly white Caucasian or Asian.

In closing, the challenge confronting the timeshare developer is that psychographic research is costly and requires time to analyze existing consumer profiles so that valid predictions can be made with minimal error as to prospects' intent to buy. However, given the predictive power of psychographic instruments such as VALS 2 and PRIZM, these are minimal issues due to long range payoffs for the developer.

Sources: http://www.tetrad.com/pcensus/usa/prizmlst.html; http://www.claritas.com/claritas/Default.jsp?ci=3&si=4

References

Adelmann, M.B., Ahavia, A., & Goodwwin, C. (1994). "Beyond Smiling: Social Support and Service Quality." In R.T. Rust and R.L. Oliver (eds.), *Service Quality: New Directions in Theory and Practice*. London: Sage.

Alpander, G. (1991). "Developing Manager's Ability to Empower Employees." *Journal of Management* 10: 13–24.

American Institute of Certified Public Accountants. (2002). *Common Interest Realty Associations*. New York: American Institute of Certified Public Accountants.

American Resort Development Association. (1998). *State of the Timeshare Industry: 1999*. Washington, DC: ARDA.

American Resort Development Association. (1999a). *The American Recreational Property Survey: 1999*. Washington, DC: ARDA.

American Resort Development Association. (1999b). *State of the U.S. Vacation Ownership Industry: The 1999 Report*. Washington, DC: ARDA.

American Resort Development Association. (Spring 1999). *Phenomenal Growth in the U.S. Timeshare Industry: The Baby Boomer Way to Vacation!* Washington, DC: ARDA.

American Resort Development Association. (2002a). *A Survey of Timeshare and Vacation Ownership Resort Developers*. Washington, DC: ARDA.

America Resort Development Association. (2002b). *The Timeshare Industry Resource Manual*, Washington, DC: ARDA.

American Resort Development Association. (2003a). *State of the Timeshare Industry: 2003*. Washington, DC: ARDA.

American Resort Development Association. (2004a). *State of the Timeshare and Vacation Ownership Industry: The 2003 Report*. Washington, DC: ARDA.

American Resort Development Association. (2004b). *Financial Performance of the Timeshare Industry*. Washington, DC: ARDA.

Anderson, B.A., Povis, C., & Chappel, S.J. (2002). Coping Strategies in the Performance of Emotional Labour. Council for Australian University Tourism and Hospitality Education: 2002 National Research Conference. Perth: CAUTHE.

Anonymous. (2004). "Wyndham Jumps into Timeshare Franchising." *Lodging Hospitality*, 60, no. 8: 23.

Argenti, P. A. (1998). "Strategic Employee Communications." *Human Resource Management* 37, no. 3–4: 199–206.

Baiman, Gail, & Forbes, Robert. (1992). *Vacation Timesharing: A Real Estate*. Burlington, Ontario: Rapport Publishing.

Balmer, S., & Baum, T. (1993). "Applying Herzberg's Hygiene Factors to the Changing Accommodation Environment." *International Journal of Contemporary Hospitality Management* 5, no. 2, pp. 21–32.

Barbee, C., & Bott, V. (1991). "Customer Treatment as a Mirror of Employee Treatment." *Advanced Management Journal* 5: 27.

Bareham, J. (1995). *Consumer Behaviour in the Food Industry*. Oxford: Butterworth-Heinemann.

Barrett, G. Vincent, & Blair, John. (1988). *How to Conduct and Analyze Real Estate Market and Feasibility Studies*. New York: Van Nostrand Reinhold.

Bateson, J.G. (1985). "Perceived Control and the Service Encounter." In J.A. Czepiel, M.R. Solomon, & C.F. Superanant (eds.), *The Service Encounter*. Boston: Lexington Books.

Baumann, M.A. (2003). "Lenders Adjust to Industry's Specialized Nature." *Hotel, Motel Management* 3: 44.

Berry, L.L. (1995). "Relationship Marketing of Services—Growing Interest, Emerging Perspectives." *Journal of the Academy of Management Science* 23, no.4: 236–245.

Bitner, J. (1990). "Evaluating Service Encounters: The Effects of Physical Surroundings and Employee Responsiveness" *Journal of Marketing* 54 (April): 69–82.

Bitner, J., Booms, B.H., & Tetreault, M.S. (1990). "The Service Encounter: Diagnosing Favourable and Unfavourable Incidents." *Journal of Marketing* 54 (January): 71–84.

Blicher, Bert. (1999). *Financing of Timeshare Resorts*. Unpublished manuscript.

Bratcher, D. (2002). "Travellers and Strangers: "Hospitality" in the Ancient Middle East." The Voice, Christian Resource Institute. http://www.cresourcei.org/travellers.html (January 25, 2003).

Bureau of Economic Analysis. (2005). http://bea.gov, February 19, 2005.

Burlingame, John. (1999 and 2001). Vacation Ownership World, Bothell, WA.

Butler, R. (1980). "The Concept of a Tourist Area Cycle of Evolution: Implications for Management of Resources." *Canadian Geographer* 24: 5–12.

Carn, Rabianski, Racster, & Seldin. (1988). *Real Estate Market Analysis*. Englewood Cliffs, NJ: Prentice-Hall.

Carper, J. (1992). "Strategies for Winning Guests in Competitive Times." *Hotels*, no. 52 (March).

Chopin, J. (1994). "TQM—Let's Get Excited." *Management Services Quarterly* 4, no 6: 44–47.

Coleman, Richard. (1983). "The Continuing Significance of Social Class to Marketing." *Journal of Consumer Research, 8*, no.3: 264–280.

Collins English Dictionary. (1993). Glasgow: HarperCollins.

Conger, J.A., & Kanungo, R.B. (1988). "The Empowerment Process: Integrating Theory and Practice." *Academy of Management Review*, no. 13: 471–482.

Cooper, R., & Sawaf, A. (1997). *Executive EQ*. London: Orion Business.

Cowell, D. (1984). *The Marketing of Services*. London: Heinemann.

Crotts, John, & Ragatz, Richard. (2002). "Recent U.S. Timeshare Purchasers: Who Are They, What Are They Buying and How Can They Be Reached." *International Journal of Hospitality Management* 21, no. 3: 227–238.

Deighton, J. (1994). "Managing Service When Service Is a Performance." In R.T. Rust and R.L. Oliver (eds.), *Service Quality: New Directions in Theory and Practice*. London: Sage.

Eaglen, A., & Lashley, C. (2001). *Benefits and Costs Analysis: The Impact of Training on Hospitality Business Performance*. Leeds: Leeds Metropolitan University.

Eaglen, A., Lashley, C., & Thomas, R. (1999). *Benefits and Costs Analysis: The Impact of Training on Business Performance*. Leeds: Leeds Metropolitan University.

Eaglen, A., Lashley, C., & Thomas, R. (2000). "Modelling the Benefits of Training to Business Performance." *Strategic Change* 9, no. 4: 35–49.

Elwell, W. (ed.) (1996). *Baker's Evangelical Dictionary of Biblical Theology*. Grand Rapids, MI: Baker Books.

Engel, B., Blackwell, R.D., & Miniard, P.W. (1995). *Consumer Behaviour*. London: Dryden Press.

Engel, B., Kollat, K., & Blackwell, R.D. (1968). *Modelling Consumer Decision Making*, London: Dryden Press.

Festinger, L. (1957). *A Theory of Cognitive Dissonance*. Stanford, CA: Stanford University Press.

Fineman, S., ed. (2000). *Emotion in Organizations*. London: Sage.

Fisher, C., & Lovell, A. (2003). *Business Ethics and Values*. London: Prentice-Hall.

Fletcher, John E. (1989). "Input-Output Analysis and Tourism Impact Studies." *Annals of Tourism Research* 16: 514–529.

Florida State Chapter 721: Vacation Plans and Timesharing, Part II. Chapter 721.11—http://www.flsenate.gov/Statutes/index.cfm?App_mode=Display_Statute&Search_String=&URL=Ch0721/SEC11.HTM&Title=-> 2004->Ch0721->Section%2011#0721.11

Florida State Chapter 720: Homeowners Associations. http://www.flsenate.gov/Statutes/index.cfm?App_mode=Display_Statute&URL=Ch0720/titl0720.htm&StatuteYear=2004&Title=%2D%3E2004%2D%3EChapter%20720.

Florida State Chapter 721: Vacation and Timeshare Plans, http://www.flsenate.gov/Statutes/index.cfm?App_mode=Display_Statute&URL=Ch0721/titl0721.htm&StatuteYear=2004&Title=%2D%3E2004%2D%3EChapter%20721

Fox, A. (1974). *Beyond Contract: Work, Power and Trust Relations*. London: Faber & Faber.

Foxall, G.R. (1992). "The Behavioural Perspective of Purchase and Consumption." *Journal of the Academy of Marketing Science* 20, no. 2: 189–198.

Francese, Peter. (2001). "The Coming Boom in Second-Home Ownership." *American Demographics* 10: 26–27.

Frechtling, Douglas C. (1994). "*Assessing the Impacts of Travel and Tourism – Measuring Economic Benefits*." In J.R.B. Ritchie and C.R. Goeldner (eds.), *Travel, Tourism, and Hospitality Research, A Handbook for Managers and Researchers*. New York: John Wiley, pp. 367–391.

Frechtling, Douglas, & Horvath, Endre. (1999). "Estimating the Multiplier Effects of Tourism Expenditures on Local Economy through a Regional Input-Output Model." *Journal of Travel Research* 37, no. 4: 324–329.

Friedman, M. (1970). "The Social Responsibility of Business Is to Increase Its Profits." *New York Times Magazine*, September 13, pp. 33, 122–26.

Gentry, R.A., Mandoki, P., & Rush, R. (1999). *Resort Condominium and Vacation Ownership Management: A Hospitality Perspective*. American Hotel Motel Association.

Gibb, Kenneth, & Hoslei, Martin. (2003). "Development in Urban Housing and Property Markets." 40, no. 5/6: 887–896.

Gilkeson, J. (2005). "Hypothecation, Sales of Receivables and Securitization." In A. Pizam, *International Encyclopedia of Hospitality Management*, London: Elsevier, pp. 615–616.

Goleman, D. (1998). *Working with Emotional Intelligence*, London: Bloomsbury.

Gose, Joe. (2003). "Capitalizing on Timeshares." *National Real Estate Investor*, March 1, 2003, pp. 1–2.

Gronroos, C. (1984). *Strategic Management and Marketing in the Service Sector*. Bromley: Chartwell-Bratt.

Gronroos, C. (1994). "From Marketing Mix to Relationship Marketing" *Management Decisions*.

Gruber, Kurt. (1999a). What Is Timesharing? Unpublished manuscript. Orlando, FL: Island One Resorts.

Gruber, Kurt. (1999b). Timeshare Glossary. Unpublished manuscript.

Gummeson, E. (1999). *Total Relationship Marketing*, Oxford: Butterworth-Heinemann.

Gunter, B., & Furnham, A. (1992). *Consumer Profiles: An Introduction to Psychographics*. New York: Routledge.

Haber, H., Leach, A., Schudy, S. & Sideleau, B. (1982). *Comprehensive Psychiatric Nursing*, 2nd ed. New York: McGraw-Hill.

Harris, A. (1991). "The Customer's Always Right." *Black Enterprise* 21, no. 11, pp. 3–7.

Hawkins, D.I., Best, R.J., & Coney, K.A. (1998). *Consumer Behavior: Building Marketing Strategy*, 7th ed. Burr Ridge, IL: Irwin/McGraw-Hill.

Hawks, John W. (1991). *American Demographics* 13, no. 5: 46–50.

Hendry, J. (2004). *Between Enterprise and Ethics: Business and Management in a Bimoral Society*. Oxford: Oxford University Press.

Herz, Robert. (2003). Accounting for Real Estate Time-Share Transaction. Memorandum. http://www.arda.org/aicpa2/hertz_letter.htm, November 2003.

Herzberg, F. (1966). *Work and the Nature of Man*. New York: Staple Press.

Heskett, James (1997). The service profit chain: How leading companies link profit and growth to loyalty, satisfaction, and value. New York: Free Press.

Heskett, S.H., Sasser, W.E., & Hart, C.W. (1990). *Service Breakthroughs: Changing the Rules of the Game*. New York: Free Press.

Heslin, P.A. (1999). "Boosting Empowerment by Developing Self Efficacy." *Asian Pacific Journal of Human Resource Management*, 37, no. 1: 52–65.

Higher Education Funding Council for England (HEFCE). (1998). *Review of Hospitality Management*. London: HEFCE.

Hochschild, A.R. (2003). *The Managed Heart: Commercialization of Human Feeling*. Berkeley: University of California Press.

Hubrecht, J. & Teare, R. (1993). "A Strategy for Partnership in Total Quality Service," *International Journal of Contemporary Hospitality Management*. Vol. 5, No. 3.

Interval International. (2001). *2001 U.S. Membership Profile*. Miami, FL: Interval International.

Johns, N. (1993). "Quality Management in the Hospitality Industry: Part 3. Recent Developments." *International Journal of Contemporary Hospitality Management* 5, no. 1: 10–15.

Johnson, P.R. (1993). "Empowerment in the Global Economy." *Empowerment in Organisations* 1, no. 1: 13–18.

Kaynak, E., & Kara, A. (1996b). "Consumer Life-style and Ethnocentrism: A Comparative Study in Kyrgyzstan and Azarbaijan." 49th Esomar Congress Proceedings, Istanbul, pp. 577–596.

Koberg, C.S. Boss, R.W., Senjem, J. S., & Goodman, E. A. (1999). "Antecedents and Outcomes of Empowerment: Empirical Evidence from the Healthcare Industry." *Group and Organization Management* 24, no. 1: 71–92.

Kotler, Philip. (1999). *Kotler on Marketing: How to Create, Win, and Dominate Markets*. New York: Free Press.

Kotler, Philip. (2003). *A Framework for Marketing Management*. Englewood Cliffs, NJ: Prentice Hall.

Langhorn, S. (2004). *The Role of Emotion in Service Encounters*. DBA Thesis. Luton: University of Luton.

Lashley, C. (2000). "Towards a Theoretical Framework." In C. Lashley & A. Morrison (eds.), *In Search of Hospitality: Theoretical Perspectives and Debates*. Oxford: Butterworth-Heinemann.

Lashley, C. (2000a). *Hospitality Retail Management: A Unit Manager's Guide*. Oxford: Butterworth-Heinemann.

Lashley, C. (2000b). "Empowerment Through Involvement: A Case Study of TGI Friday's Restaurants." *Personnel Review* 29, no. 5/6: 791–815.

Lashley, C. (2001). *Empowerment: HR Strategies for Service Excellence*. Oxford: Butterworth-Heinemann.

Lashley, C. (2004). "Rhetorics and Realities in Hospitality and Tourism Employment Practice: Observations from Some Recent Research Projects." *Tourism: State of the Art Conference Proceedings*. Glasgow: University of Strathclyde.

Lashley, C., & Best, W. (2001). "Induction in Licensed Retailing." *International Journal of Contemporary Hospitality Management* 14, no 1: 15–28.

Lashley, C., & Lee-Ross, D. (2003). *Organisational Behaviour in Leisure Services*. Oxford: Butterworth-Heinemann.

Lashley, C., & Lincoln, G. (2002). *Business Development in Licensed Retailing: A Unit Manager's Guide*. Oxford: Butterworth-Heinemann.

Lashley, C., & Morrison, A. (eds.). (2000). *In Search of Hospitality: Theoretical Perspectives and Debates*. Oxford: Butterworth-Heinemann.

Lashley, C., & Morrison, A. (2003). "Hospitality as Commercial Friendship." *Hospitality Review* 5, no. 4: 31–36.

Lashley, C., Morrison, A., & Randall, S. (2004). "More Than a Service Encounter? Insights into the Emotions of Hospitality Through Special Meal Occasions." *Journal of Hospitality and Tourism Management* 11, no. 2: 26–38.

Lashley, C., & Rowson, W. (2000). "Wasted Millions: Staff Turnover in Licensed Retail Organisations." In A. Williams, (ed.), Ninth Annual Hospitality Research Conference Proceedings, Huddersfield: University of Huddersfield.

Lashley, C., Thomas, R., & Rowson, B. (2002). *Employment Practices and Skill Shortages in Greater Manchester's Tourism Sector*. Leeds: Leeds Metropolitan University.

Leach, P. (1995). "The Importance of Positive Customer Service to Ansell's." *Managing Service Quality* 5, no. 4: 31–34.

Leidner, R. (1994). "Fast Food, Fast Talk: Service Work and the Routinization of Everyday Life." *The American Journal of Sociology*, 99, no. 6: 1663–1664.

Levitt, T. (1972). "Production Line Approach to Service." *Harvard Business Review* (September–October): 41–52.

Lovelock, C. (1981). "Why Marketing Needs to Be Different for Service." In J.H. Donnelly & W.R. George (eds.), *Marketing of Services*. Chicago: American Marketing Association.

Lovelock, Christopher. (1996). *Services Marketing*. Englewood Cliffs, NJ: Prentice Hall.

Lovelock, Christopher, & Wright, Lauren. (1999). *Principles of Service Marketing and Management*. Englewood Cliffs, NJ: Prentice Hall.

Lynch, P. (2005) "Reflections On the Home Setting in Hospitality." *Journal of Hospitality and Toursim Management*, Vol. 12, no. 1: 37–49.

Mann, S. (1998). *Psychology Goes to Work*. Oxford: Purple House.

Mann, S. (1999). *Hiding What We Feel, Faking What We Don't: Understanding the Role of Emotions at Work*. Shaftesbury: Element.

Manning, Gerald, & Reece, Barry. (2001). *Selling Today—Building Quality Partnerships*. Englewood Cliffs, NJ: Prentice-Hall.

Maslow, A.H. (1954). *Motivation and Personality*. New York: Harper.

McDermid, K. (1992). "Those in Favour of BS5750." *Hospitality* (March): 14–15.

McMahan, J. (1989). *Property Management*. St. Louis, MO: McGraw-Hill.

McMahan, John. (1989). *Property Development*. New York: McGraw-Hill.

McMullen, Edwin, & Crawford-Welch, Simon. (1999). "Looking into the Crystal Ball: Vacation Ownership 2000." *Timeshare and Vacation Interval Ownership Review* 2, no. 1: 82–91.

McMullen, Zanini, Fugleberg, and Donovan (2000). "State-of-the-Art Unit Design Means Affordable Ambience" *Developments Magazine*, American Resort Development Association.

Molinell, Harold. (1991). *Wanted Timeshare Bandits*. Carbondale, IL: Timeshare Posse Publishing.

Moon, C., & Bonny, C. (2001). *Business Ethics: Facing Up to the Issues*. London: Economist Books.

Mudie, L., & Cottam, J. (1999). "Empowering the Front Line." *Participation and Empowerment: An International Journal,* 7, no. 8.

Mullins, L. (2002). *Management and Organizational Behaviour*. London: Pitman Financial Times.

O'Mara, Paul. (1978). *Residential Development Handbook*. Washington, DC: Urban Land Institute.

O'Mahony, B. (2003). "Home and Hospitality in Australia." *The Hospitality Review*, 5, no. 4: 37–41.

Palmer, A. (2001). *Principles of Services Marketing*. London: McGraw-Hill.

Pannell Kerr Forster Associates. (1992). "PFKA Column." *International Journal of Contemporary Hospitality Management* 4, no. 2: i–vi.

Parasuraman, A., Berry, L.L., & Zeithaml, V.A. (1991). "Understanding Customer Expectations of Service." *Sloan Management Review* 32, no. 3: 39–48.

Parson, S.G. (1995). "Empowering Employees—Back to the Future at Novotel." *Managing Service Quality* 5, no. 4: 16–21.

Plouff, Kathryn (2001). "Static Pool Analysis." *Developments*. Washington, DC: American Resort Development Association, pp. 20–23.

Potterfield, T.A. (1999). *The Business of Empowerment: Democracy and Ideology in the Workplace*. Westport, CT: Quorum Books.

Pryce, Adrian. (1999). *Timeshare: Coming of Age*. Travel and Tourism Intelligence, UK.

Pryce, Adrian. (2002). "Timeshare Industry Structure and Competitive Analysis." *International Journal of Hospitality Management*, 21, no. 3: 267–275.

Putnam, L.L., & Mumby, D.K. (1993). "Organizations, Emotions and the Myth of Rationality." In S. Fineman (ed.), *Emotion in Organizations*. London: Sage.

Rafiq, M., & Ahmed, P.K. (1993). "The Scope of Internal Marketing: Defining the Boundary Between Marketing and Human Resource Management." *Journal of Marketing Management* 9: 219–232.

Ragatz & Associates. (2003a). *Resort Timesharing in the United States*. Eugene, OR: RCI.

Ratajczak, Donald. (2005). "A Look Ahead at the Economy and Investments, 2005–2015." *Journal of Financial Service Professionals* 59, no. 1: 37–43.

Rezak, Stephanie. (2002). "Consumer Research Sheds Light on All Aspects of Resort Timesharing Business." *International Journal of Hospitality Management* 21, no. 3: 245–255.

Ritzer, G. (1993). *The McDonaldization of Society*. London: Pine Forge Press.

Ritzer, G. (2000). *The McDonaldization of Society*. London: Pine Forge Press.

Ritzer, G. (2002). *McDonaldization: The Reader*. London: Pine Forge Press.

Ritzer, G. (2004). "The Inhospitable Hospitality Industry." *Hospitality Review* 6, no. 3: 40–46.

Rodwell, J.J., Kienzie, R., & Shadur, M.A. (1998). "The Relationships among Work-related Perceptions, Employee Attitudes and Employee Performance: The Integral Role of Communication." *Human Resource Management* 37, no. 3–4: 277–293.

Rust, R.T., & Oliver, R.L. (1994). *Service Quality: New Directions in Theory and Practice*. London: Sage.

Sellers, P. (1990). "What Customers Really Want." *Fortune* 121, no. 13.

Senge, P.M. (2003). *The Fifth Discipline: The Art and Practices of the Learning Organisation*. New York: Currency Doubleday.

Sherles Tracy and Marmorstone, James (1994). "How successful point systems begin: careful program design and point valuation," *Resort Development and Operations*, April, p. 32–35.

Sherles, T. and Lennon, M. (2004). Shell Vacations Systems to be offered in Second Quarter: Becomes one of the first US companies to franchise its points-based product. Shell Vacations, http://www.shellvacationsclub.com/shownews.html?id=102, Retrieved April 23, 2004.

Smeral, Egon. (2003). "A Structural View of Tourism Growth." *Tourism Economics* 9, no. 1: 77–93.

Sohn, Sung. (2005). "Sustainable Growth Ahead." *American Banking Association: Banking Journal* 97, no. 1: 68.

Sorrell, T., & Hendry, J. (1996). *Business Ethics*. Oxford: Butterworth-Heinemann.

Spaulding, Art. (2004). Financing Timeshare Vacation Clubs. http://www.hotelinteractive.com/news/articleView.asp?articleID=2783, February 11, 2004.

Statt, D.A. (1997) *Understanding the Consumer*. London: Macmillan.

Suchman, Diane. (1999). *Developing Timeshare and Vacation Ownership Properties*. Washington, DC: Urban Land Institute.

Suprenant, C.F., & Solomon, M.R. (1987). "Predictability and Personalization in the Service Encounter." *Journal of Marketing* 51 (April): 86–96.

Sweeney, M. (2003). *An Investigation into Customer Perceptions of Timeshare Product*. Unpublished B.A. (Hons) dissertation, Edinburgh: Queen Margaret's University College.

Taylor, F.W. (1947). *Scientific Management*. New York: Harper & Row.

Teare, R. (1995). *Services Management*. London: Cassell.

Telfer, E. (2000). "The Philosophy of Hospitality." In C. Lashley & A. Morrison (eds.), *In Search of Hospitality: Theoretical Perspectives and Debates*. Oxford: Butterworth-Heinemann.

Trevino, L.K., & Nelson, K.A. (1999). *Managing Business Ethics: Straight Talk about How to Do It Right*. New York: John Wiley & Sons.

TRI Consulting. (2001). *The European Timeshare Industry*. London: Organisation of European Timeshare.

Trowbridge, Keith. (1981). *Resort Timesharing*. New York: Simon & Schuster.

Tuckman, A. (1995). "Ideology, Quality and TQM." In A. Wilkinson and H. Willmott (eds.), *Making Quality Critical: New Perspectives on Organizational Change*. London: Routledge.

Upchurch, R. (2005). "A Case Study into Vacation Clubs." *Tourism Analysis*, forthcoming.

Upchurch, R. (2004). Hilton Grand Vacations: 2004 Annual Member Survey. Hilton Grand Vacations: Orlando, Florida.

Upchurch, R. (2003). Hilton Grand Vacations: 2003 Annual Member Survey. Hilton Grand Vacations: Orlando, Florida.

Upchurch, R. (2002). "Product Design Evolution in the Vacation Ownership Industry: From Fixed Points to Vacation Clubs." *Journal of Leisure Property* 2, no. 3: 239.

Upchurch, R., & Gruber, K. (2002). "The Evolution of a Sleeping Giant: Resort Timesharing." *International Journal of Hospitality Management* 21, no. 3: 211–225.

Upchurch, R. (2002). "Product Design Evolution in the Vacation Ownership Industry: From Fixed points to Vacation Clubs." *Journal of Leisure Property* 2, no. 3: 239.

Urban Land Institute. (1987). *Mixed-Use Development Handbook*. Washington, DC: Urban Land Institute.

U.S. Government Equal Credit Opportunity Law. http://www.ftc.gov/bcp/conline/pubs/credit/ecoa.htm

U.S. Government Fair Credit Reporting Law. http://www.ftc.gov/os/statutes/fcra.htm

U.S. Government Fair Debt Collection Procedures Act. http://www.ftc.gov/os/statutes/fdcpa/fdcpact.htm

U.S. Government RESPA. http://www.hud.gov/offices/hsg/sfh/res/respa_hm.cfm

Vacation Ownership World. January 2000, Bothell, WA.

Vacation Ownership World. January 2003. Bothell, WA.

Vacation Ownership World. January 2004. Bothell, WA.

Walton, J.K. (2000). *The British Seaside: Holidays and Resorts in the Twentieth Century*. Manchester: Manchester University Press.

Warde, A., & Martens, L. (2000). *Eating Out: Social Differentiation, Consumption and Pleasure*. Cambridge: Cambridge University Press.

Weinstein, W. (1994). *Market Segmentation: Using Demographics, Psychographics, and Other Niche Marketing Techniques to Predict and Model Customer Behavior*. Chicago: Probus Publishing Company.

Wells, W., & Tigert, D. (1977). "Activities, Interests, and Opinions." *Journal of Advertising Research* 11, no. 4: 27–35.

White, T., & Gerstner, L. (1991). *Club Operations and Management*. New York: Van Nostrand Reinhold.

Wilkie, W.L. (1994). *Consumer Behaviour*. London: John Wiley & Sons.

Williams, A. (2002). *Understanding the Hospitality Consumer*. Oxford: Butterworth-Heinemann.

Wood, R.C. (1992). *Working in Hotels and Catering*. London: Routledge.

Woods, Robert. (2002). "Compensation Study on the Timeshare Industry." Unpublished manuscript.

World Bank. (2000). *World Development Indicators*. Washington, DC: World Bank.

World Book. (1994). *The World Book Encyclopedia*. Chicago: World Book.

Zeithaml, V.A., Berry, L.L., & Parasuraman, A. (1993). "The Nature and Determinants of Customer Expectations of Service." *Journal of the Academy of Marketing Science* 21, no. 1: 1–12.

INDEX

Acceptance of timeshare product, sustained, 21–22
Accessibility factor, 33, 108
Accommodation market history, 61–63
Activity occasions, 106
Affinity marketing, 139
After-sales contacts, 145–146, 147
Ages of typical timeshare owner, 64, 78, 101, 102
Aggregated strategy, 284
American Hotel and Motel Association, 26
American Resort Development Association
on age and income of timeshare owners, 101, 152
Developments published by, 18
codes issued by, 261
on double-digit growth, 19, 22
establishment of, 21
ethical business practice and, viii, 253, 262, 270, 271
Financial Performance Study (2002 and 2004) by, 20, 154, 155, 293
on growth of timeshare industry, 78–79, 276
on harming guests, 260
on honesty, 258–259
hospitality management code, 199, 201
membership in, 253, 257
reciprocity and, 257
reports of, 60
on sales and marketing costs, 19
sales pyramid of, 141
Standards of Practice in Professional Hospitality Management by, 198, 260
state of the industry reports by, 38, 91
Timeshare Industry Resource Manual by, 18
on trial close stage, 143
on United States selling to non-U.S. citizens, 102
United States states and timeshare industry according to, 15

Annual percentage rate (APR), 168
ARDA. *See* American Resort
    Development Association
Asset-backed securities (ABS), 54–55
Asset relationships, 263–264
Automobile versus timeshare
    financing, 161

Balanced scorecard approach, 134,
    229, 234, 236, 237, 249
Behaviorism, 113
Benchmark factor, 36–39, 134, 239
Benefits, tangible and intangible,
    200–201
Best practice framework, 267
Boston Consulting Group (BCG)
    matrix. *See* SWOT analysis and
    BCG analysis, conducting
Branding, 22, 23
Bullying, 259–260
Bureau of Economic Analysis (BEA)
    on tourism-related employment,
    81, 82, 84
Business ethics and ethical practice,
    251–274
    asset relationships, 263–264
    association codes, 270–273
    best practice framework, 267
    bullying, 259–260
    cheating, 259
    code development, 252, 267
    conclusions about, 273–274
    discrimination, 270
    education, 267
    external review, 267
    factors affecting, 262–263
    fairness, 257–258
    feedback gathering and analysis, 267
    functional responsibility, 267
    harming, 260–261
    ingredients for success, key, 265–268
    introduction, 252–253

    issues, key, 253–262
    issues and timeshare management,
        268–273
    legal framework, 268–270
    legal versus illegal actions, 254–255
    lying, 258–259
    managing, 262–268
    mapping ethics and morality, 256
    mission statement, 267
    morality versus ethics, 253–254, 261
    performance reviews and
        standards, 267
    programs for, 265
    reciprocity and fair play, 257
    self-regulation, 252
    social development and caring, 256
    social responsibility and
        supporting, 256–257
    test for, quick, 261
    training programs, 266, 267
    Value Dynamics model, 263–264
    whistle-blowing, 266
Butler's product life cycle theory
    applying to timeshare industry, 18
    applying to timesharing, 15–18
    consolidation stage, 17
    decline phase, 17–18
    description of, 24
    development stage, 16–17
    diagram, 15
    exploration stage, 15–16
    growth phase, 16–17, 19
    involvement stage, 16
    stages, 14
    stagnation stage, 17

Canal boat timeshare, 103
Capital factor, 46–49
    cash flow level need,
        determining, 48
    operating costs estimate, 47–48
    pro-forma analysis, 47–49

Cheating, 259
Cohorts definitions, 118–123
Collection for consumer
    nonpayment, 163–164
Common Interest Realty Association
    (CIRA), 244–245
Community relationships, 264
Condominium-style
    accommodations, 29
Consolidation stage, 17
Construction loans, 50
Consumer accounting, 30
Consumer behavior and markets.
    See Markets and consumer
    behavior
Consumer decision making,
    108–116. 117
  alternative evaluation, 110
  behaviorism, 113
  brand perceptions, 116
  classic conditioning techniques, 113
  cognitive school of learning theory,
    113–114
  consumption and outcomes,
    110–111
  cooling-off period, 111
  EKB model, 108–109
  information search, 110
  motivation and need, 108, 109,
    112–113
  operant conditioning techniques, 113
  personality, 114
  reference groups, 116
  self-concepts, 114–115
  stages, 109, 111
Consumer-driven design influences,
    11–13
Consumer end-loans sales, 51–53, 54
Consumer finance, 149–170
  annual percentage rate, 168
  automobile versus timeshare, 161
  collection for nonpayment,
    163–164, 166–167

conclusions about, 169–170
developers recourse, 163–164
down payments, 153
end-loan financing, 51–53, 54,
    152, 155
flow of money, 154–155
in-house financing, 153
introduction, 150–151
loan assistance, 160–161
loan profile, consumer, 153
note receivable financing, 161
onsite financing, 153, 160, 164
overview, 151–154
point of sale financing, 153,
    160, 161
promissory notes, 161
protection legislation, 164–169;
    see also Consumer protection
    legislation
rescission laws, 161–163, 170
sales transaction, 156–159; see also
    Sales transaction
Settlement Costs booklet, 168
Consumer protection legislation,
    164–169
  Equal Credit Opportunity Act, 165
  ethical issues and, 269
  Fair Credit Reporting Act, 165–166
  Fair Debt Collection Practices Act,
    166–167
  Federal Consumer Credit
    Protection Act, 167–168
  real estate actions and, 156
  Real Estate Settlement Procedures
    Act, 168–169
  what a creditor cannot do, 165
Consumer receivables, 30
Cooling-off period, 111, 137, 143, 145,
    228, 270, 271
Customer loyalty and relationship
    marketing, 127–136; see also
    Relationship marketing and
    customer loyalty

Deeded interests, 6, 7
Demand factor, 39–41
Demographic factor, 63–65
Demographic segmentation,
  97–98, 100
  cohorts definition, 118–123
  cohorts recent timeshare purchase
    charts, 289
  current industry practices, 288–291
  Looking Glass Cohorts, 288–291
  PRIZM, 295–298
  projection models, 287–291
Design features development
    factor, 72
Design shifts and development, 10–13
  consumer-driven influences, 11–13
  industry standards, evolution of, 13
Destination factor, 31–32
Developer role, 29–31
Developer sales price per interval,
    average, 152
Development and financing, 25–57
  conclusions about, 56–57
  factors in development, 31–49; see
    also Models of resort
    development, proven
  funding resort project, 49–55; see
    also Funding resort project
  introduction, 26–27
  location importance, 31–32
  product evolution, 27–29
  proven models of development,
    31–49; see also Models of resort
    development, proven
  role of developer, 29–31
  site selection considerations, 34
  specialization areas for developer,
    29–30
  studies undertaken for
    feasibility, 36
Development stage, 16–17
DINKIES. See Double income no kids
Direct mail, 138

Disney's entry into timeshare, 9, 13,
  23, 26, 27, 294
Disney's vacation club, 4–5
Double income no kids, 98

Economic factor, 41–42
Economic impact studies, 37
Economy level of timeshare, 20
Effort reward bargain, 193
EKB. See Engel, Kollat, and Blackwell
  model of consumer decision
  making
Emotional dimensions of timeshare
  service, 173–180, 194–195, 236
Emotional Intelligence Quotient,
  179, 189
Employee empowerment, 173,
  180–184, 220, 221, 225
Employees and building customer
  loyalty, 132–133
Employees and customer satisfaction,
  209–217
Employment at timeshare resorts. See
  Human resources managing in
  timeshare operations
End loan financing, 51–53, 54, 152, 155
Engel, Kollat, and Blackwell model of
  consumer decision making,
  108–111
Entertainment programs, 146
Environmental factor, 33–35
Equal Credit Opportunity Act, 165
Escrow account, 156–157
Ethics. See Business ethics and ethical
  practice
European settings, 107
Evolution of timeshare industry, 1–24
  conclusions about, 23–24
  design shifts and developments,
    10–13
  first appearance of, 2, 7–8
  growth phase, 19–23

history, short, 2–7
industry standards, 13
introduction, 2
law, first, 8
legal forms of conveyance, basic, 5–7
macro view of industry's growth
    cycle, 7–10
product evolution, 27–29
product life cycle and timeshare
    product, 14–23
product registration, 3–5
profile of timeshare resorts, 10
public trading on stock market
    start, 9
vacation club points system, 4–5
Exploration stage, 15–16
Extrinsic rewards, 193

Factoring receivables, 53
Factors in development. See Models
    of resort development, proven
Fair Credit Reporting Act, 165–166
Fair Debt Collection Practices Act,
    166–167
Fairness, 257–258
Family holiday occasions, 106–107
Feasibility factor, 35–36, 75
Federal Consumer Credit Protection
    Act (1968), 167–168
Federal (U.S.) regulatory issues,
    43, 44
Festinger's theory of cognitive
    dissonance, Leon, 162
Financial impact studies, 37
Financial investment model
    hypothecation, 53–54
    sale of consumer end-loans, 51–53
    securitization, 54–55
Financial management knowledge
    needed by developer, 29–30
Financing, consumer. See Consumer
    finance

First appearance of timeshare resort,
    2, 7–8
Float week offering, 4
Fractional timeshare resorts, 28
Francese on second-home market,
    Peter, 77–78
Franchising agreements, 294
Funding resort project, 49–55
    asset-backed securities, 54, 55
    construction loans, 50
    consumer end-loans sale, 51–53, 54
    development loans, 50
    hypothecation, 53–54, 291–292
    mortgage-backed securities, 55
    multisource funding, 50
    preopening loan models, 50–51
    securitization, 30, 37, 51, 54–55,
        292, 293
    single-source loan, 50
    working-capital sources, 51
Future of timesharing, 275–298
    advantage, practical elements of
        competitive, 286–287
    aggregate strategy, 284
    cash cow market, 281–282
    conclusions about, 295
    current industry practices, 288–291
    demographic projection models,
        strategic application of,
        287–291; see also Demographic
        segmentation
    developer investment projections,
        291–293
    external analysis, 279–280
    franchising agreements, 294
    growth strategy, 283, 285–286
    internal analysis, 278–279
    introduction, 276–277
    market development, 285
    market penetration, 286
    niche marketing, 286
    PRIZM, 295–298
    product development, 285

Future of timesharing (*Continued*)
product differentiation, 285–286
resort life-cycle theory, 293–294
retrenchment strategy, 284
stability strategy, 283–284
strategic approaches, general,
283–284
SWOT and BCG analysis,
conducting, 277–283; *see also*
SWOT and BCG analysis,
conducting

Gender and market segmentation,
98–99
Geographical segmentation, 99
Growth cycle, macro view of
timeshare industry's, 7–10
Growth phase
acceptance of timeshare product,
sustained, 21–22
of Butler's product life cycle
theory, 16–17, 19
industry volume and growth,
sustained, 22–23, 78–79
marketing tactic refinement, 19
product design advances, 20–21
Growth strategy, 283

Harming and business ethics,
260–261
Hilton
employee empowerment
and, 181
entry into timeshare, 9, 13, 23,
26, 27
franchising and, 294
growth phase and, 294
History of timeshare, short, 2–7
Holiday packs, 103
Home from home occasions, 104–105,
108, 110, 112, 115, 126, 133

Home owners associations and
stakeholder management,
227–250; *see also* Stakeholders
balanced scorecard measures, 234,
236, 237, 249
benefit, 240
budget, 244
conclusions about, 249–250
definition of stakeholder, 230
developers knowledge of, 30
duties and responsibilities per
regulation, 246
duties of association, 243–244
duty of care, 241–242
duty of loyalty, 242
duty of obedience, 242
election board members, 242–243
Florida laws, 244, 245
focus groups, 239
image of developer and, 248
introduction, 228–229
legislative provisions and home
owners association, 241
levels of management, 247
maintenance fees, 240, 243
mission statements, 242
overview of home owners
associations, 240–249
owner committees, 239–240
responsibilities, 243
setting up, 234
stakeholders in timeshare
organizations, 229–237
techniques, 237–240
tensions in interactions, 234–237
utilities and, 74
Home ownership versus
timeshare, 40
Hotel versus timeshare
consumer, 40
Human resources managing in
timeshare operations, 171–195
appraisal systems, 192–193

attracting recruits, 186–189
case study, 190–191
concerns about, 184
conclusions about, 194–195
designing and defining job,
185–186
effort reward bargain, 193
emotional deviance, 178
emotional dimensions of service,
173–180, 194–195, 236
emotional dissonance, 178
emotional harmony, 178
emotional intelligence, 172,
179–180
empowering service excellence,
173, 180–184
extrinsic rewards, 193
functionally flexible workforce,
185–186
induction and employment,
191–194
interviewing process, 189–190
intrinsic rewards, 193–194
introduction, 172–173
job description, 186
job enlargement, 185
job enrichment, 185
job rotation, 185–186
managerial meanings of
empowerment, 181–182
managing as though people
mattered, 184–194
motivational empowerment,
181, 182
relational empowerment, 181
rewards, 193–194
selection process, 189–190
staff specification, 186, 188
training importance, 192
Hyatt and timeshare, 13, 23,
26, 294
Hypothecation, 30, 37, 51, 53–54,
291–292

Income of typical timeshare owner, 101
Industry standards, evolution of, 13
Information search, 110
Input-output models, applying,
85–86
Interval International (II)
affiliation with other resort
operators, 105–106
owner satisfaction surveys
and, 38
publications of, 18
rating system, 13
Intrinsic rewards, 193–194
Intrinsic value of location, 70
Involvement stage, 16
ISO 9000, 218

Labor factor, 44–45
Land usage classifications, 65
Land value factor, 35
Law; see also Consumer protection
legislation
discrimination, 270
ethical issues and legal framework,
268–270
first timeshare, 8, 62
home owners associations and,
244, 245–246
knowledge needed by developer,
29
regulatory, 42–44, 62
rescission, 161–163, 170, 228,
260, 270
Truth-in-Lending Law, 167–168
Leasehold agreements, 6
Legal forms of conveyance,
basic, 5–7
Life-cycle segmentation, 98
Lifestyle factor, 75–78
Loan assistance, 160–161
Loans. See Consumer finance;
Funding resort project

Location(s)
  analysis, 71
  heaviest concentration in United
      States, 91–92
  quotients (LQs), 82
  worldwide, 93, 102
Location importance, 31–32, 69–70
  intrinsic, 70
  in marketing mix, 96
  relative, 70
Looking Glass Cohorts, 288–291
Luxury market, 20
Lying, 258–259

Maintenance
  building relationships and, 131
  fees, 74
Managing service quality in
    timeshare. *See* Service quality,
    managing
Market condition factor, immediate,
    45–46
Market development, 285
Market expansion, national and
    international, 91–95
  acceptance by market, 95
  locations, 91–92, 93
  resort distribution in United States
      timeshare market, 92
  sales figures, United States, 92,
      93–94
  sales volumes, 94
  United States versus worldwide
      sales performance, 92, 93–95
  weeks owned worldwide, 94
  worldwide locations, 93
Market penetration, 286
Market segmentation, 95–108
  activity occasions, 106
  definition, 101
  demographic characteristics, 97, 100
  extravert/introvert, 99–100

family holiday occasions, 106–107
gender, 98–99
geographical, 99
home for home occasion, 104–105
leads, 95
life-cycle, 98
lifestyle choices, 99
Looking Glass Cohorts, 288–291
occasionality in timeshare markets.
    See Occasionality in timeshare
    markets
ownership, timeshare, 101–103
premises, 96
reason for, 116–117
services marketing mix table, 96
services mix table, 96
strategies, 287–291
swappers occasions, 105–106
Marketing mix, timeshare services,
    96, 97
Marketing plan importance,
    276–277
Marketing relationship. *See*
    Relationship marketing, selling,
    and beyond
Marketing tactic refinement, 19
Markets and consumer behavior,
    89–123
  cohorts definitions, 118–123
  conclusions about, 116–117
  decision making, consumer,
      108–116; *see also* Consumer
      decision making
  introduction, 90
  locations, 91–92, 93, 96
  national and international
      expansion, 91–95; *see also*
      Market expansion, national
      and international
  number of units, average, 91
  promotion, 96
  segmentation, 95–108; *see also*
      Market segmentation

Marriott Vacation Club International
(MVCI), 22
Marriott
employee empowerment and, 181
entry into timeshare, 9, 13, 23,
26, 294
franchising and, 294
purchase of American Resorts, 27
revenue gains and earnings, 155
standardization of offer, 202
McDonaldization of job skills, 185, 236
McMullen and Crawford-Welch
classification system, 20
Mission statement, 242, 267
Mixed-use timeshare resorts, 28
Models of resort development,
proven, 31–49
accessibility factor, 33
benchmark factor, 36–39
capital factor, 46–49
demand factor, 39–41
destination factor, 31–32
economic factor, 41–42
environmental factor, 33–35
feasibility factor, 35–36
immediate market condition
factor, 45–46
labor factor, 44–45
land value factor, 35
price factor, 41
proximity factor, 32
regulatory factor, 42–44
site selection considerations, 34
Money flow within timeshare
organization, 154–155
Mortgage-back securities, 54
Motivation and need to buy, 108, 109,
112–113
Multiplier effect factor, 78–84
Bureau of Economic Analysis and,
81, 82
calculating, 80
direct output indicators, 80

indirect benefits, 80
induced effect, 80
location quotients, 81
regional-input-output modeling
system and, 81–82, 83
study components, 85
Multisource funding, 50

National Timeshare Council on
ethics, 252
Need and motivation to buy, 108, 109,
112–113
Niche marketing, 286
Nondisturbance clause, 157
Nonperformance protection
clause, 157
North American Industrial
Classification System (NAICS)
importance, 82–84
Notes receivable financing, 161
Number of units in average
timeshare resort, 91

Occasionality in timeshare markets,
97, 103–107
activity occasions, 106
family holiday occasions, 106–107
home from home occasions,
104–105, 108, 110, 112, 115, 126
motives for buying and, 108
swapper occasions, 105–106, 110,
115, 126
Occupancy levels, 130
Off-premises contacts (OPCs),
137–138, 139
Operating costs estimate, 47–48
Organization Timeshare Europe
(OTE)
codes issued by, 261
ethical business practices and, viii,
252, 253, 262

Organization Timeshare Europe
  (OTE) (*Continued*)
  on growth of timeshare industry,
    276
  membership in, 253
  reciprocity and, 257
Organizational structure and
  developer, 29
Orlando, Florida drawing power, 70
Owner satisfaction surveys, 38, 151
Owners (1990–2003), number of, 22
Ownership, timeshare, 101–103

Parking factor, 73
Phasing in timeshare units, 91
Physical features development
  factors, 72
Point clubs, 106
Potential Rating Index for Zip
  Markets, 295–298
Preopening load models, 50–51
Price definition, 96
Price factor, 41
Price per interval, average developer
  sales, 152
Prices, weekly, 20–21
Private residence clubs, 28
PRIZM. *See* Potential Rating Index
  for Zip Markets
Pro forma analysis, 47–49
Product definition, 96
Product design advances, 20–21
Product development, 285
Product differentiation, 285–286
Product evolution, 27–29
Product life cycle and timeshare
  product, 14–23
Product ownership continuum
  diagram, 7
Product registration, 3–5
Profile of timeshare resorts, 10
Promissory notes, 161

Promotion, 96
Prospects, generating, 137–141
  affinity marketing, 139
  case study, 140–141
  direct mail, 138
  drive-to programs, 138
  fly-buy, 139
  home sits marketing programs, 139
  mini-vac, 139
  off-premises-contacts, 137–138, 139
  referral programs, 138
  tactics, 138–139
  telemarketing, 138
  trial membership programs, 139
Proximity factor, 32
Public utilities factor, 74
Publications, 18
Purchasing contract information
  example, 158–159

Quality level of product, 20
Quality of service. *See* Service quality,
  managing

Rating systems, 13
Real estate development, 59–88
  accommodation market history,
    61–63
  conclusions about, 87–88
  demographic factor, 63–65
  design features, 72
  Hawks on demographics and,
    John, 63
  input-output models, applying,
    85–86
  intrinsic value of location, 70
  introduction, 60–61
  lifestyle factor, 75–78
  location analysis, 71
  multiplier effect factor, 78–84
  physical features, 72

regulatory characteristics, 72, 74
relative location value, 70
resort site factor, 69–75
roadway analysis, 71
second-home market trends, 76–78
site development factors table,
    71–72
visibility analysis, 71
zoning factor, 65–69
Real estate industry as part of
    timeshare industry, 28–29
Real Estate Settlement Procedures
    Act (RESPA), 168–169
Real value added by industry
    percentage change table, 84
Receivables, selling. *See* Sales of
    receivables
Reciprocity and fair play, 257
Referral programs, 138
Regional-input-output modeling
    system (RIMS II), 81, 82, 83, 85
Regulatory
    characteristics, 72, 74
    duties and responsibilities,
        timeshare, 246
    factor, 42–44
    home owners associations, 241,
        244, 245, 246
    issues in United States, 43
Relationship building, 131–136
    customers, 133
    dimensions of, 131, 134
    employees, 132–133
    measurement, 133–136
    products, 131–132
Relationship marketing, selling, and
    beyond, 125–147
    after-sales contacts, 145–146
    conclusions about, 146–147
    definitions of relationship
        marketing, 127
    generating prospects, 137–140
    introduction, 126

selling and making the sale, 141–145
timeshare sales and selling,
    136–145; *see also* Sales and
    selling
Relationship marketing and customer
    loyalty, 127–136
    benefits, 129–131, 134–135
    building relationship, 131–136;
        see also Relationship building
    communication, 135
    dimensions, 131, 134, 135, 136
    factors, 134–135
    hospitableness, 129
    levels of loyalty, 135
    philosophical level, 128
    retention of customers, 130–131
    strategic level, 127
    tactical level, 127
    transaction-oriented marketing
        versus, 128
Relative location value, 70
Rescission laws, 161–163, 170, 228,
    260, 270
Resort Condominiums International
    (RCI)
    affiliation with other resort
        operators, 105–106
    owner satisfaction surveys and, 38
    publications of, 18
    rating system, 13
Resort life-cycle theory applied to
    timeshare, 293–294
Resort property management and
    developer, 30
Resort site factor, 69–75
Retrenchment strategy, 284
Right-to-use agreement, 6, 7, 29, 47
Roadways factor, 73

Sales and selling, 136–145
    approaches, dominant, 144–145
    be-back strategies, 144

Sales and selling (*Continued*)
  bringing customer to resort,
    136–137
  case study, 140–141
  cooling-off period, 137, 143
  counselor selling, 145
  establishing rapport, 142
  exit programs, 144–145
  greeting and prospect registration
    stage, 141
  home sits, 145
  interactive technology, 145
  making sale, selling and, 141–145
  off-premises-contacts,
    137–138, 139
  offer stage, making, 143
  offsite sales, 144
  onsite sales, primary, 144
  pre-tour activities stage, 141–142
  prospects, generating, 137–141;
    see also Prospects, generating
  relationship development, 143
  stages in sales encounter, 141
  tactics for generating prospects,
    138–139
  tour stage, 142–143
  trial close stage, 143
Sales commissions, 154
Sales of receivables, 37, 51
  reasons for, 52, 53
  with recourse, 53
  without recourse, 53
  securitization and, 54
  whom to sell to, 52–53
Sales price per interval, average
  developer, 152
Sales transaction, 156–159
  escrow account, 156–157
  first step, 156
  interval purchase, 156
  nondisturbance clause, 157
  nonperformance protection
    clause, 157

purchasing contract information
    example, 158–159
Sales volume (1990–2002), 21, 92, 93–94
Second-home market trends, 76–78
Securitization, 30, 37, 51, 54–55,
    292, 293
Security, 46
Segmentation of market. *See* Market
    segmentation
Service excellence, empowering, 173,
    180–184
Service interactions and tensions,
    234–237
Service Quality Management on
    TQM, 218
Service quality, managing, 197–225
  commercial domain, 223
  conclusions about, 224–225
  control conflicts in service
    encounter, 235
  critical incidents in service
    delivery, 210–212
  customer and employee
    satisfaction flowchart, 215
  customer expectations, 205–208
  customer loyalty, 213–214
  customization, 202, 203
  cycle of good service flowchart, 215
  cycle of poor service flowchart, 215
  definition of service, 200
  dimensions of customer
    expectations table, 206
  dimensions of service, 206
  employee responses to service
    delivery failure, 211–212
  employees and customer
    satisfaction, 209–217
  employees as internal customer,
    214, 215–216
  empowerment, 217, 220, 221
  expectation and delivery
    divergence flowchart, 208
  functional aspects, 205

goods versus services, 199–200
heterogeneity of services, 201–202
inseparability, 203
intangible aspects, 201, 224–225
introduction, 198–199
ISO 9000, 218
labor costs, 210, 216
more than service encounter,
    221–224
motives, 222, 223
perishability, 203–204
personalizing services, 212, 213
private domain, 223
SERVQUAL, 207, 208, 209
social domain, 223
social science perspective, 222
standardization, 202, 203,
    212–213, 216
tangible and intangible benefits,
    200–201
technical aspects, 205
total quality management, 217–221;
    see also Total quality
    management
training, 210, 216, 224, 231
understanding, 199–209
Settlement Costs booklet, 168
Site development factors and table,
    71–72
Site selection considerations, 34
Social development and caring, 256
Social responsibility and supporting,
    256–257
Stability strategy, 283–284
Stagnation stage (phase), 17
Stakeholders, 229–237; see also Home
    owners associations and
    stakeholder management
    balanced scorecard measure, 234,
        236, 237, 249
    business owners, 232
    customers/owners, 231, 239–240
    employees, 230–231, 239

focus groups, 239
government, 232–233
management techniques, 237–240
managers, 232
shareholders, 232
structural responses to different
    interests of, 238
tensions, 234–237
trade bodies, 233
Standard Industrial Classification
    system, 83
State of the industry reports, 38–39
State regulatory issues, 43, 44
Stock market and start of public
    trading, 9
Strengths, weaknesses, opportunities,
    and threats analysis. See SWOT
    analysis and BCG analysis,
    conducting
Superdevoluy and first timeshare
    resort, 2, 6–7
Swapper occasions, 105–106, 110, 115,
    126, 133
SWOT analysis and BCG analysis,
    conducting, 277–283, 295
    BCG growth-share matrix
        diagram, 281
    case study, 279
    cash cow market, 281–282
    dogs market, 282
    external analysis, 279–280
    internal analysis, 278–279
    modeling diagram, 278
    question marks market, 282
    stars market, 282

Telemarketing, 138
Tensions in timeshare service
    interactions, 234–237
Timeshare definitions, 2, 3
Timeshare Europe on generating
    prospects, 137

Total quality management and
   timeshare, 217–221
  customer satisfaction and, 220
  defining, 218
  employee empowerment and, 220,
     221, 225
  objective, 220
  principles of, 219
  Service Quality Management on, 218
  systems theory and, 220
Tour flow, 150
TQM. *See* Total quality management
   and timeshare
Transportation factor, 73
Trial membership offers, 139, 144–145
Truth-in-Lending Law, 167–168

United States regulatory issues, 43
United States Zoning Enabling Act
   (1926), 66
United States states and timeshare
   industry per ARDA, 15

Up-market, 20
Urban Land Institute, 26
Utilities factor, 74

Vacation club points system, 4–5
Vacation Industry Review, 18
Vacation Ownership World, 18, 22
Value Dynamics model, 263–264
Value level of timeshare, 20
Visibility analysis, 71
Volume and growth, sustained
   industry, 22–23

Weekly prices, 20–21
Weeks owned worldwide chart, 94
Working capital funding sources,
   51, 57

Zoning classifications tables, 66, 67–68
Zoning factor, 65–69